What People *
Go in Peace!

Go in Peace! was one awesome and eye-opening book! As I read this book, it was as though Cherie was with me and talking to me! You don't have to have had an abortion to understand what she is saying, as it can be used for *any* situation in life. I felt different just reading it, and it was very hard to put down. I will do my best to kneel at God's feet daily—if only for a moment—and continue to let Him use me and my family.

—Chelle Jacobsen
Reno, Nevada

I saw the tiniest little heart beat on the big screen today, and I am not afraid anymore. Thank you, Cherie, for sharing *Go in Peace!* with me.

—From a woman in an unplanned pregnancy
Oregon

This book will be an eye-opener to anyone not familiar with the grief associated with abortions. Every pastor who wants to understand the struggles of many of the women in their churches should listen to what Cherie has to say. Any servant of the Lord who invests the time to explore these biblical prescriptions will find himself or herself more readily equipped to treat the hurting in the Church.

—Pastor Peyton Jones
Lampeter Evangelical Church, Wales

I started reading *Go in Peace!* and could not put it down. So many morsels! It was filled with great, applicable, practical and simple life applications to ponder and hide in my heart.

—Theresa Redden
CC Northern Beaches, Australia

God has been waiting for one of His children to be obedient and caring enough to write this book. *Go in Peace!* is biblically based and offers Christ-centered solutions. Here is real help for the guilt, shame and deep sense of loss suffered by mothers and fathers who have bought the abortion lie.

—R. Steve Lowe
Chaplain, Pacific Youth Correctional Ministries

Go in Peace! was written to minister to women who are undergoing post-abortion trauma, but in reality it offers the wonderful healing touch of Jesus to anyone who has been in bondage. If you find yourself hopeless because of habitual sin, unforgiveness and/or lies of this world, let Jesus set you free through the timeless principles of His Word that Cherie Fresonke has captured so practically herein. Read them—believe them—and *Go in Peace!*

—Monte Sharp
Area Director Student Venture
Campus Crusade for Christ

This is a powerful book that will change the lives of the men and women who read it. Using her own story and the story of the Sinful Woman in Luke 7 as a foundation, Cherie addresses many of the issues that are brought about by the unconfessed sin in people's lives—whether that sin is abortion or any other self-destructive behavior. She also provides practical steps to help those caught in such patterns gain freedom and overcome their past. This book will truly help readers to go in peace!

—Mark Weising
Senior Managing Editor, Regal Books

CHERIE FRESONKE

Go in Peace!

A Biblical Approach to Post-Abortion

SUNFLOWER PRESS

Go in Peace!
Copyright © 2000, 2011 by Cherie Fresonke
Published by Sunflower Press
P.O. Box 813
Seal Beach, CA 90740
www.sunflowerpress.net
Printed in Bulgaria

Graphic design by Albena Tzvetkova
Cover painted by Lindsey Fresonke (when she was 14 years old)
ISBN: 978-0-9831678-1-5

First edition published in 2000.

Second revised and updated edition published in 2011.

All Scripture quotations, unless otherwise indicated, are taken from the Holy Bible, New International Version®. Copyright © 1973, 1978, 1984 International Bible Society. Used by permission of Zondervan Publishing House.

Scripture quotations marked ESV are from the Holy Bible, English Standard Version, copyright © 2001. The ESV and English Standard Version are trademarks of Good News Publishers. Used by permission. All rights reserved.

Scripture quotations marked NKJV are taken from the New King James Version. Copyright © 1979, 1980, 1982 by Thomas Nelson, Inc. Used by permission. All rights reserved.

Scripture quotations marked NASB are taken from the New American Standard Bible, © Copyright 1960, 1962, 1963, 1968, 1971, 1972, 1973, 1975, 1977, 1995 by the Lockman Foundation. Used by permission.

Scripture quotations marked NLT are taken from the Holy Bible, New Living Translation, copyright © 1996. Used by permission of Tyndale House Publishers, Inc., Wheaton, IL 60189. All rights reserved.

Internet addresses (websites, blogs and the like) printed in this book are offered as resources only. They are not intended in any way to imply an endorsement by Cherie Fresonke or Sunflower Press, nor does Cherie Fresonke or Sunflower Press vouch for the content of these sites for the life of this book.

Contents

ACKNOWLEDGEMENTS

First and foremost, I want to thank God for giving me the burden to write this book—a burden that I know was a result of His love for you. Writing this book seemed an impossible task when I created the first outline, yet I know and believe the truth of God's Word when it says:

> I can do all things through Christ who strengthens me.
> —Philippians 4:13

Likewise, I want to thank my husband, who has always supported my ministry. He is my Lappidoth,[1] my torch, who forever lights my fire. I also want to thank my precious daughters, who gave completely when they shared their mom with a laptop computer in the original writing of this book.

Thank you to my family and my accountability team, who prayed with me and encouraged me during the writing of this book. Thank you for all of your help, your insights and your prayers. Thank you to my board members, who continually challenged me beyond my view. And thank you to the staff at my church, who were always so helpful when I would come in digging (amongst your minds and your bookshelves) for more research material.

Thank you to my editor. The clarity you brought among these pages will help set the captives free.

I also want to thank the Lord for the wonderful gift of a cabin in the mountains for two weeks. It was a wonderful gift of peace and quiet. Much of the original book was written among the chatters of squirrels and the bickering of blue jays.

A special thank you to my dear friend, who gave me his laptop computer. Remember, you cannot out-give God. I know He will bless you richly for your sacrificial gift to me. What faith you have. You, a missionary living by faith, gave such a wonderful gift to me. Lives were touched beyond measure and changed by the words written in the original book with your gift. I stand in awe of God who gives abundantly more than we could ever hope or ask for.

Thank you to the worship team for allowing me to come to worship during your practice times. The Lord inspired many of the words written in this book during these worship practices, and I want to thank you all for your service to Him. Most people are unaware of the hours that each of you devote to the Lord for practice, and you will never know the lives you touch by your obedience to be faithful. Remember Paul's words in Galatians 6:9-10:

> Let us not become weary in doing good, for at the proper time we will reap a harvest if we do not give up. Therefore, as we have opportunity, let us do good to all people, especially to those who belong to the family of believers.

Thank you to each person who lifted up this work in prayer. It touched my heart so deeply each time I learned that someone I didn't even know was praying for me.

Most important, I want to give a special heartfelt thanks to each woman who was brave enough to allow me to share her life within these pages. May God richly bless you. I know many women whose lives were changed when they read your stories in the original version of *Go in Peace!* and I know there will be many more whose lives will be set free because you were brave enough to allow me to put your struggles in this book. I am sure there are rewards waiting for you in heaven for each woman to whom you have ministered. Thank you, and may you continue to walk in peace.

Last but not least, thank you to each and every woman who over the years felt I was a safe person with whom you could share your deepest pain. Your lives have touched mine, and the Lord continues to teach me through your hurt and pain. May all of you always *go in peace!*

Thank You, Lord, for all these wonderful people You have put in my life!

PREFACE

I wrote this book for two main reasons: (1) to help heal the brokenhearted, and (2) to provide a resource for post-abortion counseling that is based on God's Word and not human philosophy or human psychology. We all live in a sinful world, and most of us will not make it through it unscratched and unharmed. Whether the hurt and pain is self-inflicted or inflicted by another, it can affect us to the depths of our innermost being. If this hurt is not handled in the manner in which God intends, it can and will wreak havoc in our lives. In fact, it is this hurt that causes the many "cruddy consequences" we often suffer, including depression, anxiety, outbursts of anger and other self-destructive behaviors.

What I am about to teach you in this book is what God personally taught me many years ago. This information changed my life, and as I continue to apply it to my situation today—sometimes moment by moment—I am able to be all that God intends me to be. I had many deep heart hurts—sin that had been inflicted on me by others, and sin that, unfortunately, I had inflicted on myself. Yet God truly touched my life, just as He touched the life of the Sinful Woman:

> Then Jesus said to her, "Your sins are forgiven. . . .
> Your faith has saved you; *go in peace.*"
> —Luke 7:48,50, emphasis added

When I was ready to admit that my life was out of control, I cried out to God for help, and He met me there. He began to heal my broken heart and teach me how to give my deep heart hurts to Him once and for all. I learned that He never intended for me to carry the hurt by myself. What He taught me set me free. It enabled me to *go in peace!* Fear was replaced with strength, depression with joy, anxiety with faith, and rage with rest. Best yet, I experienced peace with God deep within my heart. That's what it means to *go in peace!* Likewise, if you have been hurt in life, this book is for you. God truly desires for you to join with me as we *go in peace!*

Note that I wrote this book specifically for those suffering with the issue of post-abortion. However, I have found over the years that God has impacted the lives of those who read this book in which abortion was not an issue just as powerfully as the post-abortive women. Therefore, if abortion is not an issue in your life, whenever you see the word "abortion," simply change it in your mind to the word "sin" and apply what is being taught to your life. God's Word is all-sufficient and has the power to change lives—including yours—if you are willing. Though it grieves me deeply to see the depth of a woman's pain, know that it grieves our heavenly Father even more. God has a love so deep for you that it is immeasurable, and His desire is for you to *go in peace!*

The burden and insight for writing this book came from many years of discipling women and teenagers in both

America and overseas. Women around the world have the same deep heart hurts, and in studying and teaching godly principles, I was blessed to witness life-changing results. I have witnessed broken and bruised, shackled and chained women become whole again. I have observed women come to the full understanding that God sees them as holy and sanctified and wants to restore them if they are willing to admit their sin to Him. Praise the Lord!

However, during these years of discipling broken women, I have also observed an emptiness and lack of substance from counseling methods based on human ways. Many women have shared with me that the counseling they received prior to this course offered them no hope and no answer to their problems. In fact, once when I was teaching a *Go in Peace* workshop, a woman shared how she had learned more in one day than she had learned during nine years of counseling. She felt a new sense of freedom that she had never before experienced. Her testimony and the testimonies of many others is evidence that God's Word is true when it states:

> There is a way that seems right to a man, but in the end it leads to death.
> —Proverbs 14:12; 16:25

This brings us to the second reason why I wrote this book. Back when I originally wrote *Go in Peace!* all the books or curriculums for post-abortion counseling—including all the material written for believers I had seen—relied on human philosophy and human psychology. Yet God was speaking clearly to my heart through verses such as Colossians 2:8, in which Paul states:

XIII

> See to it that no one takes you captive through hollow and deceptive philosophy, which depends on human traditions and the basic principles of the world rather than on Christ.

God created us and knows how to heal us, and any teaching not based solely on His Word will fall short of the healing power He wants to work in our lives. I knew this truth in my heart, but I didn't think it was possible for me to write a book. So God, with His wonderful sense of humor, took away the curriculum we were using in our ministry, forcing me to write one instead.

Please know that I did not write this book to attack those who have adopted human philosophy or human psychology. Many counselors who use materials based on these methods truly have a heart to help women heal. They saw the destruction that abortion caused in women's lives and wanted to help, and they probably thought they had nowhere else to turn. For years, I also used these same types of materials because they were the only ones available.

Many times when I taught overseas, a translator would have to interpret each word that I spoke to the audience. This gave me time to really think about what I was teaching. During these times, the Holy Spirit, in His love, would impress on my heart the areas in which my teaching fell short of God's best for the women. The Lord impressed deeper and deeper on me that there was a better way—the only real way, in fact—for complete healing. I began to question why I was giving women only partial freedom when God's Word offered them complete freedom. God truly knew what they needed to learn and apply to their lives. His Word was *all*-sufficient for their needs and life-changing, if only they were willing to apply it to their situations.

Are you willing to learn from Jesus? In Matthew 7:24-25, He said:

> Everyone who hears these words of mine and puts them into practice is like a wise man who built his house on the rock. The rain came down, the streams rose, and the winds blew and beat against that house; yet it did not fall, because it had its foundation on the rock.

Let us build on the solid foundation of the Rock so that we will never again be beat down by the storms of this world. Only then will we know how to stand firm regardless of how hard the winds blow. Even if the winds and rain from a hurricane filled with the sin of this world come our way, we will not fall.

In closing, there are two quick points that I want to address. First, throughout this text you will see many footnote references that refer to passages in the Bible. It is important for you to realize that what I am teaching is based on God's Word and not simply something I believe. For this reason, after you have read each chapter, I encourage you to go back and take the time to look up the Scriptures that are footnoted in the text. You will find a listing of all the footnotes for each chapter in the endnotes section in the back of the book.

Second, it is my prayer that you will read the entire book. The last few chapters contain material that will bring you such comfort, but it is important not to start there! The material in this book has been arranged to lay a foundation based on biblical principles so that you can fully achieve the freedom found in God's Word. It is my hope that you will grasp it all so that you may *go in peace!*

INTRODUCTION

Let the beloved of the LORD rest secure in him,
for he shields him all day long,
and the one the LORD loves rests between his shoulders.
DEUTERONOMY 33:12

O ne evening, there was a news story on television about a young woman who had committed suicide by jumping off a bridge. In her suicide letter, she wrote that she felt responsible for the death of her child through abortion and could no longer live with herself. For her, this was the only way to escape the pain.

Have you ever felt this way? Have you even been in such a deep pit of despair that there seemed to be no way out? Have you ever said to yourself that nothing or no one could ever possibly take the pain away? If so, this book is for you, for I have been where you are right now and have known a pit as deep as yours. However, as you will see, I have also discovered the way out—the way that set me free and enabled me to *go in peace.*

Dear beloved—yes, that's right, *beloved[2]* —God loves you, and He has put a burden on my heart for you. This book was penned with the prayer that you would feel as

XVII

though I were sitting by your side, going through each chapter with you. Some of what you read will bring pain and tears, while other parts will bring relief, joy and peace. At times, you may want to throw the book across the room and never pick it up again. (It's okay to throw it across the room, but do pick it up again!)

When you encounter these times, know that while I cannot be with you during these difficult portions of this book, there is Someone who is holding your hand[3] and lovingly comforting you.[4] He will never leave you or forsake you.[5] He is the Great Physician,[6] the Wonderful Counselor,[7] the Prince of Peace.[8] He calls you His beloved, and He came to set you free![9] So do not despair, and do not give up. As the prophet Isaiah writes:

> Why should you be beaten anymore? Why do you persist in rebellion? Your whole head is injured, your whole heart afflicted. From the sole of your foot to the top of your head there is no soundness—only wounds and welts and open sores, not cleansed or bandaged or soothed with oil.
>
> —Isaiah 1:5-6

If you are brave enough to turn these pages and apply what you learn to your life, you will find a peace that surpasses all understanding. The Wonderful Counselor is waiting to restore to you a joy, peace and happiness that you may not have even known was missing. The Prince of Peace will bring wholeness and wellbeing to your soul!

So be brave enough to walk away from the side of the bridge and into a brand-new life filled with love, joy, peace, patience, kindness, goodness, faithfulness, gentleness and self-control.[10] As you walk away from that ledge, you will

XVIII

discover the best that Jesus has in store for you. For as He said to the Sinful Woman in Luke 7:48,50:

> Your sins are forgiven. . . . Your faith has saved you; *go in peace* (emphasis added).

Chapter One

WHAT A SHAME

Cover their faces with shame
So that men will seek your name,
O LORD.
PSALM 83:16

*I*n 1991, the Lord called me to begin a ministry to help women who were hurting because of the choice they had made to have an abortion. Since that time, I have given my testimony hundreds of times. I have shared it in rooms full of people, and I have shared it with women on a one-on-one basis. However, each time I have given my testimony, I have always had to paraphrase it due to time constraints.

As I was praying and seeking God's will for the opening chapter of this book, I felt Him impressing on my heart that I needed to share *everything with complete honesty.* He wanted me to give my complete testimony and leave nothing out. For while I might omit a portion that I thought was unimportant, that part of my testimony may be the very thing that someone needs to hear to bring healing to his or her life. So please forgive me if this part of the book is a tad long.

I remember that when God first called me to this ministry, I would argue with Him and say, *Lord, if I do this,*

1

everyone will know my most horrible sin—the most shameful thing I have ever done in my life. What will people think of me? The Lord, in His love, showed me over and over again that people did not judge me when I gave my testimony. In fact, they appreciated my honesty. Of course, it is one thing to stand up before an audience and share my story with people and quite another to sit down and write out *everything*! So here goes another step of faith.

When I was about nine years old, I put my faith in Jesus to be my Lord and Savior at Vacation Bible School. I loved the Lord so much. He was my Best Friend. If no one were going to church, I would walk myself to Sunday School. I loved to hear all the stories from the Bible about Jesus.

One of my favorite stories was about the apostle Peter and his claim that he would never disown Jesus. The story is found in Matthew 26:

> Then Jesus said to them, "You will all fall away because of Me this night. . . ." But Peter said to Him, "*Even* though all may fall away because of You, I will never fall away." Jesus said to him, "Truly I say to you that this *very* night, before the rooster crows, you will deny Me three times."
> —Matthew 26:31-34, NASB, emphasis added

Before Peter knew it, Jesus' words came true. The rooster crowed, and Peter wept bitterly with his denial of Christ. I remember how this story affected me. I was quite upset with Peter. How could he disown Jesus? He had walked by Jesus' side and knew Him personally. He had witnessed His miracles and had heard all of His life-changing teachings. How could Peter then just deny Him? It just did not seem possible to my young heart. I remember claiming, "I will never deny You, Jesus!"

As the years went by, I continued to love my Savior. I went to church on Sundays and attended a mid-week youth group (if I could find a ride). However, looking back I realize that there were two extremely important truths that I was not taught as a teen. These were truths that I was seeking, and one would have thought I would have found them in a church setting. It is because of these two truths that the Lord has given me a heart to teach purity seminars today. Perhaps I can help someone not make the same mistakes that I did.

The first truth I was never taught was that God's Word is alive and relevant for our situation today. I always assumed that the Bible was great for my grandmother's generation but not relevant to modern life. Because I wasn't taught how to apply the Bible to my life or how to study it—or even that I needed to open it—I just assumed it was unimportant.

The second truth I was never taught was that God's Word has a lot to say about purity and sexual immorality. How I wish my youth leaders had not been afraid to open up the Bible and tell us what God had to say about sex! Youth group was more a time for us to get together and play games instead of a time to get together to learn about God and His Word. Please understand that I am not trying to make excuses for what I did or shift the blame to someone else, but I do want to lay the foundation of who I have become and why.

As I reminisce about my teenage years, one particular day stands out in my mind—the day I came to a fork in

3

the road. I was praying, and daydreaming, and asking the Lord, *Do You know who my husband is? Do I already know him? Is he someone I know, or is he a complete stranger? If he's someone I know, do I see him all the time? Does he know me?* That same day, I walked across the street to hang out at a house, which was *the place to be.* All of the guys hung out there and worked on their Volkswagens. I remember saying hello to one of them. He was a real nice guy who was quiet, and shy, and kind of cute. I greeted him and asked how he was. I remember thinking, *Lord, why don't I date a nice guy like him instead of the one I am dating?*

God loves us so much that He gives us free will. He does not want us to be little robots. Nor does He expect that from the moment we accept Him as our Savior we would follow Him and do everything perfectly. No! He loves us so much that He allows us to make our own choices—even choices He knows may hurt us. That day, I thought this cute, quiet guy would never like me, so I continued down the wrong path that would lead to some very wrong choices. I am sure that to the Lord, I sounded very much like Peter when he claimed, "Even though all may fall away because of You, I will never fall away" (Matthew 26:33, NKJV).

There was tremendous pressure on me during my teen years to be promiscuous. Schools were just beginning to teach sex education classes, and the teachers were telling us that it was natural and normal to be sexually active. Television shows and songs were encouraging people to *fall in love* and express it. Almost everyone I knew my age was sexually active, including my sister, who became pregnant at the age of 16. She had been a virgin before she met the

4

love of her life. I had always looked up to her, as she was six years older than me. (She and her boyfriend were married when she became pregnant and had the cutest little boy. Praise the Lord! She is still married to the husband of her youth—they have been married since 1969!) And, of course, my boyfriend certainly wanted me to show him just how much I loved him.

Everything and everyone were telling my friends and I that it was time to become sexually active. There was no one telling us otherwise. The leaders in our church were not telling us to remain sexually pure. Television was not telling us to remain sexually pure. Music was not telling us to remain sexually pure. No one was telling us to wait. The pressure was on, and no one was telling us the truth.

It is difficult to share this next part of my testimony with you, for I truly do love my mom, but if it can encourage even one mother to be brave enough to share the truth of God's Word with her son or daughter, then it is worth it. (My mom felt the same when she gave me her permission to share this part of the story with you.) One day, she asked me if I had been sexually active. I told her no, which was the truth at that point. I had only been thinking about it. She said to me, "If you decide to become sexually active, let me know and I will take you to the doctor and get you on the pill."

I remember thinking, *Wow, she would take me to the doctor to get me on the pill!* Looking back, I now understand that she did not want me to become pregnant like my sister, and this was the only way she knew how to protect me. She did not know what else to do or any better way to handle the situation.

A few months later, I got brave enough to ask my mom to take me to the doctor. Now, to give my mom credit, she must have thought over what she had said to me, because when I asked her this she freaked out. I remember that she asked me not to have sex, but by then it was too late.

In hindsight, perhaps the most intriguing parts of my testimony are the lies I told myself. The prophet Jeremiah warned of this deception:

> The human heart is most deceitful and desperately wicked. Who really knows how bad it is?
> —Jeremiah 17:9, NLT

I truly did not understand how deceitful and wicked I could be within my own heart and mind. It was as if I had a hole in my heart that desired to be filled with love, but I was looking for that love in all the wrong places.

Now, although our youth group did not teach us the truth of God's Word concerning sexual immorality, the Ten Commandments were posted on the wall in the youth room. So I at least was aware of the truth found in Exodus 20:14, which says, "Do not commit adultery" (NLT). One day, my best girlfriend and I decided to look up the word "adultery" in the dictionary. She was also concerned about what God's Word had to say concerning sex, but all either of us knew was this commandment.

The dictionary definition said that "adultery" meant "voluntary sexual intercourse between a married man and someone other than his wife or between a married woman and someone other than her husband."[11] I remember discussing this with my girlfriend at some length, and we decided that because we were not yet married, the commandment must not apply to us. Doesn't that sound just like a teenager's reasoning? Do you see how easily we deceive ourselves? We did not know where else to look in the Bible. We did not know that it also said to flee from sexual immorality.[12] I suppose my excuses sounded a bit like Peter when he denied Christ and said, "I do not know what you are talking about" (Matthew 26: 70, NASB).

At the age of 16, I found myself in a situation where I thought I might be pregnant. I was scared to death! I did not know what to do, but conveniently located down the street from my high school was a free clinic—a place one could go to have a pregnancy test at no charge. Back in those days, you couldn't just walk into a store and buy a pregnancy test. You had to go to either a doctor or a clinic. So I went there for the free pregnancy test.

I found out that the test was positive. I was pregnant! I remember that the woman there said I had options available to me. She said I could have an abortion and that she could even refer me to a doctor who helped women in my situation. She also told me that I could put the child up for adoption. Somewhere that thought entered my mind, but the wickedness within my own heart deepened. *Put my child up for adoption?* I thought. *Am I crazy! I could not give my baby away!* How selfish I was to think I could not give my baby away but that I could end that baby's life!

My boyfriend was a few years older than me, and he was already an alcoholic (or soon to be one). I knew I was never going to marry someone who was an alcoholic. Isn't that amazing? I would date someone who drank too much, but I would never marry someone who did. What do we think when we accept something less than what we know is

7

right in our heart? My sister had gotten married at 16, and I thought I was not going to be that dumb! Time would show that the choices she made were so much smarter than the choices I would make.

When I told my boyfriend that I was pregnant, he was scared (or perhaps selfish) and said that he did not want me to have the baby. He thought abortion was the only option. I was so afraid, and I did not want to tell my parents. I had all the excuses: *I do not make enough money to raise a child on my own. My boyfriend does not want the child. I do not want to be married so young.* On and on it went.

When I went to the doctor's office, the nurse was so sweet. She tried to get me to realize that there was a baby in my womb and not just a mass of fetal tissue or a product of conception like I so wanted to believe. She lovingly said to me, "You need to take care of yourself now. You are eating for two." She probably knew from my file that I was going to have an abortion and was hoping I would admit the truth to myself. Yet I was scared, and I did not know where I could turn. I ignored my relationship with the Lord. I am sure at this point in my life that if someone had said, "She's a believer in Christ—she knows the Lord and can trust Him with her fears," I would have replied just like Peter did when he denied Christ: "I do not know the man" (Matthew 26:72, NASB)!

Back then abortions were performed at hospitals, so I had to go in the day before the procedure to have blood work done. I just about fainted when I walked into the lab for the workup. I knew the anesthesiologist! He was a regular customer at the restaurant where I worked. How I wanted to melt into the floor in shame! I was so afraid that he would tell my parents.

I do not remember much about the abortion itself. I went in early the next morning, and the hospital staff prepared me for the operation. I remember the doctor telling me to count backward from 100, and I fell asleep. When I awoke, I was in a room with just two beds. It was like any other hospital room—just as if I had undergone any other surgical procedure. There was another girl in my room, and her family was visiting her. Of course, no one was visiting me—I was a sinful, young teen-woman.

One of the girl's family members asked me why I was there. I did not know what to reply. Even at that low point of my life I did not want to lie outright, so I just replied, "A female problem." Imagine calling a baby a "female problem"! I was so filled with shame. I cannot even describe the guilt I felt. I just wanted my life to end. No one knew I was at the hospital except for my boyfriend (and the anesthesiologist, of course). My boyfriend was out in the waiting room and would not even come into the room, so I made the nurse go get him. I insisted that he sit with me until the hospital finally released me.

The anesthesiologist began to call me frequently and ask me to play tennis with him. I was afraid to say no. *What if he told my parents?* I thought. He gave me the heebie jeebies, and I lived in such fear during that time. I could not stand him. I knew that he thought I was a loose girl—and, in reality, I was. Yet in my mind I tried to rationalize my sin away by thinking, *He does not understand. I've only had one boyfriend. I'm not loose.* Out of my shame, I allowed this man—who I knew only wanted to use me— to remain around me. He did not really care about me. I finally arrived at the place were I was brave enough to stop seeing him. *Go ahead and tell my parents,* I thought. *It*

9

would be better than anything you have planned. I thank the Lord that He protected me from whatever evil thoughts that man had in his mind. He never touched me.

At first, I was relieved that I had the abortion. My problem was solved, and my parents had not found out. I was actually *thankful* for what I had done! But I was just deceiving myself. Little did I know just how much my decision to have an abortion would adversely affect me. I was hurting so deep inside, and to numb my pain I soon turned to drinking alcohol and smoking pot. Deep within my heart, I felt like such a failure. My life was not turning out as I had expected. For most young women, life is just beginning at age 16, but I felt as if mine were ending. I did not realize how much I missed my baby. Every time I thought of him or her, I would push those thoughts away and try to think of something else. I would try to convince myself with all of the excuses I could muster that I had made the right choice. I felt so low. I was not good enough anymore, and I was out to destroy myself.

Of course, if you had said this to me at the time, I would have said you were crazy. At that low point in my life, my ears were too full of my deception to even hear the rooster crow. To possibly consider the truth would have been too painful to bear, and my deception was easier to maintain (or so I thought). It is only in spending time with the Lord and looking back over the years that He has given me clarity and understanding about this time in my life. I never went to a doctor or psychologist to figure these truths out, because that was not necessary. The one I needed was the Great Physician, the Wonderful Counselor, the Prince of Peace.

I eventually broke up with my boyfriend and began to date weirder and weirder guys. God may have protected me from the anesthesiologist, but there was no way to protect me from myself. The stories I could tell you! At 18 I found myself pregnant again. Oh, how I wanted this baby! I even told my friends that I was pregnant. My boyfriend wanted the baby as well. I was so excited, and I sometimes wonder if I got pregnant on purpose.

But then I started looking at my situation. I was in the same place as I had been during my first pregnancy. So the deception began anew. I did not want to marry my boyfriend—he had some major problems, and I was not going to make a mistake like that. So I thought, *I cannot live on my own and raise a child. What am I doing? Am I crazy? Even if I didn't marry this guy, I would be chained to him for the rest of my life, as he would be the father of my child.* I started coming up with all the same excuses and deceptions that I had for the first abortion. Finally, I decided that I was not going to have the child. By this point, I had passed up Peter with my denial of Christ! Yet truth be told, Christ is the one to whom I should have turned. He was the one who had the right answers for me.

I remember going to the doctor with my boyfriend. He tried to talk me out of having the abortion, as he really wanted to have this child. He tried to get the doctor to convince me to have the baby, but there was nothing he could do. It was not his legal "choice." Oh, the pain I must have caused him.

I went to Planned Parenthood to have my abortion. I felt as if I were on an assembly line with a number of other women. One woman after another would go into a room, give a urine sample; go into another room, change her clothes; come into another room, do something else— one right after the other. We all followed each other as if we were in a daze.

I did not want to be conscious during the procedure, so I asked to be put to sleep. I remember being so cold as I climbed up on to the table where they would apply the anesthesia. Truth be told, I never wanted to wake up again. But that was not to be. I woke up hours later with my mind confused from the medication. I remember thinking as I came to that I was a baby who had just discovered her feet. I sat on the gurney saying, "Look, oh boy! Look, there's my feet!"

As I was talking and playing with my feet, the two nurses who had been so nice and kind before the abortion began yelling at me. "Shut up, stop it! Quit doing that!" they said. The medicine they gave me had made me sick and I was vomiting, but they did not care. They just wanted me out of there because they did not want to deal with me playing with my feet. I believe it was because it brought the truth too close to home for them—a baby's life had just ended. "It's time for you to leave," they insisted. So, as I was joking around, I asked, "Can I have a to go bag so I have something to throw up in?" I was sick all the way home.

I went to a friend's house and stayed with her for a couple of days. About two days after the abortion, I began to hemorrhage. I woke up one morning and the whole bed was full of blood. When I had gone in for the abortion, they had told me not to go to the hospital if I had any complications. How stupid and naive I was! They had only said that to cover up any mistakes they made. I should have gone to a hospital, but I was afraid to do so. I still did not want anyone to know what I had done.

So, to continue to cover up my sin, I drove all the way back to the abortion clinic. I had lost so much blood that I was ready to pass out, and I still cannot believe that I actually made it there. When I arrived, the staff called in a doctor. They had to perform the abortion again to clean out everything. Apparently they had missed something during the procedure, which was why I was hemorrhaging. Because this was an emergency and did not take place during their normal hours, they did not have a full staff and could not put me to sleep. I had to stay awake. It was so awful. It was so much easier to be put to sleep and not know what was going on than to hear the sound of the suction machine. The pain I felt as they dilated my cervix was torture. There is no need to describe any more for those of you who were awake for your abortion—you know what I am taking about.

After that terrible experience, I got crazier. I was deeply depressed and never wanted to get out of bed again. I contemplated suicide at one point, but I was too chicken to go through with it. I was afraid that I would fail in my attempt and end up living through it, which would have been worse. From that time on, I started getting involved with harder drugs. It was only through God's grace that I never became addicted to any of them. I was probably high more days than I was not.

One day, I went with a friend to her friend's house. He had thrown a party the night before and had a container full of leftover pot that was all mixed together. So we sat down to smoke a joint. Something in it was bad! It really affected me. I could not walk, so I went to lie down on the bed. I was terrified to the point of paranoia—I had never experienced that bad of a trip before. I was lying on the bed, and I could not stop it from spinning and spinning. Above me was a bright white light, but I was spinning down into the dark pit of hell. I was on my way there for all the wrong I had done, and I could not stop. I remember crying out to the Lord, *Save me! I won't do any more drugs if You save me. I will change!*

I would like to say that I never touched any drugs from that moment on, but that would be a lie. I did some drugs a few more times. However, that experience got me thinking, and it eventually led to the end of my drug and alcohol use. I finally came to my senses and decided that I did not want to live like that any longer. I realized that for just a couple of hours of pleasure and being high, I could hit someone with my car and kill him or her. If that happened, I would be responsible for that person's death for the rest of my life. I started thinking that if something like that did happen, there was no way I could live with that guilt on top of everything else. It would destroy me. So I determined to quit doing drugs, stop drinking, and never date another guy in my life. I wanted nothing to do with them.

People who know me now cannot believe that I did any of these things. They always say, "You appear so innocent." I thank them for the compliment. If they only knew the gutter from which I came—the absolute deep pit of slime. But Jesus looked past all of that. He reached down, took my hand and lifted me from my pit of despair.[13] Jesus had always been my Savior, but during that time in my life He was not my Lord. I had denied Him for so many years. Like Peter, when I began to realize the depth of my denial of Christ, I wept bitterly. I began to pray again and seek God.

One night, my friend was having a birthday and everyone was going to a restaurant with a bar and disco called the Red Onion. I did not want to go. I hated those "meat markets"—places guys go to pick up girls—but this was a good friend of mine, and because it was her birthday I felt I needed to go. My plan was to go for a short while and leave early.

As I was walking through the restaurant, I passed a group of guys and heard one of them say, "Hey, I know her." I turned around and saw that nice, quiet, shy guy that I had known from five years before. This was the one whom I had seen after I had prayed and asked God if He knew who my husband would be. But now, he was one nice-looking young man!

His name was Keith, and he asked me out. When I began to really fall in love with him, I knew that I needed to tell him about my past. I was certain that when I told him the truth of who I was he would never want to see me again. However, I knew that if I waited too long, my love for him would be too deep and it would hurt too much when he left. I had never been this scared in my life. I contemplated not telling him and rationalized that he did not *really* need to know. But in my heart I knew that if I did not tell him the truth about my background, I would be living an even bigger lie. If we got married someday, I would have to live with a lie for the rest of my life.

15

I remember the moment as if it were yesterday. We were near an old white church, which perhaps got me thinking about God and gave me the courage to finally tell him. With my heart pounding loud enough to hear, I said, "Keith, I have to tell you something terrible. After I tell you this, you may not ever want to see me again. If that is the case, I'll understand." I could not even look at him because I was too scared of what his reaction would be. I slowly went on to explain how at age 16 and 18, I had undergone two abortions. Amazingly, Keith said, "Cherie, that's someone you used to be, it's not who you are now." Although he was not a believer, he modeled God's unconditional love and forgiveness to me. He loved me just as Christ loved me—unconditionally, with all of my sins and flaws.

So, in 1983 I married my closest friend. I decided that I was going to do everything right. We were married for about two years before we decided to have children, and then the Lord blessed us with two beautiful girls. They were born 13 months apart. It was at that point in my life that I really began to think about the abortions. As I held my babies, I was put face to face with what could have been. It would have worked out. It would not have been easy, but it would have worked out. The choices I had made were so wrong.

When the girls were still babies, I decided to go back to church. This time I did not want to hear what human wisdom had to say. I had listened to human philosophy, and it had only messed up my life. I had made some bad, bad choices, and now I wanted to hear what *God* had to say. So I began to look for a church that taught strictly out of the Bible, verse by verse and chapter by chapter. I don't know where I got that idea—it must have been God leading and directing me.

I soon found a church where all the people had their Bibles with them as they walked in and the pastor taught the Word verse by verse. I began attending every Sunday with my daughters, and I loved my Savior with all my heart. I rededicated my life to Christ, and He became my Lord again. Soon I began to pray that my husband would come to church with us. Keith had never really gone to church as a kid, and he didn't even know if he believed in God. I did not understand that as a follower of Christ—even a backslidden believer—I was not to marry someone who did not believe in God. I knew nothing about being unequally yoked. But I did know that the vows I made when I got married were before God and that it was for life.

Please understand that I am not saying that it was God's perfect will for me to marry a non-believer. Paul's words are true when he says:

> Do not be yoked together with unbelievers. For what do righteousness and wickedness have in common? Or what fellowship can light have with darkness?
> —2 Corinthians 6:14

God does not contradict His Word. Yet I believe that He, in His grace and mercy, blessed my marriage in spite of our ignorance.

For about two years, I walked the babies and myself to church. My husband never came with us. I prayed and prayed for him, asking the Lord to continually put believers in his path as a light. God, in His faithfulness, soon

17

began to orchestrate events and strategically placed a man in his life who was a light and witness by his actions and deeds. My husband worked in the construction field—with heavy equipment—and moved around a lot. He constantly worked with different companies and different people, but God put him on a long job where he worked with this man for several months. Partly, because of this man's influence, my husband came to church and also accepted Jesus as his Lord and Savior.

Meanwhile, I was continually being faced with the fact of what *could* have been. As my relationship with Christ deepened, I felt that I needed to know what God thought about abortion. I still believed at this point in my life that abortion was acceptable—to think otherwise still hurt too much. I was taking a college English course, and we had to write a term paper on something controversial. The moment the teacher assigned the report, I knew my subject would be about abortion.

The professor told us not to base any of our arguments on emotional responses—the arguments had to be based on hard evidence. At this point in my walk with the Lord, I did not know any of the verses that supported life in the womb. I was just an infant in my faith, so I did all of my research in a secular college library. I needed to know the truth from the depth of my being, and I remember asking God continually to show it to me. I knew that I would never be set free without it. That secular college library was one-sided, but God, in His faithfulness, led me to the right medical facts that proved to me that abortion was wrong.

Writing that term paper (and this book) were the hardest projects I have ever undertaken. But drafting that paper was also one of the most cleansing things for me to do personally. There is freedom in realizing and admitting the wrongs in our lives. Knowledge is the beginning of freedom, yet admittance and repentance of the truth of our sins are the steps we need to take to be set free. The best part of all this is that this freedom is available to any who desire it. All we have to do is admit the truth,[14] leave it behind,[15] and walk forward as a new person.[16]

Although I have titled this portion of my testimony "What a Shame" because of the depth of shame I was feeling from both my sinful actions and the corrupt actions inflicted on me by others, God's Word became real in my life when I read:

> Cover their faces with shame so that men will seek your name, O LORD.
>
> —Psalm 83:16

Because of my shame, I truly sought Him with my whole heart. In view of this, God—also known as the Lifter of My Head[17]—began to turn my life around and use my story for His glory. May my testimony encourage you to know that He can and will do the same in your life if you allow Him. Continue to turn the pages, so that you may join me as we *go in peace!*

Chapter Two

FOR HIS GLORY

Bring. . . . everyone who is called by my name,
whom I created from my glory,
whom I formed and made.
Lead out those who are blind. . . .
"You are my witnesses," declares the LORD,
"And my servant whom I have chosen."
ISAIAH 43:6-10

year or so after my husband put his faith in Christ, we moved to Temecula, California, and began to attend a Calvary Chapel. We were there for about two months when one Sunday morning, just as the service ended, my husband said, "We have to hurry!"

"What's the rush?" I asked.

"Do you remember that guy from work I used to tell you about?" he said. "Well, he's here!"

Where? I thought. I wanted to meet this man and thank him for being such an influence in drawing my husband to the Lord. We finally caught up with him, and Keith introduced me to him. His name was Phil, and he introduced us to his wife, Kathie.

Have you ever met someone with whom you immediately clicked? That was the case for Keith and I and this

21

couple. Phil and Kathie had also just moved to Temecula, and they had three little girls around the same ages as our two little girls. It is amazing to look back over the years and realize how God orchestrated events for His purpose and plans.[18]

Kathie and I became good friends. One time, our church was planning a women's retreat and I told Kathie, "I want to be your roommate, but I really want the best of what God has for me, and I want the best God has for you. So I am not going to request any roommate. I am going to leave it in God's hands." She also wanted God's best. Well, as it turns out, God put Kathie and me in the same room!

I knew that Kathie was hurting deep inside, but I did not know the cause of her pain. I thought, *Maybe she's hurting deep inside like I am*. As her friend I wanted to reach out and help her if I could, so I decided to be brave and share with her my most horrible shame and my most sinful past. I worried that she would never want to talk to me again, but I felt it would be worth the risk if I could help her. So I shared with Kathie what I had been through, and she shared with me that she had also undergone two abortions. (I have to say here, I have Kathie's permission to share her testimony with you.)

During the next year, Kathie and I would occasionally talk about how we thought the abortions were affecting us. Our children were young—they were all between the ages of three to six—and we wondered whether the abortions were affecting the way we were treating our children. We talked about how painful it still was to think about the choices we made and how it hurt deep down inside mentally, emotionally and spiritually. We wondered what our children would have looked like, and we talked about how old they would have been.

A year went by, and soon it was time for our annual women's retreat. I said the same thing to Kathie as I had said the previous year: "I would love to be your roommate, but . . ." We giggled and joked that maybe God would again put us in the same room. When we got there, we discovered that we were once again to be roommates. We were excited. It was at this retreat, in 1991, that God had given us a vision for a ministry to help women overcome the pain and guilt they were experiencing from having an abortion and to help teenagers not make the same mistakes that we had. The vision that He gave us was exactly the same.

Kathie and I decided to name the ministry the Strong A.R.M. (for Abortion Recovery Ministry). We went to the leader of the women's ministries at the church and shared with her that we believed God was calling us to start a ministry. She told us we needed to share this with our pastor, so we made an appointment and told him what God was putting on our hearts. He said, "You need to study. You need to learn all you can about post-abortion." So, for the next two years, we read every book we could find on the subject. I also began to train in how to counsel and disciple through the Biblical Counseling Foundation's course called *Self-Confrontation—A Manual for In-Depth Discipleship.*[19]

It was during this time that God began to teach me some amazing truths. He lovingly taught me that I *was* created with a hole in my heart that could only be filled by a right relationship with Him—not just a saved relationship, but a *right* relationship. He also taught me that whenever I handled hurt in a way that He did not intend, it became an infected wound deep within my heart. This unresolved hurt was what had caused the consequences in my life and had led me to make even more wrong choices. Better yet, God taught me how to give that hurt to Him so that the infection could be healed. This amazing truth is what He called me to teach you in the pages to come.

Kathie and I soon started getting bombarded like you cannot imagine with all kinds of spiritual warfare. I look back and laugh because, at the time, we did not even know what spiritual warfare was. For me, the trials were mostly health issues. I have systematic lupus, and I also had skin cancer removed on my hand, which then became infected. I could not use my hand for more than two months. On and on it went. Kathie also was going through some of the same kinds of trials that I was experiencing.

I remember at one point going to see my pastor. I had never gone for counseling before, but I needed to know what was going on. He said, "Cherie, this is spiritual warfare. God has given you a vision to help women who are hurting. He has put you on the front lines where you can help set free the captives. The enemy does not want you to do this ministry." I remember thinking, *Wow, spiritual warfare? Cool!* Knowing that there was a battle going on all around me that I could not see made my situation a little easier to handle.[20] Understanding what was actually taking place in my life totally changed my perspective.

This warfare went on for about two years (and, in many ways, it has never really stopped). God had given me the vision to begin this ministry, but up until that point, nothing had really happened except a whole lot of spiritual warfare! Finally, after two years, I got to the point where I began to ask the Lord, "God, was this vision really from You, or was it just my imagination? Do You really want Kathie and me to do this? Lord, if this was from You, I need to know. I need some answers. If this was from You, when do you want us to start?" I prayed that prayer for about two months. I knew that God, in His timing, would eventually answer my prayers.

It soon became time again for our annual women's retreat. I knew that this would allow me to finally have some peace and quiet where I could be focused on the Lord away from home and the little ones, and I went with the expectation that God was going to do great things. The retreat was somewhere near the ocean, so I dropped my kids off at my mom's house near the beach and drove down the coast alone. As I drove, I sought God and asked Him to answer my prayer. I really felt the presence of the Holy Spirit that day.

When I arrived and went to register, I asked, "Who are my roommates?" Of course, in His divine plan, God had put Kathie and me together again. When I discovered this, I knew that God truly was going to answer my prayer concerning this ministry. In fact, God did answer my prayer through His still small voice and through circumstances that He orchestrated that weekend. He basically showed Kathie and I that *this ministry was a ministry for us to do and that we were to start that ministry now!*

God did this by placing in our room a woman who had two abortions several years before. Kathie and I ended up counseling her that night and into the early morning hours.

This woman shared with us that for 15 years she had never cried about anything. After talking with us, she could now see that she had been bulimic, and she could connect the bulimia back to the time she had the abortions.

When I woke up that Sunday morning at the retreat, I was in awe of all the Lord had done. He had confirmed the work that He wanted me to do by placing this woman in our room. I had gone to be by myself and have some quiet time. I praised God and said to Him within my heart, *You are so awesome and so faithful. You have made everything beautiful in Your time.*[21] I now knew that the vision to begin a ministry to heal the brokenhearted and to help teens not make the same mistakes I had made was truly from the Lord.

As I was rejoicing, I picked up my Bible and looked down to find it opened to the first chapter of Jeremiah. I did not thumb through it to look for anything in particular—I literally opened it up to the first chapter of Jeremiah. As I began to read, the words jumped off the page and into my heart:

> The word of the LORD came to me, saying, "Before I formed you in the womb I knew you, before you were born I set you apart; I appointed you as a prophet to the nations."
>
> —Jeremiah 1:4-5

I could not believe what I was reading. I stopped in awe of God and prayed, *Lord, I am so afraid. I do not know how to counsel women. I have never gone to college to be a counselor. I do not know what to say. You, Lord, are the one who is going to have to do it through me.* I was crying as I

26

spoke with the Lord (which is what I always do when I feel the Holy Spirit speaking to my heart). I looked down to read more of His Word, and I was totally amazed by the next verse I read:

> "Ah, Sovereign LORD," I said, "I do not know how to speak; I am only a child."
>
> —Jeremiah 1:6

At this point, my heart was deeply pierced by what the Holy Spirit was saying to me. It was as if God's Word were speaking to my fear. I thought, *You are so amazing, Lord!* As I continued to read, it was if He were speaking out loud and answering my heart's cry:

> But the LORD said to me, "Do not say, 'I am only a child.' You must go to everyone I send you to and say whatever I command you. Do not be afraid of them for I am with you and will rescue you," declares the LORD. Then the LORD reached out his hand and touched my mouth and said to me, "Now, I have put my words in your mouth. See, today I appoint you over nations and kingdoms to uproot and tear down, to destroy and overthrow, to build and to plant."
>
> —Jeremiah 1:7-10

I realized that is exactly what had to be done with the issue of abortion. Women need to uproot and tear down the lies of the enemy and even the lies they had told themselves. In its place, they need to build and plant the truth of God's love, grace and mercy.

My ministry began the moment God gave me these life verses in 1993. They are new to me every morning, and the Lord has continued to be faithful to me. He has sent

27

me to places I would have never imagined going. He has told me to go to everyone He sends me to see and say whatever He commands me to say. He said that I was not to be afraid, for He would rescue me, and He has been faithful to do just that. He has gone before me everywhere He has sent me. He has kept me safe.

When I first read this passage, I thought the word "nations" meant that women of different nationalities would visit me in my hometown. But God meant it *literally*. He has literally sent me to other nations to share His message of love with hurting women and teenagers around the world. He has sent me to uproot and tear down the lies of the enemy and to build and plant the truth of His love, grace and mercy.

Just a few months after the retreat in 1993, God took me to Bulgaria in Eastern Europe. I thought I was going there to teach people how to be Sunday School teachers (at least that's why I was invited on the team), but God had greater plans. The first evening we were there, we went to a little outdoor café. Our team was made up of 13 people, of whom three were pastors, and also with us that evening was an American woman who had been living in Bulgaria for six months. She had been born in Bulgaria during communist times but had somehow escaped with her mother when she was just a child. She was speaking with the pastors about the plans for our team, and I was just sitting there, looking around, amazed that I was in Eastern Europe.

I had never really been out of America before (unless you would consider going to Tijuana, Mexico, an international trip), so I was sitting there looking around and praising the Lord within my heart. It was at that moment that I heard a word spoken within my heart and mind: *Nations, nations, nations.* I had never heard God speak to me like that before. I thought, *Lord, nations? But I'm here to teach people how to be Sunday School teachers.* He again whispered within my heart and mind: *Nations, nations, nations.* So I prayed and questioned, *Lord, You want me to teach about abortion here in Bulgaria?* Again I heard: *Nations, nations, nations.* So I began to argue with the Lord: *But I don't even know if abortion is legal here in Bulgaria.* The whisper became even louder: *Nations, nations, nations.* One word, "nations," repeated over and over again within the depth of my heart and mind. It was a call from God that I could not ignore.

Miraculously, the Lord opened a door the next evening for me to teach about abortion at a church meeting. During a question and answer time, a man stood up and asked, "In Bulgaria most people have one child; some have two. My wife and I have four, and she is pregnant again. What do we do?" I wish I could share the complete story with you. It's amazing. But to make a long story short, that evening the couple decided to keep their baby. Because of this miraculous event, the Lord began a work in my heart that night for the women and teenagers of Eastern Europe. I began going, every year thereafter, on short-term trips.

As time marched on, and God expanded this ministry, many women would come up to me and say, "I've never had an abortion, but I heard about your workshop. Can I come?" Because God's Word is all-sufficient, I knew that He could help them with any issue they were experiencing. In this way, the Lord began to expand this ministry into other areas besides post-abortion, and before long the name was changed to the Truth and Hope Ministry. Soon others wanted to be trained in how to help women heal. Today, the work we do covers all kinds of issues, including abortion, abuse, rape, abandonment—you name it, we've heard it.

Over the years, I have discovered that hurt—no matter what kind of hurt it is—that is not handled in the manner God intended will turn into anger, anger over time will turn into bitterness and bitterness will turn into a bitter poison that will infect a person's whole life. This is what causes guilt, shame, fear, anxiety, bad memories, depression, rage, over-protectiveness, relationship difficulties and self-destructive behaviors. It doesn't matter what the issue was that originally caused this hurt; what matters is how the person handles the hurt deep within his or her heart.

Statistics show that each year in Bulgaria there are more abortions than live births. In 1996 alone there were more than 98,000 abortions, compared to only 72,743 live births. Yet in the midst of a sinful world, God is so good and so faithful. At one particularly low point of my ministry in Eastern Europe, when I was wondering if everything I was doing was all in vain, I saw a man whom I had not seen for five years. It was, unbelievably, the same man who had asked the question about abortion that night during my first trip to Bulgaria. I had never seen him again during all my trips. I looked at him, and playing around his legs was a five-year-old little boy!

I went up to him and asked, "Do you remember me?" He replied, "How could I ever forget you? This is my son. He is an angel sent by God. And I have two more!" I thought, *Seven kids—what have I done?!* He went onto say, "I want you to know that your ministry is not in vain. I still have the little 'feet pin' you gave me that night." (The pin he was speaking about is a little lapel pin that shows the actual size of a baby's feet at 10 weeks after conception). "In fact," he went on to say, "I teach the truth about abortion here in Bulgaria whenever I have the opportunity. I just taught at a national convention for women." I forget the exact number of women with whom he said he shared, but it was in the hundreds!

Since the original writing of this book, God has done even greater things in and through my life. In 2000, my family and I moved to Sofia, Bulgaria, to live as missionaries. It was my desire to go and make disciples. During that first year, a Bulgarian pastor asked us to open a pro-life pregnancy center in Sofia. In 1998 I had opened a center in Shumen, but the concept hadn't really worked out, so my husband and I were a little confused as to why we would open another one. Yet, after much prayer, God impressed the following Scripture our hearts:

> These are the words of him who is holy and true, who holds the key of David. What he opens no one can shut, and what he shuts no one can open. I know your deeds. See, I have placed before you an open door that no one can shut.
>
> —Revelation 3:7-8a

We knew that we were to open another center although this time it would not be a crisis pregnancy center, but a center to help women and teenagers heal. So, in July 2001, the Truth and Hope Foundation was legally registered as a non-profit foundation in Sofia, Bulgaria. Our vision for this work is to biblically teach and disciple women and teenagers so they can become all that God intends them to be. As of the writing of this revised version of this book, the Truth and Hope Foundation will soon be celebrating their tenth anniversary.

Since 2000, my family and I have lived in both the United States and Bulgaria. Since 2006, I have been on staff at Calvary Chapel Murrieta as the overseer of the women's biblical counseling ministry where, in addition to training women how to minister to those who are hurting, I biblically counsel and disciple women and teenagers. I want to teach them the truth that God has taught me and be a part of the work that God desires to do in and through their lives. God truly has the answers for our hurts to the very depths of our beings.

In 2010, we moved back to our hometown in Seal Beach, California. We found a great little church we love. Guess where they meet? The church is in the old Red Onion building, the same place (the "meat market") where my husband picked me up more than 30 years ago. Isn't God amazing! He is a God who restores and redeems.

My husband and I continue to travel back and forth between the United States and Eastern Europe, where we desire to be used by God in whatever manner He sees fit— whether that is by discipling, teaching or writing. I am ready to go to whomever God sends me and say whatever He commands me to say, as the Lord instructs us to do in Jeremiah 1:7. I cannot count—nor do I want to—the number of people whom God has touched through my life. God is the one who healed me of my most horrible sin and shame, and He is the one who works all things together for good in my life. He is the one who set me free, and I stand in awe of Him today. He is the one to whom I give the glory. He is the One who said:

> Your sins are forgiven. . . . Your faith has saved you; go in peace!
>
> —Luke 7:48,50

Jesus is the one who can do all these things in your life. So take courage beloved, and turn to the next page. It's time to learn how God wants to set you free! Join me as together we *go in peace!*

Chapter Three

A SINFUL WOMAN

Come to me,
all you who are weary and burdened,
and I will give you rest.
MATTHEW 11:28

y prayer as I write this chapter is that you will fully understand the beautiful words penned in the following verses. These verses are so fundamental to your healing that I cannot leave it to chance that you will find a Bible and read them. For this reason, I am going to include the full text here. As you begin, I want you to ask the Wonderful Counselor to prepare your heart. He loves you more than you can imagine! He knew, in His infinite wisdom, that you would need to hear the testimony of the Sinful Woman, so He preserved the following passage throughout the ages out of His love for you:

> Now one of the Pharisees invited Jesus to have dinner with him, so he went to the Pharisee's house and reclined at the table. When a woman who had lived a sinful life in that town learned that Jesus was eating at the Pharisee's house, she brought an alabaster jar of perfume, and as she stood behind him at his feet weeping, she began to wet his feet with her tears. Then she wiped them with her hair, kissed them and poured perfume on them.

When the Pharisee who had invited him saw this, he said to himself, "If this man were a prophet, he would know who is touching him and what kind of woman she is—that she is a sinner."

Jesus answered him, "Simon, I have something to tell you."

"Tell me, teacher," he said.

"Two men owed money to a certain money-lender. One owed him five hundred denarii, and the other fifty. Neither of them had the money to pay him back, so he canceled the debts of both. Now which of them will love him more?"

Simon replied, "I suppose the one who had the bigger debt canceled."

"You have judged correctly," Jesus said.

Then he turned toward the woman and said to Simon, "Do you see this woman? I came into your house. You did not give me any water for my feet, but she wet my feet with her tears and wiped them with her hair. You did not give me a kiss, but this woman, from the time I entered, has not stopped kissing my feet. You did not put oil on my head, but she has poured perfume on my feet. Therefore, I tell you, her many sins have been forgiven—for she loved much. But he who has been forgiven little loves little."

Then Jesus said to her, "Your sins are forgiven."

The other guests began to say among themselves, "Who is this who even forgives sins?"

Jesus said to the woman, "Your faith has saved you; go in peace."

—Luke 7:36-50

I know many women who have prayed and prayed and asked God to forgive them for their sin of abortion. They continually ask, over and over again, for forgiveness for the same offense. Some come to the point that they realize God has truly forgiven them, but they cannot forgive themselves.

Notice that Jesus did not say to the Sinful Woman, "Your sins are forgiven, your faith has saved you, but I want you to beat yourself up for the next 20 years." No! He said that her sins were forgiven, that her faith had saved her, and that she was free to go in peace. Likewise, Jesus, the Wonderful Counselor, Mighty God, Everlasting Father, Prince of Peace, wants you to fully understand this gift He has for you. He wants you to understand and receive His gift to go in peace.

Because these verses in Luke are the foundation of what we will be discussing, we will be examining them in depth throughout the book. We will take a look at exactly what these verses mean to you and me. But first, let me prepare the canvas of the portrait of the Sinful Woman.

We will begin by taking a look at where this story falls chronologically in the life of Jesus. Although the Gospels—Matthew, Mark, Luke and John—record the life of Christ, they are often not presented in chronological order, which means that they are not written in such a way as to follow Jesus' day-by-day life. Yet if we take the time to put the events of His ministry in daily order, it's interesting to note what took place just before He went to the Pharisee's house that evening for dinner. Pastor Warren Wiersbe, in his commentary on the book of Luke titled *Be Compassionate*, claims that just before this event, Jesus had given the gracious invitation found in Matthew 11:28-30: "Come to me, all you who are weary and burdened, and I will give you rest. Take my yoke upon you and learn from me, for I am gentle and humble in heart, and you will find rest for your souls. For my yoke is easy and my burden light."[23]

Was this woman in the crowd? Did she hear Jesus say these words? Did she long for what He had to offer—for something she had never found anywhere else in all her life? I believe that she was there and that she heard Jesus' words. I believe that when she heard Jesus describing Himself as being gentle and humble in heart, she knew she could approach Him. When He gave the invitation for all who were weary and burdened to come to Him and find rest, I think she realized within the depths of her heart that He had the answers she was seeking. How could she refuse to accept this offer to come and find the rest and peace she deeply craved—the rest and peace that she had found nowhere else?

In the same way, how can we, beloved, refuse to accept so gracious a gift?

There is something else of great importance in this passage that we must not overlook. As Wiersbe goes on to warn: "Do not confuse this woman with Mary of Bethany, and do not identify this woman with Mary Magdalene as many continue to do."[24] Mary of Bethany was the one who constantly sat at the feet of Jesus.[25] Her relationship with the Lord was extremely close. She loved Jesus deeply, and she anointed Him with ointment. But, unlike the Sinful Woman, she did not anoint Jesus' feet. Mary of Bethany anointed Jesus' head with ointment, and the ointment ran down His body and onto His feet. She then took her hair and wiped His feet.

According to Pastor Jon Courson, "This woman [the Sinful Woman] did not feel the openness to be so presumptuous [to take the liberty] as to anoint His head, but rather in humility and brokenness anointed His feet. . . . Mary anointed Jesus' head because she knew Him well. This woman [the Sinful Woman], having never yet met Jesus, couldn't have that same freedom."[26] Likewise, we must not confuse the Sinful Woman with Mary Magdalene, who was a woman Jesus set free from seven demons.[27]

So, with this background information in place, let me paint the scene for you. Earlier in the day, perhaps while she was shopping in the marketplace for her daily bread, the woman had heard Jesus speaking to a crowd. She had heard Him plead with those who were hurting to come to Him and find rest. I believe that when she heard these words, they resonated throughout her entire being and reached into the depths of her heart. Most important, she craved what Jesus had to offer. As she followed this man to see where He was going, she discovered that He was to dine that evening at the house of Simon, the Pharisee. So she began to plan how she would meet Jesus.

When the woman entered the courtyard of Simon's house, she was filled with shame, but in her heart she knew that Jesus was her only hope. Imagine what she would have been feeling at that moment. She approached Jesus from behind, afraid to come into His presence, but knowing that He was the only one who could set her free. For He is the one who fulfilled the prophecy of Isaiah:

> The Spirit of the Sovereign LORD is on me, because the LORD has anointed me to preach good news to the poor. He has sent me to bind up the broken-

hearted, to proclaim freedom for the captives and release from darkness for the prisoners, to proclaim the year of the LORD'S favor.

—Isaiah 61:1-2a

In those days it was customary to recline on a couch, at the table, with your legs tucked off to the side and back. Weeping bitterly, much like Peter wept, she began to wet the feet of Jesus with her tears. In humility and brokenness, she bowed down and began to wipe His feet with her hair. She kissed them and poured perfume on them. Look how this scene is described in the *New Living Translation*:

> Then she knelt behind him at his feet, weeping. Her tears fell on his feet, and she wiped them off with her hair. Then she *kept* kissing his feet and putting perfume on them.
>
> —Luke 7:38, emphasis added

According to Ralph Earle in *Word Meanings in the New Testament*, in the original language in which this passage was written, "The three Greek verbs [in verse 38] are the imperfect tense—kept."[28] In other words, she *kept* wiping His feet with her tears, she *kept* kissing His feet, and she *kept* anointing them with perfume.

Now, this was no ordinary bottle of perfume. This was an expensive alabaster jar made of marble that she had to break to open. Wiersbe points out that the woman's "tears, her humble attitude, and her expensive gift all spoke of a changed heart."[29] A repentant heart! But Simon did not see this. All he saw was a sinful woman at Jesus' feet. In his judgmental attitude, he thought:

> If this man were a prophet, he would know who is
> touching him and what kind of woman she is—that
> she is a sinner.
>
> —Luke 7:39

I so enjoy Jesus' answer. God always knows what we are thinking, and we cannot fool Him! "Simon," Jesus said, "I have something to tell you" (Luke 7:40). He was busted! Jesus then went on to tell him the parable of the moneylender. As Wiersbe notes, "Simon's real problem was blindness: he could not see himself, the woman, or the Lord Jesus. It was easy for him to say 'She is a sinner!' but impossible for him to say 'I am also a sinner!' Jesus proved that He was indeed a prophet by reading Simon's thoughts and revealing his needs."[30]

Let's not make the same mistake that Simon did when he believed he had no sin. There is no one who is without sin. As Paul says:

> For *all* have sinned and fall short of the glory of
> God.
>
> —Romans 3:23, emphasis added

I have discovered in my many years of discipling women that there are typically two types who come into my office for help: those who are like Simon and those who are like the Sinful Woman. Those like the Sinful Woman can be helped. Those like Simon, on the other hand, cannot be helped, because they don't *want to be helped*. They think there is nothing wrong with them and that all their problems are a result of someone else's actions. This is what Simon thought, but, as the story clearly shows, he was wrong! He was the one who went away from Jesus unchanged and hopeless.

It is my prayer that you will have a heart like the Sinful Woman. For if you have such a heart, your life will be miraculously changed when you take what you read in this book and apply it to your life. As the author of Hebrews states, God's Word has the power to change every person's heart:

> • For the word of God is full of living power. It is sharper than the sharpest knife, cutting deep into our innermost thoughts and desires. It exposes us for what we really are.
>
> Hebrews 4:12, NLT

When we get to the point where we are willing to allow God's Word to expose the ugliness found in the depths of our beings, we are ready to allow Him to clean our hearts and change our lives. That's the place where the Sinful Woman was in her life, and that is why she went away changed. In view of this, let's gaze a bit deeper into our portrait of the Sinful Woman so we can learn more from this illustration.

Look at the passage again. Do you see Simon in the background? In fact, Simon did not offer Jesus even the most common of courtesies. According to the *NIV Study Bible*, "Simon's motive may have been to entrap Jesus rather than to learn from him."[31] As Pastor Jon Courson shared, "You see Simon's mind was curious about Jesus, but his heart was not touched."[32]

Back in Jesus' time, it was customary for a servant to wash the guests' feet.[33] In fact, according to the *Illustrated Encyclopedia of Bible Facts*, "An important Hebrew custom was the washing of guests' feet, a gesture of welcome in a hot, dusty country where stony roads often made foot travel a painful experience."[34] Pastor Chuck Smith explains that it was also "customary to greet your friends with a kiss, a kiss on each cheek. This was just common. It was common to anoint with oil, to pour oil on the head of the guest, which was a symbol of the joy you hoped to share together that evening."[35]

Yet Simon offered none of these most common of courtesies. I like what Wiersbe writes: "Simon was guilty of sins of omission. He had not been a gracious host to the Lord Jesus. Everything that Simon neglected to do, the woman did—and she did it better!"[36]

Did the Sinful Woman know the Hebrew custom of anointing with oil in hope of the joy to be shared? Did she understand this symbol of joy and therefore come kneeling before Christ to have her joy restored? From what she had heard Jesus say earlier in the day, she knew that He would give her rest. But little did she know she would go away with a peace that surpasses all understanding.[37]

There is one more extremely important point that we must not overlook in the detail of our portrait—a fact that is obvious. As the woman's name implies, she was a sinner. Many Bible commentaries and Bible teachers claim she was a harlot (a prostitute), but God's Word does not tell us what kind of sin in which she was involved. In fact, I believe that God, in His infinite wisdom, left her sin a mystery. The reason? Because each one of us is a sinner. It does not matter what our sin is—whether it is the sin of abortion, adultery, prostitution, pride, anger or whatever. Each of us is just like this sinful woman. Our sins are many, and we have no right or ability to enter into Jesus' presence. It is only by His grace and His love that we can accept His invitation to come unto Him.

So don't be like Simon. On the day we die, we will all stand before the Lord. We will not be able to point or compare ourselves to another, as Simon tried to do. Just as Jesus knew Simon's thoughts and the depths of his heart, God knows *our* thoughts and the depths of *our* hearts. He knows each of us individually. It will be just you or just me standing before the Lord.

Dear beloved, there is so much to learn from the Sinful Woman! If we, like her, come to Jesus in humility and with a broken and repentant heart, He will be faithful to cleanse us from *all* unrighteousness.[38] Our only way to be restored—to be healed and receive joy and peace—is to kneel at the feet of Jesus. There is nothing that we can do or ever hope to do on our own that will bring us to a place of being restored. It is only by receiving the gift that Christ has to give that we can find peace.

It is my prayer that you will come and kneel at Jesus' feet just as the Sinful Woman did. May His invitation, "Come to me, all you who are weary and burdened" (Matthew 11:28), resonate within the depths your heart. May your heart be ready to hear His precious words:

> Your sins are forgiven. . . . Your faith has saved you; *go in peace.*
> —Luke 7:48,50, emphasis added

Chapter Four

ARE YOU RIGHT WITH GOD?

God demonstrates his own love for us in this:
While we were still sinners,
Christ died for us.
ROMANS 5:8

By now, you have probably come to the realization that this book is written to believers. However, I cannot go on just assuming that every person who picks up this book is saved and right with God. There may be some of you who are not followers of Christ, but even if you have not accepted Jesus Christ as your Lord and Savior—or perhaps you don't even believe that there could possibly be a God—*please do not put down this book.* My goal in this chapter is not to change your opinion, which I respect, but to simply share the love of Christ with you, as this is what this book is truly about. So continue to read on, and allow God's gentle Spirit to reach deep within you. He loves you more than you know.

Before I write more on that subject, I want to take a moment to discuss some basic beliefs I had when writing this book. First, as I have alluded to earlier, I want you to understand that the principles in this book are not based on human philosophy or human psychology. In fact, in many ways, it is just the opposite. Maybe you are at a point in your life (much like I was) where you no longer want to hear what modern psychology and psychotherapy have to say. Humans, in all of their wisdom, have only caused you pain and confusion. A verse that is repeated twice in Proverbs states this same viewpoint:

> There is a way that seems right to a man, but in the
> end it leads to death.
> —Proverbs 14:12; 16:25

In fact, it wasn't until hundreds of years after the Bible was written that the term "psychology" was even coined. According to Wikipedia, "The first use of the term psychology is often attributed to the German scholastic philosopher Rudolf Gockel . . . in 1590."[39] And it wasn't until the middle of the nineteenth century in England when the term "psychology" overtook "mental philosophy" in common usage.[40]

The point I am trying to make here is that psychology is a relatively new concept when compared to human history. However, all the issues with which humans struggle today—fear, anxiety, depression, rage, relationship difficulties and self-destructive behaviors including the *so-called* new issue of the day, cutting—are all found within the Bible. Best of all, because God is the creator of the universe, He is the One who understands human nature better than any human ever could. He chose to preserve His Word and address these issues within it. Therefore, if we are willing to search, we can discover the answers to all of these issues within the Bible. This is why I wrote this book—to share with you the truth that I saw become a reality in my own life when God and His Word set me free. Listen to what Jesus said:

> The Spirit of the LORD is upon Me, because He has anointed Me to preach the gospel to the poor; He has sent Me to heal the brokenhearted, to proclaim liberty to the captives and recovery of sight to the blind, to set at liberty those who are oppressed.
>
> —Luke 4:18, NKJV

God sent His Son—Jesus Christ—to set the captives free and to heal the brokenhearted. His Word enabled me to *go in peace*, and He wants to do the same for you.

I would also like you to know that I have had no training in the world's way of counseling. In fact, that was one of my biggest arguments with the Lord when He called me to this ministry. I told the Lord that I did not know how to counsel people and that I was only a woman without a degree. Again, my life verses in Jeremiah came true, because it was as if I were saying the same words that Jeremiah had spoken to the Lord when God had called him to his ministry: "Sovereign LORD . . . I do not know how to speak; I am only a child" (Jeremiah 1:6).

What I realized, however, is that God wants us to be dependent on Him in any work we do for Him. He doesn't want us to rely on our own education or our own ideas or our own strength. He wants us to rely 100 percent on Him. He wants us to turn to Him so that He can do His work through us. That is why He answered Jeremiah with these words:

> Do not say, "I am only a child." You must go to everyone I send you to and say whatever I command you. Do not be afraid of them, for I am with you and will rescue you. . . . Now, I have put my words in your mouth. See, today I appoint you over nations

47

and kingdoms to uproot and tear down, to destroy
and overthrow, to build and to plant.
—Jeremiah 1:7-10

In view of this, it is God on whom I am relying as
I write this book. It is Him whom I am asking for the
perfect words to reach your heart as I share the truth of
His love—His love, which has the power to heal even
the deepest hurt. It is Him whom I am asking to speak
through me, because I know without a doubt that just as
He called Jeremiah, He has called me to write this book of
love to you.

More important, as I work on this revised addition, I
know that this message has literally touched thousands of
women's lives around the world with the truth that God
truly does care about their deepest hurts and that His
Word truly does have the power to heal. I know this because I've watched God change many women's lives and I
hear from many readers who offer words of encouragement
to me. I thank God for their prayers and uplifting words,
which always seem to come when I am the weariest.

So I write this book to simply share with you what God
taught me as He healed my broken heart. As the apostle
Paul states:

> Praise be to the God and Father of our Lord Jesus
> Christ, the Father of compassion and the God of all
> comfort, who comforts us in all our troubles, so that
> we can comfort those in any trouble with the com-
> fort we ourselves have received from God.
> —2 Corinthians 1:3-4

It is this comfort that I received from God that I am
now able to share with you. So, dear beloved, are you at the

place where I have been? If so, are you tired of hearing all of the empty answers that human wisdom has to say? Are you ready to go to Someone who really knows the truth and can really set you free? Have you come to the place where you recognize that Jesus Christ is the only one who has the answers you seek?

In researching information on the parable of the Sinful Woman, I found a viewpoint from Jon Courson, a pastor and Bible teacher, that was so interesting I felt it was worth noting here. In a message titled "Their Couch or His Table," Courson compared the Sinful Woman to a person who went to sit on a psychiatrist's couch. He noted that even psychoanalysts today are questioning the premise and bases of psychiatry[41] and shared an article in which a study was done on people who were suffering from neurosis and depression.[42]

In this study, one group of subjects was treated for their depression and neuroses for three years, while another group was left untreated. After three years, 43 percent of the subjects who had received treatment had been cured, while 47 percent of the other group—those who had received no psychoanalysis or professional care—were cured. In other words, this study revealed that a person who did nothing to treat his or her depression or neuroses had the same or even slightly better chance of being cured than the person who had his or her condition treated by a professional therapist.[43]

I wonder what the results would have been if they had researched a third group who kneeled at the feet of Jesus, just as the Sinful Woman did. I wonder how many of those individuals would have gotten over their neuroses and depression. I know of many women who have done just that—the Sinful Woman and me, to name just two.

With this in mind, I would like to comfort you with the same comfort I myself received from God—a comfort that does not include any form of psychotherapy but is solely based on the foundation of Jesus Christ.[44] To become victorious over any issue—whether it is the issue of abortion, the issue of abuse, the issue of whatever—will depend strictly on your response to God's truth. As Jesus said in Matthew 22:37, the greatest command of all is to "love the Lord your God with all your heart, with all your soul, and with all your mind." And as God said through the prophet Jeremiah:

> You will seek me and find me when you seek me with all your heart. I will be found by you . . . and will bring you back from captivity.
> —Jeremiah 29:13-14

Perhaps you have been in the captivity of guilt, shame, fear, anxiety, depression, rage, over-protectiveness, relationship difficulties, and/or self-destructive behaviors such as alcohol, drugs, eating disorders, self-harm or even suicidal thoughts. If so, God desires to bring you back. He wants to set you free. In view of this, let's look again at the Sinful Woman. In reading her story, do you realize that she became a believer? How do I know? Because Jesus said to her, "Your faith has saved you" (Luke 7:50).

I want to take a moment to look at what it actually means to be "saved." Some of you, I know, truly are saved. Others of you assume that you are saved, perhaps because you go to church or went as a child or your mother was a follower of Christ. There are many reasons why people believe they are saved, but I would be remiss in the ministry the Christ gave me if I just assumed you had accepted Him as your Lord and Savior.

When Jesus told the Sinful Woman that her sins were forgiven, the guests at the Pharisee's house were amazed. They began to wonder among themselves, "Who is this who even forgives sins?" (Luke 7:49). The reason the guests were so amazed at Jesus' statement was because He was claiming to be God.[45] These men—the Pharisees who knew God's law well—knew that only God can forgive sins.

Jesus Christ is God in the flesh. As John says in his Gospel:

> In the beginning was the Word, and the Word was with God, and the Word was God. . . . The Word became flesh and made his dwelling among us.
> —John 1:1,14a

Because Jesus Christ is God, He has the authority to forgive sins. He had the authority to save the Sinful Woman. That is why Jesus said to her:

> Your faith has saved you, go in peace.
> —Luke 7:50

But what does it mean to be saved? Let's first address a few misconceptions. I like what Wiersbe has to say on the subject: "We must not conclude that this woman was saved by her tears and her gift. Jesus made it clear that it was her faith alone that saved her. . . . Nor should we think that lost sinners are saved by love, either God's love for them or their love for God. God loves the whole world (John 3:16), yet the whole world is not saved."[46]

51

We try to complicate matters by finding formulas and magic words or doing tricks and deeds to be saved. But the way this woman was saved was actually quite simple: she accepted God's gift.[47] God loves us so much that He gave us the choice to accept Him or reject Him. Wiersbe goes onto say, "The woman [speaking of the Sinful Woman] accepted God's free offer of salvation and expressed her love openly. Simon [on the other hand] rejected that offer and remained unforgiven. He was not only blind to himself, but he was blind to the woman and [blind] to his honored guest!"[48]

In view of this, let's look at a story of a man named Nicodemus, who had questions about salvation. As the story reveals, he was looking for true answers:

> Now there was a man of the Pharisees named Nicodemus, a member of the Jewish ruling council. He came to Jesus at night and said, "Rabbi, we know you are a teacher who has come from God. For no one could perform the miraculous signs you are doing if God were not with him."
>
> In reply Jesus declared, "I tell you the truth, no one can see the kingdom of God unless he is born again." "How can a man be born when he is old?" Nicodemus asked. "Surely he cannot enter a second time into his mother's womb to be born!"
>
> Jesus answered, "I tell you the truth, no one can enter the kingdom of God unless he is born of water and the Spirit. Flesh gives birth to flesh, but the Spirit gives birth to spirit. You should not be surprised at my saying, 'You must be born again.'"
>
> —John 3:1-7

When Nicodemus questioned how this could possibly be, Jesus went on to say:

> For God so loved the world that he gave his one and only Son, that whoever believes in him shall not perish but have eternal life. For God did not send his Son into the world to condemn the world, but to save the world through him. Whoever believes in him is not condemned, but whoever does not believe stands condemned already because he has not believed in the name of God's one and only Son.
>
> —John 3:16-18

Jesus explains very clearly in this passage what we must do to be saved: trust Him as our Lord and Savior in faith just like the Sinful Woman did. Jesus said, "You *must* be born again" (John 3:7 emphasis added), once of the flesh and once of the spirit.

Some people say that there are other ways to God and that all roads lead to heaven. Sounds great, but what does God's Word say?

> Jesus answered, "I am the way and the truth and the life. No one comes to the Father except through me."
>
> —John 14:6

Those are Jesus' words, not mine. The only way to be saved for all eternity is through Jesus Christ. He is the Way, the Truth and the Life. There is no other way.

So, what exactly is involved when we accept Jesus Christ as our Lord and Savior? What does that mean? First, we must acknowledge that *we are sinners separated from God.* Remember Paul's words in Romans 3:23: *all* have sinned and fallen short of God's glory. As my sister wrote in a letter to a friend, "In other words, we are not perfect. The only perfect man was Jesus, and that is because He was fully God and fully man.[49] When Adam, the first man, chose to disobey God in the garden, sin entered the human race.[50] We, as descendants of Adam, are born into sin.[51] Sin resides in our physical body. . . .[52] When we receive Jesus Christ as our Savior, we are 'born again'—our spirit is made alive and our relationship with God is restored.[53]"[54]

In view of this truth, we must believe that *"Jesus is God the Son, the eternal God in the flesh.* He came to this earth for the express purpose of dying for our sins.[55] From the very beginning, when Adam and Eve first sinned, a sacrifice was required. God performed the first sacrifice in that He killed an animal to provide a covering for Adam and Eve after they had eaten from the tree of the knowledge of good and evil.[56] All sacrifices were a temporary covering for sin until the perfect sacrifice—Jesus—came.[57]"[58]

It is important for us to accept and understand that *"Jesus died for our sins*; that He died for our sins past, present and future;[59] that through the covering of His blood, we now have access to God the Father, and to eternal life.[60]"[61]

In addition, it is important to acknowledge that *"Jesus rose again.* The bodily resurrection of Jesus Christ is the ultimate proof that there is life after death.[62] The apostle Paul tells us that without the resurrection, our hope is in vain.[63]"[64]

The bottom line is that all you need to do to be saved is *accept God's free gift of salvation through faith.* Faith and trust implies action. "You must agree with God that there is nothing you can ever do that will get you to heaven because Jesus did it all.[65] The Bible states over and over again that we are saved by *grace* and *not* by our good works.[66] We can be the nicest, kindest person in the world, but without Jesus we are destined for eternal separation from God."[67]

To sum up, I believe that Paul provides the best instructions for what we need to do to receive God's salvation in Romans 10:9-10:

> If you confess with your mouth, "Jesus is Lord," and believe in your heart that God raised Him from the dead, *you will be saved*. For it is with the heart that you believe and are justified, and it is with your mouth that you confess and are saved (emphasis added).

Look what the Sinful Woman did. She came into His presence and knelt at His feet, broken and in humility. With her actions, she asked Jesus to forgive her sins. Jesus was faithful, and He forgave her and saved her from the punishment her sins deserved, which would have been eternal separation from God. That is what it means to be saved. That's why He told her that her sins were forgiven and that her faith had saved her.

Dear beloved, if you have not done so already, won't you accept His wonderful gift? As Paul states:

> God demonstrates his own love for us in this: While we were still sinners, Christ died for us.
> —Romans 5:8

Today, kneel at Christ's feet in humility, brokenness and repentance. Ask for His forgiveness. Allow Him to anoint you with His joy and peace. If you are not sure what to pray, just pray something like this from your heart:

> *Dear God, I know that I am a sinner. I know that I*
> *cannot save myself. I ask Your forgiveness for the things*
> *that I have done wrong. Lord, please help me to change*
> *my sinful ways. I believe Jesus is God. I know that You,*
> *Jesus, died on the cross for me so that my sins could be*
> *washed away. I believe that You rose from the dead to*
> *live through me. I now receive You, Jesus, as my Lord*
> *and Savior. I accept Your offer of forgiveness and eternal*
> *life. Lord, I thank You for the wonderful free gift that*
> *You have given me! In Jesus' precious name, Amen.*

If you prayed that prayer, listen to what God's Word says is taking place in heaven at this moment:

> I tell you that in the same way there will be more rejoicing in heaven over one *sinner* who repents than over ninety-nine righteous persons who do not need to repent.
>
> —Luke 15:7, emphasis added

When the Sinful Woman humbly came before the Lord, kneeled at His feet in reverence and respect, and washed His feet with her tears, she was saved. She was born again. She was given new life. It is interesting to note that the italicized word "sinner" in the above verse is the same Greek word used to describe the Sinful Woman, "that she is a sinner" (Luke 7:39). Yet, at the moment we repent, no matter how bad we have been, there is rejoicing in heaven. Isn't God great?

At this point, some of you may be saying, "When I was a child I trusted Jesus as my Lord and Savior, but I have walked far away from Him." Dear beloved, God never took away His gift of salvation! He wants you to return and come home to Him. Just read the story of the Prodigal Son in Luke 15:11-31, and you will see that your heavenly

Father is waiting with open arms to receive you back to Him. You, too, can pray a prayer to rededicate your life to Him, such as the following:

> *Dear God, I know that I have walked far away from You and lived life according to my own selfish wants and desires. I was wrong. I believe that I am Your child, and I now turn from the way that I have been living. I ask You to be the Lord of my life. I ask You to live Your life through me—to help me make the right choices and carry out Your plans for my life. In Jesus' precious name. Amen.*

There is one more group of people that I must address: those who are like Nicodemus before he came to see Jesus. You are worried what others will think if they see you approach Jesus and accept His salvation. You are too afraid to come into His presence and are fighting and struggling deep within your heart. Beloved, if this describes you, do not give up. Please continue to read this book and allow God's love to wash over you as you read each page. However, you need to realize that not all of the promises of God, which you will read about in this book, will apply to you. I'm sorry to say that they only apply to those who have accepted Jesus Christ as their Lord and Savior. Until then, remember the words in Jeremiah:

> "You will seek me and find me when you seek me with all your heart. I will be found by you," declares the LORD, "and will bring you back from captivity."
>
> —Jeremiah 29:13-14

Although others may have offered you empty answers, God never will. When you get to the place in your life, much like the Sinful Woman, where you seek Him with all your heart, you will find Him. At that moment, simply pray and ask God to be your Lord and Savior, and all the promises of God will be yours! Until you are ready to make that decision, remember that God loves you more than you know and that He desires you to discover His truth. So turn the pages and continue on so that you may *go in peace.*

Chapter Five

Do Not Be Deceived

Do not be deceived,
God is not mocked;
for whatever a man sows,
that he will also reap.
Galatians 6:7, NKJV

*D*ear beloved, do not be deceived: there are consequences to sin! I believe that God preserved these inspired words, which the apostle Paul wrote to the Galatians, throughout the generations out of His love for us. He wants to warn us and to teach us so that we can make wiser choices with our lives.

The Sinful Woman realized that whatever she sowed she would also reap, and I believe by the simple fact that you are reading this book that you know this to be true as well. How do we know the Sinful Woman knew this truth? Let's gaze a little deeper into her portrait. Let me again paint the background. Look at how she approached Jesus. She went up to Him from behind—in timidity and with humility. She was filled with shame and knew that she was not worthy enough to approach Him from the front, or even to talk to Him for that matter. What could she possibly mutter to explain away her sin? She knew she had no excuse. Yet she also knew that Jesus was her only hope. Once again, Luke 7:37-38 describes the scene:

> She brought an alabaster jar of perfume, and as she stood behind him at his feet weeping, she began to wet his feet with her tears.

To bring some depth to this portrait, let's examine two of the words in this passage in more detail: "weeping" and "wet." The word translated as "weeping" means to sob or to wail aloud.[68] When the Sinful Woman stood behind Jesus and reflected on the sins she had committed, she was not crying silently (there's a completely different word in the Greek for that action) but loudly sobbing and wailing. In addition, according to Ralph Earle in *Word Meanings in the New Testament*, the word for "wet" used in this passage in its other occurrences in the New Testament is translated as "rain."[69]

Can you see the scene? This woman not crying silently but sobbing uncontrollably. She was broken and raining down tears at Jesus' feet. She knew that her life was out of control and that there were consequences to her sin. She knew that Jesus was her only hope, and she realized that her hope was in Him. As Paul writes:

> Hope does not disappoint us, because God has poured out his love into our hearts.
> —Romans 5:5a

Jesus wants to pour out His love into our hearts! All we have to do is accept His gift. Hope is a precious word that means "to cherish a desire with expectation of fulfillment."[70] Do you cherish the desire to be set free from the guilt, the shame, the hurt and the pain of having chosen to have an abortion? Do you wait in expectation for God to heal your broken heart? In John 8:31-32, Jesus promises the following:

> If you hold to my teaching, you are really my disciples. Then you will know the truth, and the truth will set you free.

This same truth applies to us today. Do you believe what Jesus is saying to you in this passage? Are you ready to hold onto His teaching like the Sinful Woman did so that you can also *go in peace*? If so, then understand that knowledge is the beginning of freedom. In view of this, we are going to look at the consequences of our sin. As we do, it is important to realize that the consequences we are suffering in our lives—the depression, the anxiety, the outbursts of anger—are all tied to what is taking place deep within our hearts.

As I mentioned previously, hurt not handled in the manner God intended will turn into anger, anger over time will turn into bitterness and bitterness will turn into a bitter poison which will infect every aspect of your whole life. This infection is what is fueling the depression, the anxiety, the outbursts of anger or any of the other consequences you are suffering in your life. However, as you look at this list of consequences, realize that there is hope. Jesus has the answer. He came to set you free, and He loves you more than you know. Remember this as you read the next few pages. Don't ever forget that *there is hope*.

During my many years of working with women, I have seen over and over again the consequences that have taken place in women's lives because of the sin that was occurring deep within their hearts. Now, before we take a look at these consequences in greater detail, I want to make one more important point. This point especially applies for those who are reading this book who are not struggling with the pain associated with an abortion. Perhaps the issue you are dealing with is something as tragic as rape or abuse. If so, it is important to realize that you were sinned against, that it was out of your control, and that what happened to you was not your fault. However, during my years of discipling, I have found that the same consequences will apply in the life of a person who was sinned against as in the life of a person whose sins were self-inflicted.

I wondered about this and asked God, *Why do I see the same consequences in people's lives when they were the ones who were sinned against? Where are those consequences coming from?* The Lord taught me through His Word that the consequences occurring in the life of a person who had been sinned against were stemming from an infection deep within that person's heart, just as was the case with the person whose sins were self-inflicted. With this in mind, it is important to ponder this point: *When did the sin first enter the heart of the person who was sinned against?*

To answer this question, we need to again remember that hurt not handled in the manner God intended will turn into anger, anger over time will turn into bitterness and bitterness will turn into a bitter poison that will infect our entire lives. Each of us must be aware of the sin that is in our *own* hearts. Even though the anger may be justifiable (such as in the case of rape or abuse), if we do not handle the anger in the manner God intended, it is sin. It is this sin in the depths of our hearts that causes the consequences. Take a look at what Paul says in Ephesians 4:26:

"In your anger do not sin:" Do not let the sun go down while you are still angry.

With this in mind, we can now take a closer look at the specific consequences of sin. The first of these is *guilt*. We see this consequence occurring in the life of King David after he committed the sin of adultery with Bathsheba. Listen to what he wrote in Psalm 38:4-10:

> My guilt has overwhelmed me like a burden too heavy to bear. My wounds fester and are loathsome because of my sinful folly. I am bowed down and brought very low; all day long I go about mourning. My back is filled with searing pain; there is no health in my body. I am feeble and utterly crushed; I groan in anguish of heart. All my longings lie open before you, O LORD; my sighing is not hidden from you. My heart pounds, my strength fails me; even the light has gone from my eyes.

The guilt from David's sin affected him physically, emotionally, mentally and spiritually. And, dearly beloved, even though we don't like to admit it, the guilt of our sin, which is hidden in our hearts, affects us as well.

I want you to take a moment and do an exercise. Get out a piece of notebook paper and fold it in half, lengthwise. Draw a line down the middle. At the top of the page on one side write the title "guilt." That's right, "GUILT." Now make a list of everything you do when you feel guilty. Because it is often difficult to remember back to the abortion that occurred in your life, think about something else that you did wrong recently, and consider what you did after you committed that sin. Most likely you did not want anyone to find out, so you began to lie to cover it up. This is one of the things people do when they feel guilty, so write "lie" on the list. Sometimes when I feel guilty I feel sick to my stomach, so you can add the word "sick" to the list also if this is something you experience as well. Continue making the list of all the things you feel (the emotions) and all the things you do (the actions) when you feel guilty.

Make a complete list, and do not forget to consider the spiritual aspect of your sin. For instance, do you stop praying when you feel guilty? Do you stop reading the Bible? Do you avoid going to church? Do you stop fellowshipping with other believers? When people sin, they often feel as if God does not love them anymore and that their actions have separated them from Him. If this is true in your situation, you can also add these items the list. Usually, you will end up with a list with about 20 to 30 items. When you are finished, fold the paper again and stick it in the back of this book. In a later chapter, we will take a look at this list again.

Let's examine the passage King David wrote in Psalm 38. Notice how the guilt from his sin affected him physically, emotionally, mentally and spiritually:

- Physically: David described that there was no health in his body and that even his strength had failed him. Likewise, it's important for us to realize that sin can cause physical consequences in our lives.

- Emotionally: David described the intense feelings he was experiencing because of his guilt. He said that his guilt had overwhelmed him like a burden that was too heavy for him to bear. In the same way, even though we try to deny the sin we have hidden deep within our hearts, it too becomes a burden too heavy for us to bear.

- Mentally: David described how his heart pounded and that all day long he went about mourning. In this case, He was describing both the anxiety and depression he was experiencing because of his sin. How many of us also struggle with anxiety and depression because of the sins that we have committed?

- Spiritually: David wrote, "Even the light has gone from my eyes" (Psalm 38:10b). His fellowship with God had been impacted because of his actions. Why do we think that we will not reap the same consequences for our sin? Remember, "Whatever a man sows, that he will also reap" (Galatians 6:7, NKJV).

If you are unsure of whether you have experienced any of these consequences associated with sin, let me explain it this way. If you have done something wrong, you may struggle with *fear* that your sin will be found out, *fear* that something bad will happen, *fear* that nothing good will ever happen . . . *fear, fear, FEAR!*

Another consequence we can experience as a result of not dealing with the deep hurt in the manner God intended is *depression*. Depression is basically a prolonged state of feeling sad,[71] and it will typically continue until we are willing to deal with the root cause of our pain. This means that until we stop denying the hurt and anger—which we have stuffed deep within our inmost being—and give that hurt and anger to God in the manner He intended, we will suffer with depression.

Many times, depression is a result of an "anniversary reaction." In other words, the person feels depressed around the same time each year when he or she first suffered the traumatic event. For example, a post-abortive woman may experience depression around the same time of year as when she had the abortion or what would have been the due date of the child.

One time, a woman shared that she had undergone an abortion five years ago to the month and claimed that she had suffered no ill effects from it. She continued talking of other subjects for a few minutes, and then she shared how she had been feeling so depressed during the last couple of weeks that her doctor had to put her on anti-depressants. However, she did not relate the depression with her abortion, because the abortion had occurred five years before. The Lord, in His love, was prompting her to deal with the root cause of her depression, but she could not admit to herself it could possibly be stemming from the abortion. This is not an isolated case—I see this continually in women's lives.

In Psalm 42:5a, the Sons of Korah wrote, "Why are you downcast, O my soul? Why so disturbed within me?" In Psalm 32:3-5, David wrote, "When I kept silent, my bones wasted away through my groaning all day long. For day and night your hand was heavy upon me; my strength was sapped as in the heat of summer." Don't these passages of Scripture accurately describe what it feels like to be depressed? But do not give up, beloved—remember that there is hope! As the prophet Isaiah states:

> Those who hope in the Lord will renew their strength.
> They will soar on wings like eagles: they will run and
> not grow weary, they will walk and not be faint.
> —Isaiah 40:31

You will *soar on wings like eagles* if you take the truth of God's Word and apply it to your life. Even though you are suffering the consequences of the sin hidden deep within your own heart, remember that knowledge *is* the beginning of freedom. When you uncover the source of your hurt and begin to deal with it in the way God intended, the process of healing will begin and you will be set free.

Another consequence we often experience as a result of not dealing with our sin is *anxiety*. Anxiety means abnormal uneasiness, worry and fear and is often accompanied by physical signs such as sweating and a rapid heartbeat.[72] Remember that David described such a feeling in Psalm 38:10 when he wrote, "My heart pounds, my strength fails me; even the light has gone from my eyes." Many of us struggle with anxiety attacks. However, when everything presses in and we feel as if we cannot breathe, we can call on the Lord, and He will be faithful to answer. Cry out as the psalmist did:

> Send forth your light and your truth, let them guide me; let them bring me to your holy mountain, to the place where you dwell. Then will I go to the altar of God, to God, my joy and my delight. I will praise you with the harp, O God, my God.
>
> —Psalm 43:3-4

Have you ever let God's light and truth shine during an anxiety attack? How fast the darkness flees when the light is revealed! Learn from King David's life. When he went to the Lord, kneeled at the altar and confessed his sin, his joy returned and he was able to praise God. The same is true with the Sinful Woman: when she went to Jesus and kneeled at His feet, He forgave her and told her to *go in peace*! So ask the Lord to reveal to you the root of the anxiety you are feeling. He will be faithful to show you.

Then do what King David and the Sinful Woman did so that you can be set free.

Another common consequence of not dealing with sin is outbursts of *anger* or *rage*. Rage means "to be furiously angry, [and/or] to continue out of control.[73] A prime example of this is the woman who is going about her day and seems happy as can be, and then all of a sudden something happens and her anger is let loose. While she is yelling and raging she may realize that the situation does not call for this kind of anger, but she cannot stop herself.

A consequence specific to the sin of abortion (which doctors never warn about) is *compensatory pregnancy*. After many women have an abortion, they miss their baby tremendously in their hearts, even if they felt relief immediately after the procedure. When I counseled at a pro-life crisis pregnancy center, I would frequently see women coming in for pregnancy tests around the due date of their aborted child. In many cases, the woman would shared that she had undergone an abortion six months before when she was three months pregnant—for a total 9 months, or full term. Although most of the women I counseled were not pregnant, they deeply desired to be. Deep down, they wished to replace their aborted baby.

However, regardless of how deep the woman's desire is to have another baby, if she is in the same situation as she was with the first abortion, it is likely that she will again choose abortion. According to one study by the Alan Guttmacher Institute, "Forty-three percent of all abortions are performed on women who have had at least one previous abortion."[74] This desire to replace the baby is one of the main reasons why we see so many women with multiple abortions. The woman desires to replace the baby and becomes pregnant, and then the fear sets in because the situation is the same. So she once again chooses abortion, and the cycle repeats over and over. This cycle can quickly spin out of control if the woman does not get help or change her lifestyle.

Many women who have undergone abortions also struggle with *terrible memories*. These memories can be triggered by something as simple as a song, a flower, a smell or even a certain time of year. It is as if the memories were always there, lurking, waiting to return when they least expected them. As Jeremiah wrote:

> I remember my affliction and my wandering, the bitterness and the gall. I well remember them, and my soul is downcast within me.
> —Lamentations 3:19-20

Such memories can cause *nightmares* and *difficulty in sleeping*. It is amazing how many women suffer from nightmares for years after an abortion. In fact, during all my years of biblical counseling, I honestly cannot think of one woman who has had an abortion who said she did not have nightmares. What is even more amazing is that these women never knew that other women suffered from the same thing. They suffered with nightmares and difficulties in sleeping for years all on their own.

Now, you may be thinking, *Come on, everyone has nightmares at some point during his or her life.* This is true, but what is interesting is that the nightmares these women experience are almost always the same. I continually see women who say their nightmare is of a small child, baby or animal that is hurt or in danger, and they cannot save it. In my case, I had nightmares about a newborn baby. I went to run errands and did not realize that I had forgotten the baby at home until I was about an hour away, and when I tried to get back home to get the baby, I could not. It was rush hour, and I was stuck. I was fearful that there would be a fire or the baby would wake up crying and I would not be there to help.

The saddest dream I ever heard a woman describe was how she held in her hands the smallest little baby she ever had seen. She was amazed at how perfectly formed this baby was. As she looked at its tiny fingers and toes, she opened her hands and the baby fell into the toilet, which had just been flushed. She could not save it.

If you are experiencing these types of nightmares, you might fear that they will never end. However, I want you to remember that there is always hope. Notice in my story that I said I *had* nightmares about this newborn baby. My nightmares occurred in the past—I don't suffer from them anymore! I have not had that dream for years. In fact, most women who hear the truth—that the enemy works the same in other women's lives—never have their nightmare again. As a case in point, when I contacted the woman who had the dream of the baby who fell into the toilet to get her permission to share her story, she had forgotten that she had ever had that dream! God is so good. There is hope for you as well. Memorize this promise from God's Word:

> I will lie down and sleep in peace, for you alone, O LORD, make me dwell in safety.
>
> —Psalm 4:8

Another consequence associated with the sin of abortion is *being overprotective* of oneself or one's children. Many women who have had an abortion are extremely overprotective and also *manipulating* and/or *controlling*. The reason? Because they never want anything or anyone to hurt them again as deeply as they have been hurt. Therefore, they will do everything within their power to protect themselves and/or their loved ones from ever being hurt again that deeply.

I struggled with this one! The joke in my house when I was getting the kids ready for bed was, "Are the doors locked?" My husband would reply, "Triple locked, and I parked the car in front of the door!" I was so afraid that something terrible would happen to my family or myself. But God is so faithful. Did you notice that I again put my testimony in the past tense? God has done such a miracle in my life that I am no longer overprotective. He gave me such a perfect peace that I was able to take my two daughters (who were ages 11 and 12 at the time) to Bulgaria by myself! We lived there for two months as we opened our first center in Shumen. I dragged them all over the country and even into Romania.

Now, I am not foolish. I realize the terrible things that could have happened to me and my daughters while we were there. But I knew that God wanted me to take them with me. He gave me this verse as comfort:

> You will keep in perfect peace him whose mind is steadfast.
>
> —Isaiah 26:3a

As long as I kept my mind on Him, I had perfect peace every moment of every day. But the moment I took my mind off of Him, all the fears would flood in. When I felt this happening, I would stop and take my eyes off the things around me and then repeat this verse to myself. When I did, God's peace would return within my heart. Oh, what an amazing time the four of us had—my two daughters, myself and my God. Dear beloved, He can perform the same miracle in your life.

Relationship difficulties are another consequence of not properly dealing with sin. This could best be described as a detachment from friends, family and other loved ones. In fact, many women sabotage good relationships and choose unhealthy or abusive ones in order to reinforce their feelings of unworthiness. If this is true of you, you need to realize that if you have accepted Jesus Christ as your Lord and Savior, you are the daughter of the King of kings, and God would *never* want His daughter to stay in an abusive relationship. In the back of this book there is an appendix titled "Profile of an Abuser." Please read it and get help!

A final consequence includes various *self-destructive behaviors*. These are any type of behaviors that have a negative affect on a person's life and can include actions such as over-eating, over-sleeping, over-cleaning, over-spending or over-anything else. They can also include the opposite, such as under-eating, under-sleeping, under-cleaning or under-anything else. Many women develop eating disorders such as anorexia and/or bulimia, while others turn to drugs and/or alcohol as a means to numb their deep heart hurt. Abuse of prescription drugs can also fall into this category. Some even go so far as to cut or harm themselves just to feel something or as a means of punishing themselves. Other self-destructive behaviors include suicidal thoughts or suicide attempts.

Did you see any of these consequences in your life? Has guilt, fear, depression, anniversary reaction, anxiety, rage, compensatory pregnancy, nightmares, overprotectiveness, manipulation, issues with control, relationship difficulties, and/or self-destructive behaviors (such as anorexia, bulimia, cutting or harming yourself, drugs, alcohol or suicidal thoughts) been a part of your life? If so, allow these consequences to bring you to the foot of the cross. Kneel at Jesus' feet, just as the Sinful Woman did. In the same way that God used the consequence of sin in her life to draw her to Him, He uses the consequences in our lives to cause us to want His help. As the psalmist wrote, "Cover their faces with shame so that men will seek your name, O LORD" (Psalm 83:6). The prophet Isaiah also stated these words:

> Surely it was for my benefit that I suffered such anguish. In your love you kept me from the pit of destruction; you have put all my sins behind your back.
>
> —Isaiah 38:17

God truly can use the consequences that we suffer as a result of our sin to draw us to Him. He wants to free us completely so that we can *go in peace* just like the Sinful Woman did after she went to Jesus. Remember the words of the apostle Paul:

> Do not be deceived, God is not mocked; for whatever a man sows, that he will also reap. For he who sows to his flesh will of the flesh reap corruption, but he who sows to the Spirit will of the Spirit reap everlasting life.
>
> —Galatians 6:7-8, NKJV

73

Do not be deceived any longer. Do not continue to sow to the sinful nature, the flesh, by holding on to the hurt, pain and anger. Instead, sow to the Spirit, and you will be a new woman—guaranteed! The consequences will stop if you grab hold of the promises of God's Word and apply them to your life. I can truly say that *I suffer no more*, and the same can be true in your life. So continue to turn the pages to learn how to give the hurt, the pain, and the anger to Jesus once and for all so that you too can *go in peace!*

Chapter Six

Take Every Thought Captive

And we take captive
every thought
to make it obedient to Christ.
2 Corinthians 10:5

*I*n the last chapter, we saw how God's Word shows us that there are always consequences to our sin. What's more, when our sin is horrendous, the consequences will be greater and we will have more difficulty coping with them. Of course, none of us like consequences, so we will always try to find ways of not having to deal with them. Psychologists will often describe these methods as "defense mechanisms," and they can include suppression, rationalization, denial and reaction formation. Those who embrace psychological teachings will tell you that once you recognize that you are using these defense mechanisms, they can help you move on with your life.

However, in studying God's Word over the years and seeking Him for guidance on this issue, He clearly showed me that this is just another form of sin—plain and simple sin—that goes all the way back to the Garden of Eden. Dear beloved, I do not want to lead you astray by giving you any false teaching. As Paul teaches:

> See to it that no one takes you captive through hollow and deceptive philosophy, which depends on human traditions and the basic principles of this world rather than on Christ.
>
> —Colossians 2:8

You must know the truth if you are to be completely healed by God's love, grace and mercy. It is time to rely on Christ, just as the Sinful Woman did, so that you can be set free. For the truth is that God's Word teaches us that we are to take every thought captive:

> And we take captive every thought to make it obedient to Christ.
>
> —1 Corinthians 10:5

God does not want us to hold on to the hurt any longer. He wants us to deal with the painful things in our past so we can move forward. The consequences we discussed in the previous chapter will continue to go on for years until we are ready to take every thought captive and make it obedient to Christ. Jesus came to set us free, and freedom can be found in His Word. So let's go back to the Garden of Eden to see where the root of sin began. Although the entire story of Adam and Eve can be found in Genesis 2–3, we will look at just a few of the verses that illuminate specific principles.

> The LORD God took the man and put him in the Garden of Eden to work it and take care of it. And the LORD God commanded the man, "You are free to eat from any tree in the garden; but you must not eat from the tree of the knowledge of good and evil, for when you eat of it you will surely die."
>
> —Genesis 2:15-17

76

Now, there was no suitable helper for Adam, so God created Eve out of Adam's rib. I so enjoy true love stories, and here we find the first wedding in history:

> He [God, the Father] brought her to the man. The man said, "This is now bone of my bones and flesh of my flesh; she shall be called 'woman,' for she was taken out of man." For this reason a man will leave his father and mother and be united to his wife, and they will become one flesh. The man and his wife were both naked, and they felt no shame.
>
> —Genesis 2:22-25

Adam and Eve had no shame because at this point there was no sin in their lives. In the same way, when we are in God's perfect will, there is no guilt and no shame in our lives. However, the moment we step out of His will, we will experience both guilt and shame and—even worse— many other consequences.

The villain in this love story was the crafty serpent, who said to Eve, "Did God really say, 'You must not eat from any tree in the garden?'" (Genesis 3:1). The enemy always takes the truth of God's Word and twists it just enough to cause us to doubt. (In a moment, we will discuss how these often appear as defense mechanisms.)

The drama continues. Eve ate the forbidden fruit and then gave some to her husband, Adam, who also ate the fruit, even though he knew it was forbidden. Watch what happens the moment they chose to do that which they knew they were not to do:

> Then the eyes of both of them were opened, and they realized they were naked; so they sewed fig leaves together and made coverings for themselves. Then

77

> the man and his wife heard the sound of the LORD
> God as he was walking in the garden in the cool of
> the day, and they hid from the LORD God among
> the trees of the garden. But the LORD God called
> to the man, "Where are you?" He answered, "I heard
> you in the garden, and I was afraid because I was
> naked; so I hid.
>
> —Genesis 3:7-10

Adam and Eve's sin caused them to feel shame and they "realized they were naked" (Genesis 3:7b). Then, to cover their sin, they "sewed fig leaves together and made coverings for themselves" (Genesis 3:7c). They immediately reaped the consequences of the sin they had sown. Adam told God, "I was afraid because I was naked; so I hid" (Genesis 3:10b). Do you see the consequences of guilt, fear and avoidance in what Adam described? Because Adam was afraid to deal with the consequences of his sin, he tried to avoid the truth and hide from God.

But this story is not yet over. There is no happy ending for this love story in the Garden of Eden—at least not for a few thousand years. As you read the following passage, take a moment to ask God to reveal to you any areas of your life where you may be saying the same types of things that Adam and Eve said:

> And [God] said, "Who told you that you were na-
> ked? Have you eaten from the tree that I command-
> ed you not to eat from?"
> The man said, "The woman you put here with me—
> she gave me some fruit from the tree, and I ate it."
> Then the LORD God said to the woman, "What is
> this you have done?" The woman said, "The serpent
> deceived me, and I ate."
>
> —Genesis 3:11-13

Did you see how both Adam and Eve tried to place the blame on anyone but themselves? They both denied responsibility for their actions and tried to hide from the consequences. But God knew that they needed to deal with their sin immediately. In the same way, dear beloved, we must not try to hide from the consequences of our sin by pushing away our guilty thoughts, or by being afraid of dealing with the hurtful issues, or by avoiding the truth of our sin buried deep within our hearts. The longer we try to deny feelings or actions associated with issues such as abortion, the longer we will reap the consequences of our sin.

This type of behavior is known as *suppression* and, like all other defense mechanisms, is a sin—plain and simple. The word "suppression" means the "conscious exclusion of unacceptable desires, thoughts, or memories from the mind."[75] In other words, suppression is just a fancy word for *covering* our guilt, shame and nakedness. Every time we try to *suppress* our hurt, pain and anger by pushing it deep within our inmost being, or we try to *cover* the truth of just how much we are hurt or angry we are over a situation, "we lie and do not live by the truth . . . we deceive ourselves and the truth is not in us" (1 John 1:6b,8). Thus, we are living in sin. It is this sin of covering up the truth in the depths of our hearts that causes all of the negative consequences we saw in the last chapter. It's exactly what Adam and Eve tried to do.

> Then the eyes of both of them were opened, and they realized they were naked; so they sewed fig leaves together and made *coverings* for themselves.
> —Genesis 3:7, emphasis added

The next defense mechanism that Adam and Eve used was *rationalization*. "Rationalization" means "to provide

79

plausible but untrue reasons for [our] conduct."[76] This is just a politically correct word for *blame*. Look once again at what Adam and Eve said:

> The man said, "The woman you put here with me—
> she gave me some fruit from the tree, and I ate it" . . .
> The woman said, "The serpent deceived me, and I
> ate."
>
> —Genesis 3:12-13

Adam blamed both the woman and God for his actions, while Eve rationalized that the serpent had deceived her. Every time we provide plausible but untrue reasons for our conduct, it is the same as blaming a situation or a person for our own actions. This is a sin to God. It is this sin that causes depression, anxiety, outbursts of anger and many other negative consequences in our lives.

Let me share an example from my own life. My plausible but untrue reasons for choosing abortion were because I was too young to have a baby, because I couldn't afford to raise it, and because I rationalized that it was just a fetal tissue mass and not a true living being. In reality, the truth was that I was afraid to have the baby and was only thinking of myself. I was selfish. It is time to stop rationalizing and blaming our situation on others and take responsibility for our own actions.

Denial is another defense mechanism. *The Collins English Dictionary* defines "denial" as follows: "A psychological process by which painful truths are not admitted into an individual's consciousness."[77] Another definition for "denial" is a "refusal to admit the truth or reality of our behavior and consequence on ourselves and others."[78] In other words, denial is just a six-letter word for *hide*. When we choose to not admit the truth to ourselves, we are hiding, just as Adam and Eve did. They hid from God and the truth.

> Then the man and his wife heard the sound of the LORD God as he was walking in the garden in the cool of the day, and they *hid* from the LORD God among the trees of the garden.
> —Genesis 3:8, emphasis added

Like Adam and Eve, we are also good at hiding. We don't want to admit that our choices have hurt us or that the hurt, pain and anger deep within our hearts have brought consequences to ourselves and/or others. We hide from God and the truth and refuse to admit the truth to ourselves or accept responsibility for our actions. This is a sin in God's eyes, and it also causes many of the negative consequences we discussed in the last chapter.

Finally, notice in the story of Adam and Eve that they employed the defense mechanism of *reaction formation*. This particular defense mechanism is a bit harder to describe, but basically it is just an important-sounding word for being *afraid*. A definition of "reaction formation" is as follows: "If two motives are antithetical [the direct opposite] to each other, the system [meaning the person] may respond by doing all it can to build up the strength of one [motive], usually the more acceptable one, so that the other motive is safely contained."[79]

Perhaps the best way to explain this *fear* or reaction formation in layman's terms is by giving an example. A woman who has had an abortion may become either strongly pro-choice or strongly pro-life. For the woman who becomes strongly pro-choice, it is safer for her to believe this point of view and try to convince others to have an abortion than it is to admit the truth. By doing so, she can better justify her own decision to abort her child. Admitting that abortion is wrong hurts too much, and she is afraid of how she may react emotionally if she admits this to herself.

I know this as a fact! Even as a follower of Christ, I believed that abortion was a woman's choice, because to believe otherwise hurt too much. To change my point of view, I would have had to admit that what I had done was wrong and that I was responsible for the death of my two children. So, by choosing to believe the pro-choice lies, I safely contained the other motive, just as the definition of reaction formation states. Therefore, I did everything I could to build up the strength of one point of view (being pro-choice) so I would not have to deal with the other point of view (that abortion is wrong). I did this all out of fear of what I would do with my emotions if I admitted the truth that abortion was wrong. I was just like Adam, who told God, "I was *afraid* because I was naked [that the truth in the depth of my heart would be revealed]; so I hid (Genesis 3:10, emphasis added).

On the other hand, reaction formation (or fear) can cause many post-abortive women who have not received full healing to become strongly pro-life. This woman adopts this position to atone for the life of her baby. She comes to believe that if she can save *just one* baby from being aborted or save *just one* woman from going through what she went through, she will be set free from her hurt and pain. Her motive is to build up the strength of one point of view (being pro-life to atone for her sin) so she will not have to deal with the other point of view (that she deserves punishment for her sin). This is not to say that her thinking is correct—God's Word teaches that all we have to do is confess our sins and He is faithful to forgive us.[80] At that moment, we are set free from the punishment we deserve. I am just pointing out the motivating factor—the underlying fear—that is within the depths of her heart.

Unfortunately, if this woman has not been fully healed by the Lord, she can do more harm than good. Why? Because if another woman is considering abortion, she may come on too strongly to the woman she is counseling and push or demand that woman to keep the child. If the woman she is counseling goes ahead with the abortion, she may blame herself for the child's death. She will think, *I did not say enough to convince this woman to keep her child. I should have said this. I should have done that.* Deep within her heart, she will feel as if she failed.

If this unhealed post-abortive woman is then given another opportunity to talk to a different woman who is considering abortion, she will come on even stronger due to her past failure for atonement. (It is because of this very issue that a local crisis pregnancy center in my town requires all post-abortive women who desire to be counselors to attend a post-abortion workshop, even if that woman *claims* to have been healed over this issue in her life.) The truth is that this woman is living in fear, and she will never be able to atone for her child. It is only by accepting the gift that Jesus offers that she will be able to *go in peace.*

Let me step away from the issue of abortion for a moment and share a different example to hopefully give you a clearer picture of reaction formation. Consider a woman in an abusive relationship. Because of her fear or insecurity, she will make excuses or cover up for an abuser instead of admitting that there is a problem. Remember the definition of reaction formation: If two motives are opposite each other, a person will respond by doing everything he or she can to build up the strength of one particular motive—the one most acceptable to that person—so that he or she can contain the other motive. In this case, it is safer for the woman to build up the strength of the motive that there is no problem—that he is not an abuser—than it is for her to deal with her own fear and insecurity. Many times, the woman will even allow the abuse to continue to herself and/or her children to keep this fear and insecurity safely contained. Do you see how reaction formation is just a fancy word for being afraid?

So, within this issue of reaction formation and fear, where does the sin enter? Of course, there will be issues in our lives that will cause us fear and insecurity, and these *feelings* are not sin—God created us to have emotions. However, sin enters into the picture when we choose to make decisions *based* on our fear and insecurity instead of turning to God, trusting Him and putting His Word into action in our lives. Thus, many times we react out of fear instead of truth. When we do this, it is sin.

The enemy will take the truth and twist it. He will change the wording of something basic to make it more vague and confusing. He doesn't want us to see what is taking place in the depths of our own hearts. He doesn't want us to realize that *suppression* is covering up our sin, or that *rationalization* is just another word for blaming, or that *denial* is simply hiding from the truth, or that *reac-*

84

tion formation is just a fine-sounding word for fear. This is because when we get down to the nitty-gritty in all of this, we realize that covering, blaming, hiding and being afraid is simply not dealing with the truth, and that not dealing with the truth is sin.

The enemy is afraid that if we realize we are sinning in this area, we might deal with our sin and move on in our lives. He doesn't want us to become all that God intends for us to be, so he will seek to keep us in bondage to our sin. In view of all this, God wants us to be honest with ourselves. He wants us to run to Him with our fears and insecurities. He desires truth in our innermost being—not lies, denial and deception. As King David declared:

> Behold, You desire truth in the innermost being, and in the hidden part You *will* make me know wisdom.
> —Psalm 51:6, NASB, emphasis added

It is painful to deal with the hurt caused by abortion that we have stuffed deep within our innermost beings. We are so good at pushing these thoughts away and suppressing them to cover them up. We are excellent at rationalizing and blaming others or a situation for our decision to have an abortion. We have become proficient at denying and hiding the truth that the abortion affects us in any way today. We even use reaction formation out of fear and claim all kinds of half-truths as a means of not having to deal with what is really taking place deep within our inmost beings. We need to learn from Charles Spurgeon, who said, "Rest assured, dear hearer, that you will never attain to a well grounded freedom by trying to make your sins appear little."[81]

So, what do we do? Where do we go from here? David again provides some guidance for us:

> Listen to my prayer, O God, do not ignore my plea; hear me and answer me. My thoughts trouble me and I am distraught.
>
> —Psalm 55:1-2

God truly wants us to take every thought captive. He wants us to stop pushing away, stuffing or covering the hurt, pain and anger we are feeling. If we take our hurtful and angry thoughts captive and bring them to the foot of the cross, the moment they pop into our minds, we can deal with them in the manner God intended. If we do this, we will no longer be suppressing (covering), rationalizing (blaming), denying (hiding) or using reaction formation (fearing). In other words, we will no longer be sinning! We will then be able to move on with our lives and become the person that God always intended us to be.

In Psalm 139:13a, David says, "For you [God] created my inmost being." When I shared my testimony earlier in the book, I described how I felt as if I had a hole in my heart and that I had tried to fill up that hole in all the wrong ways. I believe that God created our inmost being as a hole in the depths of our heart that can only be filled by a *right relationship* with Him. This means more than just having a saved relationship—although that is important, for we must be saved to get to heaven. Rather, what I mean by a *right relationship* is that God truly wants to be our everything. He wants to meet with us daily and have an intimate relationship with us. I believe that it is in the depths of our heart, in our innermost being, where God meets with us.

86

We have both conscious[82] thoughts (thoughts we are aware of at a specific moment) and subconscious[83] thoughts (thoughts that we are not aware of consciously). In a sense, our subconscious thoughts are hidden. We cannot consciously keep every thought we have in the part of our mind where we are aware of them continually—if we did, we would be on overload. Therefore, we store many of our thoughts in our subconscious mind.

Now, the words "conscious" and "subconscious" are relatively new to our society. The word "conscious" first appeared in the 1600s,[84] while the word "subconscious" first appeared in the 1800s.[85] In view of this, the Bible does not use the word "subconscious," but this does refer to our inmost part. Look at the following verse that is repeated twice in God's Word:

> The words of a gossip are like choice morsels; they go down to a man's inmost parts.
> —Proverbs 18:8; 26:22

This describes an interesting truth. When someone says or does something to hurt us deeply, we can't stop thinking about it. We keep replaying the words or hurtful acts over and over again in our heads. Then, when we can't stand it any longer, we stuff that hurt deep within our hearts, deep within our inmost beings. It is as if we had swallowed it. And once we have swallowed it, we think it is gone away. We think that we are over the hurt, and so we *try* to move on with our lives.

The scary part of all this is that when we continue to stuff the hurt, pain, excuses and blame deep within our inmost being, it becomes infected and changes form. Remember, hurt not handled in the way God intended will turn into anger, anger over time will turn into bitterness and bitterness will turn into a bitter poison that will infect our entire lives. Remember Paul's words in Ephesians 4:26: "'In your anger do not sin': Do not let the sun go down while you are still angry." Instead, God wants us to take every thought captive. When hurtful and painful thoughts come to our conscious minds, He wants us to bring them to the surface and address them so we can be healed. Remember these words in Job 13:9:

> Would it turn out well if He examined you? Could you deceive Him as you might deceive men?

We cannot deceive God. He wants us to deal with these thoughts. But how do we do that? We do it in the same way the Sinful Woman did. She took all of her hurts and pain to Jesus. She took all of her excuses and knelt at His feet. In the same way, we are to take everything that is sinful in our lives to the foot of the cross. We are to kneel at Jesus' feet and leave them there forever!

> For a man's ways are in full view of the Lord, and He examines all his paths. The evil deeds of a wicked man ensnare him; the cord of his sin holds him fast. He will die for lack of discipline, led astray by his own great folly.
>
> —Proverbs 5:21-23

The Lord examines all of our thoughts, and I believe that when we continue to cover the hurt or deny that we have any hurt, pain or sin in the depths of our heart, He will try to get us to look at these things. He does so through dreams (nightmares), disturbing thoughts, anxiety, depression, outbursts of anger and overprotectiveness, to name

88

just a few means. The Lord wants to set us free. He wants to unshackle the cord of sin that holds us fast. In His love, He tries to get us to deal with the hurt and the pain because He is a jealous God and does not want to share the place He created within us—our innermost being—with anyone or anything else.

If there is sin in the depths of our innermost being, God will not come to meet with us. Listen to what the prophet Isaiah warned:

> Surely the arm of the LORD is not too short to save, nor his ear too dull to hear. But your iniquities have separated you from your God; your sins have hidden his face from you, so that he will not hear.
> —Isaiah 59:1-2

Previously, I mentioned a woman whom Kathie and I had counseled until the early morning hours at our church's annual women's retreat. When I telephoned her to get permission to include her testimony in this book, she said, "Don't you want to include the part about the nightmare?" That night when we had finally gone to sleep, this woman awoke in terror, screaming at the top of her lungs. Kathie and I realized that the nightmare she was having was a result of what we had talked about earlier in the evening. It was a repeated nightmare that she had been experiencing for many years. This woman described the dream as being a crushing feeling of overwhelming terror, as if she were trapped and unable to move.

That evening, the Lord, in His love, revealed to this woman that the nightmare was His way of showing her that the abortions still affected her. He wanted her to stop hiding from the truth. He wanted her to stop claiming that the decision she had made to have an abortion was not affecting her in any way. It was time for her to admit the truth and give the hurt, the pain and all the sin to Him. As a result of dealing with the truth, she no longer has these nightmares.

> Stripes that wound scour away evil, and strokes reach the innermost parts.
> —Proverbs 20:30, NASB

Dear beloved, the Lord wants to reach into the innermost parts of our being. He wants us to give Him permission to unlock the hidden chambers of our hearts. We can do so without fear, for God loves us and will be with us. He only wants the absolute best for us, and we can trust Him. He is gentle and humble, and His burden is light.

Let's look once again at the Sinful Woman to see just how we can go about giving our hurts over to Jesus. It is a moment-by-moment choice we make as the Lord gently and humbly reveals to us the depth of our hurts. I like to call these moment-by-moment decisions *faith choices* or *flesh choices*. A faith choice is a decision to give our hurts completely to the Lord, whereas a flesh choice is a decision to stuff our pain back down into our innermost being. I believe that it is best to make a faith choice, because it is only by making these types of decisions that we will be set free.

The Sinful Woman, by faith, made a choice to go to Jesus. First, she confessed her sin through her action of approaching Christ. Second, she repented of her sin by crying and weeping at His feet. She gave the sin in the depths of her heart to Jesus by laying down the hurt and pain at the foot of the cross. Third, she did something important— something we must never forget to do—she filled her heart with His Word. I am sure that she never forgot Jesus' instructions to "go in peace" (Luke 7:50b).

When we follow her example and confess, repent and fill our hearts with God's truth and the promises we memorize in His Word, there will be no weapons that can prosper against us in our lives. As the apostle Paul writes:

> The weapons we fight with are not the weapons of the world. On the contrary, they have divine power to demolish strongholds. We demolish arguments and every pretension that sets itself up against the knowledge of God and we take captive every thought to make it obedient to Christ.
> —2 Corinthians 10:4-5

In view of this, it's time to stop arguing and pretending that there is *no* sin within our hearts. It's time to fight the enemy with the truth of God's Word by taking every hurtful thought captive. We must pick up the spiritual weapons of warfare every time we pray and give the hurtful issues in our lives over to God. We must choose to hide God's Word within the depths of our hearts instead of our hurt and pain. When we do this, we can and will demolish the strongholds.

This is why the Sinful Woman could *go in peace* after her encounter with Christ. She took the hurtful thoughts captive and made them obedient to Christ. Imagine how hard it must have been for her to step into His presence. But, dear beloved, until we follow her example and stop covering, blaming, hiding and being afraid, we will never get over the consequences of our sin.

Do you want to be rid of all the negatives consequences of sin in your life? Then kneel at Jesus' feet today, and continue to turn the pages so that you may *go in peace!*

Chapter Seven

DEPRIVED OF PEACE

I have been deprived of peace. . . .
I remember my affliction and my wandering,
the bitterness and the gall.
I well remember them,
and my soul is downcast within me.
LAMENTATIONS 3:17A,19-20

𝒞an you relate with Jeremiah's words in this passage? Have you ever been deprived of peace?
Many women who have had an abortion cry out to God.
Over and over again, they ask God to forgive them for their terrible sin, yet they still do not feel free—their peace has not been restored. Why is that? Have you ever pondered the reason why you are deprived of peace?

Let me suggest to you that there are other sins wrapped up in the abortion package. In fact, Jesus said of the Sinful Woman, "I tell you, her *many sins* have been forgiven" (Luke 7:47, emphasis added). As sinful women, we also have many sins that require forgiveness. In the last chapter, we read this passage in Isaiah:

> Surely the arm of the LORD is not too short to save,
> nor his ear too dull to hear. But your iniquities have
> separated you from your God; your sins have hidden
> his face from you, so that he will not hear.
> —Isaiah 59:1-2

93

Our sin *separates us from God*. When we have unconfessed sin in our lives, it is as if a wall has been built between God and ourselves. God did not build the wall—we
did—and we are the ones who must tear it down. So, what
other sins do we have that are wrapped up in the abortion package? To uncover these, I am going to share with
you some tough verses. Remember that it is only when we
come to truth in our lives and see it for what it is that we
can be set free. We will begin with the following passage
in Isaiah:

> For your hands are stained with blood, your fin-
> gers with guilt. Your lips have spoken lies, and your
> tongue mutters wicked things. No one calls for jus-
> tice; no one pleads his case with integrity. They rely
> on empty arguments and speak lies. . . . We look for
> justice, but find none; for deliverance, but it is far
> away.
> —Isaiah 59:3-4,11b

Perhaps I can illuminate what Isaiah is saying here by
adding the following insights. "For your hands are stained
with blood, your fingers with guilt" refers to our sinful actions. "Your lips have spoken lies, and your tongue mutters
wicked things" refers to our sinful words. "No one calls
for justice; no one pleads his case with integrity" refers to
our replaying the events in our minds, and sometimes even
changing the facts of what really happened. "They rely on
empty arguments and speak lies" refers to our sin as we try
to deceive ourselves into believing our own lies and making ourselves appear good.

It is true; the sin of abortion has stained our hands with
blood and our fingers with guilt. But what lies have we spo-

94

ken? What case did we not plead with integrity? Dear beloved, is there someone, maybe in your family, with whom you are still angry? Someone who perhaps talked you into the abortion or forced you to go through with it? Perhaps it was the baby's father, or your own mother? For those who are reading this book and abortion is not an issue, with whom are you angry? Is it your father, your mother, your sister, your brother, your boyfriend, your husband or your abuser?

Again and again I see women who have hurt and anger locked and guarded tight in a box within their innermost being. The hurt and anger is often locked up so tight that they don't even realize it is there. Perhaps this person is someone in our family whom we love deeply, and we don't even realize that the feelings are there. Dear beloved, it is only when we are able to take that anger out of the box and place it at Jesus' feet—like the Sinful Woman did—that we will be set free. Then we will know a peace that surpasses all understanding.

Let me explain what I mean about this anger. It's as if we have taken our case to court, but the case was not pleaded with integrity. As Jon Courson states:

> [This is] not a legal court on earth, nor an eternal court in heaven. Your sins, my sins were forgiven, praise the Lord; never more to be remembered by Him. So what court? It is the court that takes place in your *own* mind. You build a case daily, you bring in new witnesses, you gather more evidence, you build this case against him, against her, against them. You build this case; it's in your mind. . . . It grows bigger. You hold the court case over and over

> and over again [as you replay the event in your mind]
> and here's the kicker—every time you hold court in
> your mind, *you win*! The other guy *never* wins. *You
> always win!* You always conclusively conclude, I'm
> right, they're wrong."[86]

The sad part is that even though in our mind we have
won, we are still the ones in prison. Our empty arguments
offer us no justice, and our pleadings have no merit. The
walls we built in our relationships are made of prison bars
and shackles, including the wall we built between ourselves
and God. We can never set our hearts free by trying to
deny our sins—even the sin of anger hidden in the depths
of our being that we think no one can see. God sees all! As
Proverbs 20:27 states:

> The lamp of the LORD searches the spirit of a man;
> it searches out his inmost begin.

God sees all that is within our hearts—our anger toward our mother, our father, our sister, our brother, our
boyfriend or husband, the doctor, the nurse, the govern-
ment for making it legal, or whomever else (and yes, we
can even be angry at God) deprives us of peace. This anger
will continue to deprive us until we give it all to Jesus, just
like the Sinful Woman did. This is true even if we were the
ones sinned against.

Maybe abortion is not an issue in your life. Perhaps
you were abused or raped. Perhaps you were hurt deeply
by someone or something that was completely out of your
control. The important point to understand is that the hurt
and anger locked within your innermost being is something over which you *do* have control. You have a choice!
You can choose to give the anger to God so that you will

know and understand that you are forgiven and set free, or you can choose to hold onto the anger and be deprived of peace. But I must warn you: If you choose to hold on to the anger, it will cause all the consequences we talked about previously to continue in your life.

Let me share a story with you. In one of our post-abortion workshops, there was a woman who continued to blame everyone around her for pushing her toward having the abortion. No one stood by her side and told her to keep the baby. She cried and shared how she wanted her baby, but everyone was urging her to make the decision to have the abortion. She felt out of control and hopeless. We taught her that it was time to stop blaming others for her decision.

I know how much that hurts, but blaming is an empty argument. Remember, we can no longer offer "empty arguments and speak lies" (Isaiah 59:4). Each one of us made the ultimate decision to have the abortion. In almost every case, no one drugged us or tied us to the table. We walked into the abortion clinic of our own will and went through with the procedure. In view of this truth, we must take responsibility for our actions. We can no longer place the blame on another, as Adam and Eve tried to do. After we accept what we did, we must then take our hurt and anger toward others to the feet of Jesus, just as the Sinful Woman did. If we don't, we will continue to hold on to the other sins that are wrapped up in the abortion package.

The woman in the workshop made the decision to take these hurts and her anger to the foot of the cross. About two weeks after the workshop, she came to see me. She was so excited. She shared how she had found letters that

97

she had written to the father of the baby and how in those letters *she* had been the one who wanted the abortion. She had held court in her mind for all these years. As she brought in new evidence and new witnesses to support her court case she had always won, but she was still serving a prison sentence. It wasn't until she unlocked the chamber that held the hurts and anger that the prison doors were thrown open and she was set free.

Dear beloved, my prayer is that you would take a moment to sit at Jesus' feet and ask Him to help you unlock the hidden hurts and the hidden anger in your heart. Remember that He is gentle and humble in heart. He is the Prince of Peace, and He wants to unshackle the chains that hold you fast. He loves you so much that He gives you a free will. It's your choice to make the decision to be honest with yourself and admit the truth. You must decide to trust in God and let go of the hurt, the pain and the anger. You have to choose to give up your rights and follow Jesus. When you do, He will meet you there and, best yet, He will set your free!

For this reason, let's look at the issue of anger and how it keeps us in bondage. Remember that in Ephesians 4:26-27, the apostle Paul tells us not to sin in our anger:

> Do not let the sun go down while you are still angry,
> and do not give the devil a foothold.

Notice that Paul does not say that we cannot be angry; rather, he says that we must *not sin* in our anger. God has created us with emotions, but He also knows that holding on to anger over a period of time will hurt us and cause problems.

Being angry over time will cause an infection deep within our hearts—deep within our inmost beings—that will cause all the consequences we learned about previously. Worst yet, this infection of sin in our hearts *will* separate us from Him. As we have stated, God is a jealous God and wants nothing to separate us from the love He has for us. In view of this, we are called to deal with our anger correctly—the same day, before the sun goes down. In fact, we are to search our hearts each night before we go to sleep. Look at what the psalmist wrote:

> In your anger do not sin; when you are on your beds, search your hearts and be silent. Offer right sacrifices and trust in the LORD.
>
> —Psalm 4:4-5

Let me explain what happens if we choose *not* to follow God's Word concerning our hurt, pain and anger. Each night that we go to sleep and do not deal with our hurt and anger in the manner God intended, we will stuff it into our inmost beings where it will begin to fester. Many times, we are hurt and angry toward someone we have to be around all the time, but because we care for him or her (or have to live with that person or work with him or her), we stuff down the hurt so we can cope and move on with our lives. We choose not to deal with the problem, and so it festers deep inside and becomes infected. Later, when we least expect it, the consequence of our sin—our sin of stuffing hurt, pain and anger—suddenly manifests itself in an outburst of anger. Unfortunately, these outbursts of anger are not usually directed toward the person with whom we are angry, but at someone we love deeply (usually our children or our husbands).

I am sorry to say that this was a difficult area in my life. The anger that I had kept hidden under lock and key for years began to manifest itself toward my children. Years later, when I least expected it, I would find myself shouting uncontrollably at my precious children over something as unimportant as a spilt glass of milk. While I knew at the time that I was overreacting, I could not stop myself. I had sinned in my anger by keeping it hidden and later using it against those I loved. But, praise the Lord, He brought me to the place where I realized there was something I needed to give to Him. He wanted to carry my burden. He knew that it was too heavy for me to bear.

Many times, we are deprived of peace because of hurtful and angry thoughts that we have never taken captive. But there is good news: God has made a way for us to be set free from the consequences of our sin. All we have to do is take every thought captive and make it obedient to Christ. This means *every* thought—all the hurt, all the pain, and all the anger—and being totally honest with ourselves. We are to take all of this captive and make it obedient to Christ.

One of the definitions of "captive" is "to capture one's mind."[87] It is as if we capture all of the hurtful and angry thoughts in our minds one last time by honestly admitting to ourselves that those thoughts were there. Then we make them obedient to Christ by confessing them to Him. The word "obedient" means to be submissive to authority. So, once we take the hurtful thoughts captive by admitting that they are there, we give them to Jesus by confessing them. We place them at His feet, just like the Sinful

Woman did, and leave them there forever! When we do this, we are being submissive and obedient to the authority of Christ.

One time, a woman said to me, "Giving my anger to the Lord is not tangible." What she was saying was that she could not touch or see the anger as she gave it to the Lord. It was just in her imagination, and therefore it seemed unreal. What she said to me was true. In fact, the definition of "tangible" is "able to be touched."[88] Something that is not tangible is unable to be touched. I think many women struggle with this fact when they are told to take the hurt, pain and anger captive and make it obedient to Christ. In view of this, I want to teach you a practical way to touch and see your anger. I want you to spend some time alone with God, search your heart and write a letter. Begin by asking Him to reveal any hurt, pain and anger that you have stuffed deep within your heart. Honesty pray the following verse:

> Search me, O God, and know my heart; test me and know my anxious thoughts. See if there is *any offensive way in me*, and lead me in the way everlasting.
> —Psalm 139:23-24, emphasis added

It is interesting to note that the word "offensive" in this passage can also be translated as "hurtful," "wicked" and "grievous." Think about this for a moment. As you have stuffed your hurt, pain and anger in your heart, have you allowed it to become so hurtful to yourself that it has become not only offensive to God but also wicked and grievous to Him? In Ephesians 4:30-31, Paul says:

> Do not grieve the Holy Spirit of God, with whom you were sealed for the day of redemption. Get rid of all bitterness, rage and anger.

101

If that doesn't convince you to let go of your anger, then consider this: according to *Strong's* concordance, one definition of the Hebrew word for "offensive" is "idol."[89] An idol is anything you put before God or in place of God. Is it possible that you have allowed the hurt, pain and anger to become an idol in your life? Remember, God is a jealous God, and He does not want to share His rightful place in your heart with anyone or anything. When you choose to hold on to hurt, pain and anger, it can become a disgusting idol that you worship and protect within your heart.

After you have prayed the above verse in Psalm 139, ask God to unlock the hidden chambers of your heart and reveal *any offensive way* in you that has become an idol in your life. Next, begin to write whatever He puts on your heart. Use the letter as a tangible tool to unlock the anger that you have hidden deep inside. Address the letter to whomever God puts on your heart, and begin to write whatever comes to your mind. Remember that this letter is between you and God only—no one else will ever see it. So do not hold back! Note that you may need to write more than one letter. One time when I was teaching about this tool at a retreat, a woman came up to me after the quiet time and said, "I just wrote 26 pages, and I've been set free!"

This is why I want to encourage you to have a quiet time with the Lord. As you ask the Lord to reveal any offensive ways in you, do not hold anything back—including tears! If you begin to cry, just let the tears flow, because it means that God is washing your heart. If you stop the tears, you will stop what God is softly trying to say to you.

I want to stress that *this letter is never to be mailed*. If you were to mail it, in most cases it would only cause more hurt and pain. Therefore, keep the letter *between you and God*. It is just a tool to allow you to uncover any hidden hurt or pain inside of you—to see if there is *any offensive way* locked deep within your heart.

After you write the letter, the next step is to offer right sacrifices and trust in the Lord by giving the anger to God. Remember what David says in Psalm 4:4-5:

> In your anger do not sin; when you are on your beds, *search your hearts* and be silent. *Offer right sacrifices* and trust in the Lord (emphasis added).

According to God's Word, you are not to let the sun go down while you are still angry, and you are to offer right sacrifices and trust in the Lord. You can do this in a practical way by destroying the letter as you offer the anger to God as a right sacrifice. One of my favorite ways to do this is by burning it in a fireplace. A dear friend of mine once shared that after she burned her letter, she felt the Lord impress the following verse on her heart:

> It is a burnt offering, an offering made by fire, an aroma pleasing to the Lord.
> —Leviticus 1:13b

If there is no fireplace available, just tear the letter into tiny little pieces. If you are feeling creative, you can even put some of the little pieces into a helium balloon and offer the anger as a right sacrifice to God by letting go of the balloon and watching it rise to Him. Burning, tearing or sending the letter up in a helium balloon is another visual and tangible way of giving the hurt, pain and anger—along with *any offensive way*—to God once and for all.

103

After many years of discipling people, I have seen that those who are brave enough to be honest with themselves and take a step of faith by going through this exercise come to a place in which they truly know and understand that they are forgiven and set free. Those who choose not to write the letters, or who do not choose to give the anger to God, stay in the vicious downward spiral of sin, sin and more sin. Their lives continue to be filled with consequences for years to come. The choice is yours! Which will it be: forgiven and set free, or afflicted with consequences for years to come and being deprived of peace?

This exercise is so freeing to me that I continue to do it whenever I feel the need. Whenever I realize that I am dwelling on something that is not pleasing to God, I write out a letter to help me discover what is really taking place deep within my heart. I want to encourage you to take every thought captive and make it obedient to Christ. The moment that you do, "you will know the truth, and the truth will set you free" (John 8:32). So, what are you waiting for? Do it! Let it go so that you may *go in peace!*

Chapter Eight

FORGIVENESS IS NOT AN OPTION

Be kind and compassionate to one another,
forgiving each other,
just as in Christ God forgave you.
EPHESIANS 4:32

*N*ow that we have learned how to give the hurt, pain and anger to God so that we will no longer be deprived of peace, it is time to discover another important aspect to our walk with Christ. As you may recall, hurt not handled in the manner God intended will turn into anger, anger over time will turn into bitterness and bitterness will turn into a bitter poison which will infect every aspect of our lives. So although we learned how to deal with our hurt, pain and anger it is now time to learn about the bitterness and bitter poison which is also known as unforgiveness.

Lamentations 3:19-20 warns about this bitterness:

> I remember my affliction and my wandering, the bitterness and the gall. I well remember them, and my soul is downcast within me.

In the original Hebrew, the word "bitterness" in this verse comes from the word "wormwood," which was a bitter herb that the Hebrew people considered poisonous.[90] Just as our bitterness stuffed deep within our inmost being

105

will become poisonous, and in time will cause our souls to be downcast within us, if we don't learn how to give it to God once and for all. It is also interesting to note that in the original Greek of the New Testament, the word "bitterness" can mean extreme wickedness, a bitter root which produces a bitter fruit, and even bitter hatred.[91] This is why I believe God's Word warns us to make sure there is no root among us that produces such bitter poison.[92]

The only way for us to get rid of this unforgiveness is to learn how to forgive others. In the Greek, the word "forgive" can be translated as "to let go, to give up, [and] to keep no longer."[93] In other words, it's time for us to not only let go of the hurt, pain and anger we learned about in the last chapter, but also to give up the bitterness and unforgiveness. It's time to keep these things no longer and move on with our lives.

In view of this, it is time for us to let go of every aspect of the wrong that has been done to us, so that we can lay down the bitterness and unforgiveness at the feet of Jesus just like the Sinful Woman did. It is time for us to forgive so that we too can *go in peace*, because if we do not learn how to deal with our unforgiveness we will soon be back to where we were at the beginning of this book. Listen to what God's Word warns in Acts 8:23:

> For I see that you are full of bitterness and captive
> to sin.

If we choose to *not* let go of the bitterness and unforgiveness we will be captive to sin. This is not where we want to be! Ephesians 4:31a clearly states what we need to do:

> Get rid of all bitterness, rage and anger.

In view of this truth, let's discuss what Jesus taught about forgiveness, because He wants us to become victorious in this area of our lives. He wants us to be set free from all the consequences and be more than conquerors over this issue of bitterness and unforgiveness. And He wants us to be at peace with God!

In Matthew 6:15, Jesus prayed:

> But if you do not forgive men their sins, your Father will not forgive your sins.

Jesus' prayer warns that if you and I are unwilling to forgive others, our own hearts are in no condition to ask God the Father to forgive us.[94] Think about it: If we are unwilling to forgive others, what right do we have to ask God to forgive our sins? God knows that unforgiveness will destroy you and me. He knows that unforgiveness in our hearts will cause us to harden our hearts. That is why, dear beloved, forgiveness is not an option. That is why, as we learned in the last chapter, it is time for us to let go of not only the anger, but also the bitterness.

For this reason, it might be a good idea to look at what forgiveness is and what forgiveness is not, so that we can completely forgive the person who hurt us.[95] We will begin by looking at what forgiveness is.

First, *forgiveness is modeled after God's forgiveness of us.* Because God has forgiven you and me, we need to forgive others. In other words, we are called to be imitators of God. In Ephesians 4:32–5:1, Paul admonished:

> Be kind to one another, tenderhearted, forgiving one another, as God in Christ forgave you. Therefore be imitators of God, as beloved children
>
> —ESV

Second, *forgiveness is a step of obedience.* We are to take every thought captive—even thoughts of unforgiveness—and make them obedient to Christ. Otherwise, we are living in disobedience to God. In 2 Corinthians 10:5b, Paul teaches this important principle:

> We take captive every thought to make it obedient to Christ.

Third, *forgiveness is leaving the revenge to God.* If we make plans to get even with someone, we are only letting that person continue to hurt us. It is similar to what Proverbs 26:27 warns:

> Whoever digs a pit will fall into it, and a stone will come back on him who starts it rolling.
>
> —ESV

In Romans 12:19, Paul also warns:

> Do not take revenge, my friends, but leave room for God's wrath, for it is written: "It is mine to avenge; I will repay," says the Lord.

Fourth, *forgiveness is expensive.* In Matthew 18:21-22, Peter came up to Jesus and asked Him:

> "Lord, how often shall my brother sin against me, and I forgive him? Up to seven times? Jesus replied, "I do not say to you, up to seven times, but up to seventy times seven."
>
> —NKJV

According to Jewish teaching, a person was to forgive an offender four times. Peter, though more generous with his willingness to forgive up to seven times, was still setting a limit beyond which he did not need to forgive. When Jesus said, "seventy times seven," He was telling Peter that he should forgive without limit.[96]

Fifth, *forgiveness is a heart issue*. In Luke 17:3-4, Jesus said:

> Pay attention to yourselves! If your brother sins, rebuke him, and if he repents, forgive him, and if he sins against you seven times in the day, and turns to you seven times, saying, "I repent," you must forgive him.
>
> —ESV

You may have heard it said that you do not need to forgive someone if he or she does not repent—in other words, if the offender does not come to say that he or she is sorry. However, it is important to realize that just because the verse says *if he repents*, forgive him, it does not say that if the person doesn't repent, we don't forgive him or her. We cannot add what we like to God's Word. What this verse means is that forgiveness is *a heart issue*. We must have a heart that is always ready to forgive.

In Psalm 86:5a, David writes:

> For You, Lord, are good, and *ready* to forgive.
>
> —NKJV, emphasis added

If we are to model our forgiveness after God's forgiveness of us, we must also be ready to forgive. In other words, we cannot hold a grudge against a person just because he or she has not repented or asked for our forgiveness. If we are holding onto grudges and unforgiveness, the truth is not in us. We are just living by excuses and blaming others for our unwillingness to forgive. In other words, we are living in sin.

We need to remember that before we repented and asked God to forgive us for our sins, He still loved us and was waiting to say, "You are forgiven!" He was *ready* to forgive the moment we repented. We must therefore have hearts that have already done the deep work of forgiveness by letting go of the hurt and are *prepared* and *ready* to say, "I forgive you." It is only then that we will have no unforgiveness in our hearts, because we have already let it go and given it to God. In Mark 11:25, Jesus explained it this way:

> And when you stand praying, if you hold anything against anyone, forgive him.

Sixth, *forgiveness is a promise.* In his book *From Forgiven to Forgiving*, Jay Adams states, "When our God forgives us, He promises that He will not remember our sins against us anymore. That is wonderful!"[97] When we are forgiven, God treats us as if we had never sinned. Again, if we model our forgiveness after God's forgiveness, we will also promise to treat the person who has wronged us as if he or she had never hurt us. Proverbs 19:11 shares a proverb to live by:

> A man's wisdom gives him patience; it is to his glory to overlook an offense.

Finally, *forgiveness is for our own sake.* We need to forgive the offender for our own sake. Ignoring this fact will cause us to dwell in the pit of despair. Listen to what God said in Isaiah 43:25:

> I, even I, am he who blots out your transgressions, for *my own sake*, and remembers your sins no more (emphasis added).

If God blots out our sins for His own sake, then this must be best for us as well. Forgiveness may or may not change the other person, but it will change us!

Now that we have looked at what forgiveness is, let's look at what forgiveness *is not*. It is important for us to know this distinction, because sometimes we can get feelings and emotions all wrapped up and confused when dealing with this issue. It's important to know dear beloved that we are not to live by feelings, but by the truth of God's Word.

First, *forgiveness is not a feeling.* Forgiveness is not something you or I feel like doing, but rather a step of obedience to Christ. As Jay Adams states, "Unlike modern discussions of forgiveness, there is nothing in the Bible about 'feelings of forgiveness' or 'having forgiving feelings' towards another."[98]

During World War II, Corrie ten Boom and her family hid Jews in their home. When they were discovered, they were arrested and put in a German concentration camp, where many of Corrie's family died. After World War II, God used Corrie to share His love with many who were hurt during the war. One of her main messages was about forgiveness.

After one particular meeting, an SS officer from the camp where Corrie and her sister Betsie had lived came up to Corrie and said, "Isn't it wonderful! Jesus has washed away my sins." He then reached out his hand and asked Corrie for forgiveness. Corrie did not have it in her heart to forgive. She did not *feel* like forgiving. In fact, she felt just the opposite. But she was obedient and asked God to give her the strength to forgive the man. "I can do all things through Christ who strengthens me" (Philippians 4:13, NKJV).

Corrie later stated that though she prayed for strength, her right hand remained limp by her side. She just couldn't bring herself to shake the hand of the man who had once stood by mocking, while she and her sister were forced to strip off their clothes and enter the shower room. "I can't do it, Lord," she said. "Don't ask me for this; it's too much." Her thoughts were angry and hurtful, yet she realized that she herself had demanded such an action from others who had suffered during the war. "Forgive your enemies," she had told them.

"Then help me, Lord," Corrie prayed. "I can't do it on my own." As she prayed, she suddenly felt power rush along her arm and generate warmth and forgiveness for the man who stood before her. Even now, he was eagerly shaking her hand. God had answered her prayer and provided.[99] Even though Corrie did not *feel* like forgiving the SS guard, she took the step of obedience, and God was faithful.

Dear beloved, if you and I wait until we *feel* like forgiving, it will never happen. If we continue to hold on to our bitterness and unforgiveness we will again be reaping the consequences we learned about in chapter five and our lives will be out of control and captive to sin.

Do you really want that to happen? Remember, forgiveness is not a feeling. For this reason, we need to ask God to give us the strength to forgive, just like Corrie did. When we do, we will discover that we truly are strong in the Lord and more than conquerors. In 1 Corinthians 13:4-5, Paul explains it this way:

> Love is patient, love is kind. . . . it keeps no record
> of wrongs.

Second, *forgiveness is not holding onto grudges.* The word "grudge" means "a feeling of deep-seated resentment or ill will."[100] In Hebrew, the word "grudge" means "to keep."[101] However, as we discussed at the beginning of this chapter, the word "forgive" in the Greek of the New Testament can actually be translated "to let go, to give up, [and] to keep no longer"—which is the exact opposite of keep. We just discussed how forgiveness is not a feeling. It is time to let go of any and all wrong feelings associated with our deep heart hurts. It is time to let go of any and all grudges that we may be hanging on to. Leviticus 19:18 says it clearly:

> Never seek revenge or bear a grudge against any-
> one, but love your neighbor as yourself. I am the
> LORD.
>
> —NLT

Third, *forgiveness is not necessarily understanding why we were hurt.* In *Forgive and Forget*, Lewis B. Smedes notes, "We will probably never understand why were hurt. . . . Understanding may come later, in fragments, an insight here and a glimpse there, after forgiving. But we are asking too much is we want to understand everything at the beginning."[102] In the Bible, a man named Joseph suffered incredible betrayal and hurt at the hands of his brothers. However, when he later reflected on all that he had been through, he told his brothers:

113

> You intended to harm me, but God intended it for
> good to accomplish what is now being done, the sav-
> ing of many lives.
>
> —Genesis 50:20

Fourth, *forgiveness is not accepting the bad behavior.* Forgiveness is sometimes confused with accepting a person's
wrongful actions. However, there is a difference between
accepting a *person* and accepting that person's *behavior.*
Forgiveness is not an acceptance of destructive, bad behavior, but an acceptance of the person regardless of his or her
behavior. We learn this example from God, who accepts
us and loves us but He does not accept our *sinful behavior.*
Even though we hate the person's bad behavior—the sin—
we are still called to forgive the sinner. In Ephesians 4:32,
Paul states:

> Be kind and compassionate to one another, forgiving
> each other, just as in Christ God forgave you.

Fifth, *forgiveness is not tolerating something unpleasant.*
To "tolerate" means "to put up with something or somebody unpleasant."[103] We do not have to tolerate or put up
with something wrong or unpleasant when we forgive a
person for the hurt he or she has caused. For example,
imagine there was a man who lived on your block who
had sexually assaulted you. He was arrested and sent to
jail. Years later he was released and moved back into the
house on your block. You had, through Christ's love, forgiven him years before for the hurt he caused you. But now
you notice him inviting a young teenager (about the age
you were when the assault happened) into his house. You
would never accept or tolerate that kind of behavior. The
man should be held accountable for the wrong he does,

and you would protect another from suffering the harm that you suffered.

In Luke 23:41a, one of the criminals who hung on a cross next to Jesus said:

> We are punished justly, for we are getting what our deeds deserve.

The criminal realized that he deserved the punishment for his crime. It is good that there were people around who did not tolerate his criminal activity.

Sixth, *forgiveness is not forgetting.* Jay Adams states, "The Bible never commands 'forgive and forget.' This is one of those old, unbiblical statements by which people often try to guide their lives that is (sic) utterly incorrect. If you try to forget, you will fail. In fact, the harder you try the more difficult you will find forgetting."[104]

Some people get confused by passages in Isaiah and Jeremiah in which God states He promises to forgive our sins and remember them no more.[105] But "forgetting" is not the same as "remembering no more." Adams states, "Obviously, the omniscient [all-knowing] God who created and sustains the universe does not forget, but He can [choose to] 'not remember'. . . . To 'not remember' is simply a graphic way of saying, 'I will not bring up these matters to you or others in the future. . . . I will never use these sins against you.'"[106] The apostle Paul wrote:

> But one thing I do: forgetting what lies behind and straining forward to what lies ahead, I press on toward the goal for the prize of the upward call of God in Christ Jesus.
>
> —Philippians 3:13b-14, ESV

115

"Forgetting what lies behind" does not mean that we will fully forget the hurt that another has caused us—especially if the hurt was horrendous, as in the case of rape or abuse. But we can *choose* to let it go and leave it behind. Then, we can move forward because we have not allowed that hurt to destroy our lives any longer. The choice is ours! God sets a wonderful example of this in Jeremiah 31:34b when He states:

> For I will forgive their wickedness and will remember their sins no more.

Finally, *forgiveness is not an option.* God knows that unforgiveness will destroy us. This is why forgiveness is not an option. So what do we do, beloved? We do what God's Word commands us to do:

> Bear with each other and forgive whatever grievances you may have against one another. Forgive as the Lord forgave you.
>
> —Colossians 3:13

Many of us desire to be rid of unforgiveness but have no idea how to go about it. For years, we have held on to our bitterness, which has now turned into the bitter poison of unforgiveness. Although we are tired of it, the unforgiveness is comfortable to us, much like an old security blanket. However, we can discover the key in how to let go of the unforgiveness in our lives by once again listening to what Jesus said:

> . But I say to you who hear, love your enemies, do good to those who hate you, bless those who curse you, *pray for those who mistreat you.* . . . Be merciful, just as your Father is merciful.
>
> —Luke 6:27-28,36, NASB, emphasis added

116

Remember, beloved, you and I need to model our lives after Christ's life. Praying for those whom we have bitterness and unforgiveness against is the key that will set us free. As we see from the life of Jesus, even as He was being crucified He prayed over and over again.

> Then Jesus said, "Father, forgive them, for they do not know what they do."
> —Luke 23:34a, NKJV

The tense of the verb "said" indicates that Jesus repeated this prayer. As the soldiers nailed Him to the cross, He prayed, "Father, forgive them." When they lifted the cross and placed it in a hold in the ground, He prayed, "Father, forgive them." As He hung on the cross between heaven and earth and heard religious people mocking Him, He repeatedly prayed, "Father, forgive them."[107] We, too, need to pray like Jesus prayed.

If there is bitterness and unforgiveness in your heart, Satan, will use this as a stronghold in your life. He will shoot fiery darts aimed at the poisonous infection of bitterness and unforgiveness. When this happens, use prayer as a weapon to extinguish the fiery darts. Every time you are reminded of the past hurt, instead of dwelling and chewing on all the thoughts and feelings associated with it, *pray*. Pray just as Jesus taught:

> Pray for those who mistreat you.
> —Luke 6:28, NASB

Or, as the *English Standard Version* puts it:

> Pray for those who abuse you.

No matter how horrendous the hurt you suffered, God calls you to let it go so that you may *go in peace*! If the person who injured you is not saved, pray for his or her salvation. If the person is saved, pray for him or her to draw closer to God. Now, it is true that you will not *feel* like praying this prayer. You may feel like Jonah felt—he did not want God to spare the Ninevites. You, too, may not want those who have caused you pain to be forgiven. However, forgiving that person is a step of obedience, not a feeling.

I have learned over the years that every time I was reminded of a past hurt, the key was to pray for the person who hurt me. As I was obedient to pray for that person, forgiveness came. Soon, I came to a point where I realized that whenever I thought of the person who hurt me, I really was praying from my heart for his or her salvation or for that person to draw closer to God. When this happened, I knew that the forgiveness in my heart was complete.

In 2 Corinthians 10:4, Paul teaches:

> The weapons we fight with are not the weapons of the world. On the contrary, they have divine power to demolish strongholds.

Use prayer as a mighty weapon to demolish the stronghold of bitterness and unforgiveness in your life.

Before moving on to the next chapter, write a letter of forgiveness to the same person or persons to whom you wrote the letter(s) of anger. This time, the letter must be one of *forgiveness*, not anger. Even if all you can do is write, "So and so, I forgive you" that is okay. Remember dear beloved, forgiveness is not an option. It is a step of obedience, not some big gushy feeling. It is all right if you don't *feel* like forgiving. Just do it! Just let it go! You can do all things through Christ who strengthens you, because you are more than a conqueror.

After you write the letter, *keep* it, because God wants you to keep your forgiveness. As you forgive others and live your life according to His Word, you will be at peace with God and be all that He intends you to be. Once you take this step of obedience and forgiveness, you will *go in peace!*

Chapter Nine

THE WEAPONS OF VICTORY

*The weapons we fight with
are not weapons of the world.
On the contrary,
they have divine power to demolish strongholds.*
2 CORINTHIANS 10:4

Now let's go back to our story of the Sinful Woman. When she was willing to come to Jesus in humility and truth, He met her in the midst of her despair. Better yet, He forgave her and restored her. Imagine what she must of felt when she heard these words:

Your sins are forgiven. . . . Your faith has saved you;
go in peace.
—Luke 7:48,50

Can you imagine being in Jesus' presence, burdened with guilt and shame, and hearing Him speak these same words of freedom to you? What joy and peace the Sinful Woman must have felt when the burden of her sin was lifted off her shoulders! Has a burden been lifted off of your shoulders as you did the deep heart work God called you to do? So many have shared with me the peace and freedom they now feel after being obedient to the Lord to do this type of deep heart work. Many wonder why they waited so long. If you don't feel this same freedom and peace, then please reread chapters 7 and 8 and do what God is calling you to do, because you are missing out.

Now that you have learned how to recognize what is taking place deep within your heart—how to give anything that is unpleasing to God in a tangible manner and let go of the unforgiveness—it is time to learn how to walk the walk that God has for you so that you can be like the Sinful Woman and move forward in peace. For the truth is that just because you give the hurt, pain, anger, bitterness and unforgiveness in your heart to God, it doesn't mean that you will never be hurt again. We live in a sinful world, and it is for this reason that the principles you learned so far *must* become a way of life.

In addition, I must warn you that the enemy wants you to stumble and fall and to take all the hurt and pain back again. Remember, he does not want you to *go in peace*. In view of this, you need to understand the spiritual battle that is being waged all around you and learn how to fight the good fight.[108] This is a battle to keep you shackled and chained in sin. It is a battle to keep you from living a triumphant life which will glorify God. But you can have the victory, because you have powerful weapons at your fingertips that you can use to demolish the strongholds in your life.

I love what Warren Wiersbe writes in his book *The Strategy of Satan*: "You are not fighting *for* victory, but *from* victory, for Jesus Christ has already defeated Satan!"[109] We already know the end of the story. We know that God wins. But until that time, there is a battle—a spiritual battle—

that must be fought. In view of this, it is important for you to be properly equipped so that you can survive this battle, and one of the most important ways for you to do this is by obtaining knowledge. Therefore, I want to teach you about Satan and how he operates, along with the spiritual armor that God has for you so that you can walk victoriously. To begin, read the following passage from Ephesians 6:10-18:

> Finally, my brethren, be strong in the Lord and in the power of His might. Put on the whole armor of God, that you may be able to stand against the wiles of the devil. For we do not wrestle against flesh and blood, but against principalities, against powers, against the rulers of the darkness of this age, against spiritual hosts of wickedness in the heavenly places.
>
> Therefore take up the whole armor of God, that you may be able to withstand in the evil day, and having done all, to stand. Stand therefore, having girded your waist with truth, having put on the breastplate of righteousness, and having shod your feet with the preparation of the gospel of peace; above all, taking the shield of faith with which you will be able to quench all the fiery darts of the wicked one. And take the helmet of salvation, and the sword of the Spirit, which is the word of God; praying always with all prayer and supplication in the Spirit, being watchful to this end with all perseverance and supplication for all the saints.
>
> —NKJV

The apostle Paul wrote these words while he was in prison. He realized that believers are in the midst of a spiritual battle, and God gave him this word picture to teach them that they can fight the good fight, be victorious and walk worthy of their calling. As you take up this spiritual armor, you will also learn how to guard against all of Satan's schemes. You will learn how to be prepared and equipped for battle so that you can live out who you are in Christ.

The first item you need to understand in fighting this spiritual battle is the nature of your enemy and how he operates. In Scripture, Satan, the devil, has many different names. In Hebrew, the word "Satan" literally means "accuser"[110] ("the devil" in Greek carries the same meaning),[111] for he accuses you day and night before the throne of the King.[112] However, God loves you so deeply that even though what Satan says may be true, He covers you with the blood of Jesus Christ.

Satan also means "adversary,"[113] or "one to contend with." Satan is the archenemy of God and contends with him, and for this reason he is your enemy as well. He is also known as the tempter. He tempted Jesus Christ,[114] and he will tempt you. He is the chief sinner, for he "has been sinning from the beginning" (1 John 3:8). He is the father of all lies and a murderer, as Jesus says in John 8:44:

> He was a murderer from the beginning, not holding to the truth, for there is no truth in him. When he lies, he speaks his native language, for he is a liar and the father of lies.

Satan is compared to a serpent[115] and a roaring lion.[116] He is known as the god of this age,[117] for he is the unseen power behind all unbelief and ungodliness. Perhaps his most effective disguise, however, is that he masquerades as an angel of light.[118]

All of this might cause you to despair and wonder how you could ever possibly hope to overcome the devil. But take heart! God is much more powerful than Satan, and He promises to give you the victory. In Scripture, we find many wonderful names for our Lord, including the Alpha and the Omega,[119] the First and the Last,[120] the Almighty God[121] and the King of Glory.[122] His attributes far outweigh those of Satan. He is known as our protector,[123] our strength, our fortress, our deliverer, our rock, our shield, our salvation and our stronghold.[124] And do not forget that He calls you His beloved. Perhaps Paul says it best in 1 Timothy 1:17:

> Now to the King eternal, immortal, invisible, the only God, be honor and glory for ever and ever. Amen.

Now, to be properly prepared for this battle, you need to know some strategic facts about your enemy. The first item you need to know is where Satan came from and how he operates. In Isaiah 14:12, the prophet indicates that in God's original creation, Satan was the "morning star, son of the dawn." According to the *NIV Study Bible*, "The Hebrew for this expression is translated 'Lucifer' in the Latin Vulgate."[125] Many believe, as Weirsbe describes, "that he was cast down [from heaven] because of his pride and desire to occupy the King's throne."[126] A crucial fact you must not overlook is that he is a *created* being, not an *eternal* being like our King. He is *limited* in his knowledge and is not *all-knowing* like our Savior. He is *limited* in his activity and is not *all-powerful* like our Lord. He is even *limited* in that he can only be in one place at one time—not *omnipresent* (everywhere-present) like our King.

Notice the word that is repeated in this description of Satan: *limited*. Satan has boundaries, and you should never forget that fact. Do not make him into something bigger than he is, for that is just what he would like you to do. However, to live your life as if he does not exist is also playing into his hands. Either of these two extremes can be dangerous to your walk. In view of this, the true knowledge of who he is and how he operates is of strategic importance. And though he is limited, he has been given authority over the earth from the time of the fall. Thus, another name he has been given is the prince of this world.[127]

You may be wondering how, if Satan is limited, he is able to accomplish so many things in different parts of the world. Remember what Paul says in Ephesians 6:12:

> We do not wrestle against flesh and blood, but against principalities, against powers, against the rulers of the darkness of this age, [and] against spiritual hosts of wickedness in the heavenly places.
>
> —NKJV

Who are these principalities, powers, rulers and spiritual hosts? They are Satan's cohorts. There is a vast army of fallen angels (also known as demonic beings) that assist Satan in his attacks against you and against me. In the book of Revelation, John states that when Satan rebelled against God, he took one-third of the angels with him.[128] Daniel states that these fallen angels struggle against God's angels for control of the affairs of nations.[129]

Now, I do not believe that Satan, or any of his cohorts, can read your mind. Remember, he is a created being and is limited in his power. However, I do believe that he can read your body language—he can hear your words and even watch your actions. He studies you to find ways to keep you shackled and chained. That's why Paul says in Ephesians 4:26-27:

> "In your anger do not sin": Do not let the sun go down while you are still angry, *and do not give the devil a foothold* (emphasis added).

This is why it is so vitally important for you to continually take your thoughts captive—especially the hurtful, painful, angry thoughts—and make them obedient to God. For if you do not, Satan, or one of his many cohorts, can gain a foothold and use these things against you. In view of this, you need to be equipped with the spiritual armor that God has given to you so that you can fight the good fight. Let's take a look at each piece of this spiritual armor.

The first item is the *belt of truth*, which represents the truth of the Word of God. When you gird your waist with the truth, you allow the Word of God to govern your actions and motives. This is why it is so vitally important for you to read God's Word on a daily basis—so that you will be able to make wise and godly choices. The belt of truth must fully surround, encircle and encompass every aspect of your life, just as a normal belt would. As God's Word fully encircles every aspect of your being and you begin to make wise choices, you will discover true victory in your life.

Let me give you an example of making wise choices based on God's Word. Say that Satan shoots his fiery darts at you and you begin to again dwell on the hurt, pain, anger, bitterness or unforgiveness of your past situation. But then you immediately remember what you learned in this book, and instead of dwelling on the hurt and the pain, you choose to "pray for those who mistreat you" (Luke 6:28, NASB). That is what having your waist girded with the belt of truth is all about. Isn't that cool! That's how easy it is. You allow God's Word to fully encircle this aspect of your life.

The next essential piece of armor is the *breastplate of righteousness*, which guards the heart. Proverbs 4:23 warns:

> Above all else, guard your heart, for it affects every-thing you do.
>
> —NLT

Remember, it is in your heart—in the depths of your innermost being—where God wants to meet with you and whisper the truth of His Word. As you meet with Him, you move the truth of His Word from your head to your heart so that you can make wise choices. When you choose to believe in your heart and make decisions based on His truth instead of your feelings and desires, you will be wearing the breastplate of righteousness.

Let me give you an example of a practical way to put on the breastplate of righteousness. Say that you are single and that all of your life you were told that you were a mistake. One day, a guy walks up to you and asks you for a date. You think, *He's sort of a loser, but no one else will ever ask me out.* So you accept the date. In this instance, you made a decision based on your feelings and desires and not on the truth of God's Word. Thus, you weren't wearing the breastplate of righteousness.

Now let's say the same thing happens and the guy asks you out on a second date. Your thoughts start going in the same direction, but all of a sudden you think, *Wait a minute—I'm the daughter of the King of kings. God loves me, and He knows the plans He has for me.* So you turn down the date, because you know the truth is that God has someone better for you (if you are to marry). In this case, you made a decision based on the truth of who you are in Christ—the daughter of the King of kings—and thus moved the truth from your head to your heart. That it what it means to put on the breastplate of righteousness.

The next piece of armor is the *sandals of peace*. Peace is only achieved by learning to take every hurtful and angry thought captive and making it obedient to Christ. This is what will protect you from the disabling wounds that are inflicted in life and what will keep Satan from setting up strongholds. Once you make it a habit to take the hurtful and angry thoughts captive, you will walk forward in peace, and *your feet will be shod with the preparation of the gospel of peace.*

In other words, as you walk worthy of your calling by making wise choices with your thoughts, you will be a light unto God and reflect His glory. Actions speak louder than words, and people will watch how you live. Sometimes, your life will be the only Bible they will ever read. Thus, as you take your thoughts captive and walk forward in peace, you will prepare the way for others to come to know Christ. People will want what you have. This is what it means to have your feet shod with the preparation of the sandals of peace. You are *prepared*—you did the deep heart work to be a cleansed vessel—and thus can be a light to those who are watching.

I have seen this happen on many occasions. One time, a young woman I knew went through *Go in Peace*, and it so impacted her life for the better that people started to notice the change in her. Soon her mother came to me and said, "I saw such a change in my daughter that I asked her what had happened. She told me that she was being discipled by you through *Go in Peace*. I want what she has. Will you disciple me too?" Pretty soon, the amazing work that God was doing within their hearts impacted their whole family.

Another important piece of armor is the *shield of faith*. As you begin to live your life based on the truth of God's Word, Satan will attack you in an attempt to destroy your faith and your relationship with God. He will shoot his fiery darts at you and try to provoke you to *take back* all the hurt, pain, anger and bitterness that you have given to God. Satan hopes that these fiery darts will hit their target, burst into flames, and start a wildfire within your mind that will be almost impossible to extinguish. It is your faith in God that will give you the confidence to live your life based on the truth of His Word and resist Satan's attacks. It is your faith in God that will quench these fiery darts and give you the strength to walk worthy of your calling.

Hebrews 11:1 defines "faith" as "being sure of what we hope for and certain of what we do not see." Having faith means trusting God and His promises.[130] Therefore, when you begin to worry about everything around you—just stop! As the prophet Isaiah states:

> You will keep in perfect peace him whose mind is steadfast.
>
> —Isaiah 26:3a

Instead of focusing on everything that is causing you to worry, or all the hurt, pain, anger and bitterness, pick up the shield of faith and stay focused on God and His Word. When you decide by faith to keep your mind steadfast on God and His promises instead of the fiery darts that Satan shoots your way, you will be using the shield of faith effectively.

The next piece of armor is the *helmet of salvation*. As a believer, you are called to protect your mind. Satan wants to destroy your thought life, and he will do this by playing on your feelings and desires in an attempt to hold your mind captive. Many times, your thoughts will trigger your emotions, your emotions will trigger your desires, and your desires will trigger your actions. Therefore, if you do not protect your mind—and especially what you choose to think about or dwell on—you will allow Satan to influence you to make bad choices. It is important to remember that sin includes not only your wrong *actions* but also your wrong *thoughts*.

In Philippians 4:8, Paul provides the key to using the helmet of salvation effectively in order to protect your mind and your thought life:

> And now, dear brothers and sisters, let me say one more thing. . . . Fix your thoughts on what is true and honorable and right. Think about things that are pure and lovely and admirable. Think about things that are excellent and worthy of praise.
>
> —NLT

These are the types of things on which you are to think and dwell. If something is *not* true, honorable, right, pure, lovely, admirable, excellent and worthy of praise, you should *not* be thinking about it—and especially *not* be dwelling on it! You must keep your thoughts away from anything that pollutes your mind. If you begin to think on discouraging, disgusting and/or polluted things, it is time to change your thinking. This may take some practice at first, and you may have to change your thinking hundreds of times a day, but as you do, you will be wearing the helmet of salvation.

The *sword of the Spirit* is the next piece of equipment in the believer's arsenal. Like the belt of truth, it also represents the Word of God, but there is an important distinction. In the New Testament, there are two Greek words used to describe the Word: logos and rhema. "Logos" speaks of the general knowledge of the Word, which represents the belt of truth. "Rhema," on the other hand, speaks of specific words or phrases. It is the piercing, double-edged sword of the Spirit that defines specific truths and allows you to apply these truths when Satan attempts to attack you. It is more than a general knowledge of the Word of God; it is a precise weapon that is meant to yield the truth of God's Word in specific situations to help you overcome temptations—even temptations to dwell on hurt, pain, anger and bitterness. As mentioned previously, just because you gave something to God doesn't mean you won't be hurt again or desire to take an old hurt back again. This is why it is vitally important to read God's Word daily and to memorize key verses. You need to know how to wield this incredible weapon.

Psalm 119:11 holds the key to effectively using the sword of the Spirit:

> I have hidden your word in my heart that I might
> not sin against you.

Therefore, a great passage to memorize (in fact, the best out of all of the ones I have given to you) to help you avoid the temptation to dwell on something unpleasing to God is Psalm 139:23-24:

> Search me, O God, and know my heart; test me and know my anxious thoughts. See if there is any offensive way in me, and lead me in the way everlasting.

As you take the time to memorize God's Word, you will actually be hiding it within your heart. Then, when you find yourself in a situation where you are being tempted, God will bring His Word to your memory. All of a sudden, a verse will come to you that will be applicable to that specific situation. When you take action based on God's Word, you will be using the sword of the Spirit effectively.

The final weapon in the believer's arsenal is *prayer*. This is perhaps one of the most important weapons that you can use to remain victorious. Through prayer, you can continue to give all the hurt, pain, anger and bitterness to God and defend against any other fiery dart that Satan tries to send your way. Through prayer, you can also receive God's strength, guidance and wisdom to walk worthy of your calling in any situation. However, you have to make the choice to use the weapon. As Charles Spurgeon wrote, "Look upward, and let us weep. O God, You have given us a mighty weapon, and we have permitted it to rust."[131] Prayer is a top-secret weapon with which God has equipped you for battle, so don't allow it to rust. Use it every time you find yourself in a situation that you need God's strength, guidance and wisdom.

Let's conclude by looking at the story of the Sinful Woman once again to see how we can use the weapons of victory to our advantage. Remember, it was earlier in the day that Jesus taught the following to a crowd:

> Come to me, all you who are weary and burdened, and I will give you rest. Take my yoke upon you and learn from me, for I am gentle and humble in heart, and you will find rest for your souls. For my yoke is easy and my burden light.
>
> —Matthew 11:28-30

As I mentioned, I believe that the Sinful Woman was present and heard these words of Jesus. This message spoke to the depths of her heart, and she became single-mindedly focused. She picked up the *shield of faith*, without even realizing it, and chose to do what Jesus was calling her to do. He said, "Come!" and she followed, knowing that He was her only hope. She chose to use the *sword of the spirit* all the way to Simon's house as she battled all the warfare in her heart and mind. Imagine the fiery darts of unworthiness, guilt and shame that Satan was sending at her, yet the craving to receive rest for her soul drove her to stay focused on Jesus' words. Without realizing it, she was using the shield of faith in the manner in which God intended. By faith, she chose to throw caution to the wind and ignore the fiery darts. She chose to run to Simon's house in spite of all the conflicting emotions raging within her, because her soul craved the rest that Jesus spoke about.

It was when she chose to obey God's Word that the Lord met her there and performed one of the most amazing events in her life. Many times, God does the same thing in our lives—He calls us to walk the walk according to His Word and *then* meets us there. The principals of His Word are simple, but that does not mean they are easy to do. We must choose by faith to be single-mindedly focused on the Word of God. We must choose by faith to pick up the weapons of victory. We must choose by faith to fight the good fight so that we may be set free. As we do, we will take every thought captive to Christ and make it obedient to Him.

Now, continue to turn the pages so that you can *go in peace.*

Chapter Ten

A BROKEN AND CONTRITE HEART

The sacrifices of God are a broken spirit;
a broken and contrite heart.
PSALM 51:17A

*N*ow that you have dealt with your hurt, anger and unforgiveness and also learned how to fight the good fight, there is another issue that you need to address: repentance. Is your heart broken, as mine was, over the issue of abortion? God can heal your broken heart if you give Him all the pieces. He is waiting for you to run to Him. He desires for you to approach Him in the same manner that the Sinful Woman approached Jesus. Perhaps King David wrote it best when he penned these vivid words in Psalm 51:17a:

The sacrifices of God are a broken spirit; a broken and contrite heart.

Do you remember the way in which the Sinful Woman came to Jesus? She was broken and had a contrite heart. By "contrite," I mean that she was remorseful for her past sins and resolved to avoid future sin.[132] In other words, she had repented. But what exactly does repentance mean?

According to Ralph Earle in *Word Meanings in the New Testament*, "The Greek noun *metanoia* [in English,

137

"repentance"] literally means 'a change of mind.' It is more than emotional sorrow, which too often does not produce any change of life. Rather, it is a change of mind, or attitude, towards God, sin and ourselves. Deep repentance involves a real turnabout in life."[133] Deep repentance involves a changed life. We see this in the Sinful Woman's case. She entered the room broken and weeping, but left with peace and faith in a Savior.

Dear beloved, God loves you so much that He desires the same for you. He wants you to *repent* of your sin, which means to change your mind. Let me give you an example. As I mentioned, for years I was pro-choice, meaning I believed that abortion was a woman's choice and that nothing was wrong with a woman making such a decision to abort her baby. Of course, I had great reason to take this position, for to believe otherwise was just too painful to bear. It would have meant that I had to admit that what I had done was wrong.

Yet God, in His timing and love, showed me the error of my ways. It is God's kindness that leads us toward repentance. Once I understood the truth, I had to repent of my ways and change my mind. So I changed my viewpoint and now, of course, I am pro-life. (By this point, I am sure you figured that out!)

I learned that according to the *New Unger's Bible Dictionary,* "repentance contains three essential elements. First, a genuine sorrow towards God on account of sin."[134] When I looked closely at how a baby is knit together in the mother's womb and learned what God's Word said about the baby in the womb, I had a genuine sorrow toward God on account of my sin. I pray that you too, dear beloved, have the same kind of genuine sorrow. If so, you have accomplished the first element of repentance. Listen to what the apostle Paul wrote to the Corinthians:

> Even if I caused you sorrow by my letter, I do not regret it. . . . I see that my letter hurt you, but only for a little while—yet now I am happy, not because you were made sorry, but because your sorrow led you to repentance. For you became sorrowful as God intended and so were not harmed in any way by us. Godly sorrow brings repentance that leads to salvation and leaves no regrets.
> —2 Corinthians 7:8-10

The second element of repentance is to see your sin as God sees it. In other words, you have to have "an inward repugnance to sin necessarily followed by the actual forsaking of it."[135] The word "repugnance" means to have a strong dislike or distaste for something.[136] If you look in a thesaurus for other terms to use in replace of "repugnant," you will find the words "repulsive" or "disgusting" among the list.[137]

Think about this for a moment. In the case of abortion, you only have to look at what an abortion actually is to feel repugnance for it. Knowing the medical facts of abortion and how an abortion is performed it is repulsive and disgusting. With the knowledge I now have, I find it amazing that abortion is even allowed by human intelligence. In America, the abortion industry calls the baby a "product of conception" or a "fetal tissue mass," or some other dehumanizing term. The abortion industry is trying to make such a disgusting and repulsive thing appear to be not so ugly, thereby encouraging people to believe the lie that it is not a baby. However, when you search God's Word, you *will* know the truth. I pray that you, dear beloved, have joined me in this second element of repentance by feeling repugnance and repulse for this sin.

There is another aspect to this second element. Remember that repentance means you have "an inward repugnance to sin necessarily followed by *the actual forsaking of it*."[138] If you have truly repented of the sin of abortion, than you can no longer be pro-choice. Remember the definition of "contrite"? It not only means to be remorseful for past sin but also to be *resolved* to avoid future sin.

It's time to *change your mind* and become pro-life. In addition, if for some reason you find yourself in an unwanted pregnancy, then you need to be resolved to avoid future sin and not choose to have an abortion. In Matthew 3:8, John the Baptist warned the religious leaders of his day to "produce fruit in keeping with repentance." Likewise, in Acts 26:20, Paul states that he "preached [to the Jews and Gentiles] that they should repent and turn to God and prove their repentance by their deeds." Dear beloved, you cannot change the past, but you can change the future!

"Repentance" means to change your mind and change your life by your deeds. In fact, as a repentant woman, you are changed. You could compare your life to a drama. The person you played in act one (the bad guy) is not the same person you are today. Paul, with wisdom inspired by God, wrote:

> One thing I do: Forgetting what is behind and straining towards what is ahead, I press on toward the goal to win the prize for which God has called me heavenward in Christ Jesus.
> —Philippians 413b-14

So press on toward the goal. You have learned, you have grown, and you have matured. Praise the Lord! You are a new creation in Christ. As Paul again states:

> Therefore, if anyone is in Christ, he is a new creation; the old has gone, the new has come!
>
> —2 Corinthians 5:17

So, what is the third element of repentance? You will need to continue to turn the pages to find the answer, for we will discuss that in a later chapter. Until then, you need to ask yourself if is there something that God is putting on your heart for which you need to repent. If so, come and kneel at Jesus' feet, just like the Sinful Woman did, so you can *go in peace!*

Chapter Eleven

THE PRICE IS PAID

And He himself bore our sins in His body on the cross,
that we might die to sin and live to righteousness;
for by His wounds you were healed.
1 PETER 2:24, NASB

$\mathcal{O}$ver the years I have heard many people say, "I know and understand that God forgives me for my sins, but I cannot forgive myself." What these individuals are truly saying in making such a statement is that Christ did not pay a large enough price for their sins. Do you *feel* as if you cannot forgive yourself? Do you *feel* as if your sins are so reprehensible that they are unforgiveable? If so, you need to understand that Jesus paid the price and that the price He paid is sufficient! The apostle Peter states this clearly:

> He Himself bore our sins in His body on the cross,
> that we might die to sin and live to righteousness; for
> by His wounds you were healed.
> —1 Peter 2:24, NASB

It is by Christ's wounds, dear beloved, that you and I have been healed and set free from our sins. However, what you are struggling with is normal. Not that it is right or good, mind you, but it is normal. As the apostle Paul states:

> Even when Gentiles, who do not have God's written law, instinctively follow what the law says, they show that in their hearts they know right from wrong. They demonstrate that God's law is written within them, for their own consciences either accuse them or tell them they are doing what is right.
>
> —Romans 2:14-15, NLT

It is your conscience that is accusing you and causing you to *feel* as if your sins are unforgiveable, because deep down you know right from wrong. God's law is written deep within your heart, and because of this truth you know deep within your innermost being that your sins deserve punishment. In fact, because God's law is written within your heart, you know that "the wages of sins is death" (Romans 6:23). As the writer of Hebrews states:

> [God's] law requires that nearly everything be cleansed with blood, and without the shedding of blood there is no forgiveness.
>
> —Hebrews 9:22

Yet God made a wonderful way for you and I to be set free from the penalty of sin. In Romans 6:23, Paul goes on to say:

> For the wages of sin is death, but the free gift of God is eternal life through Christ Jesus our Lord.
>
> —NLT

With this in mind, it is important to learn and understand the price that Christ paid for your sins, for it is in understanding and accepting God's gift that you can be set free and get to the place where you can forgive yourself. In view of this, let's learn more about the One who paid the price. In Philippians 2:8, Paul writes:

And [Christ] being found in appearance as a man, he
humbled himself and became obedient to death—
even death on a cross!

It was love that sent Jesus Christ to the cross—a love
so deep for you, a love so deep for me. I want you, dear
beloved, to feel, touch and grasp just how deep and immeasurable this love was that Christ had for you. I want
you to see, hear and picture the most important event in
all of history—the death and resurrection of our Lord and
Savior, Jesus Christ—and know without a doubt that the
price He paid for you and for me is sufficient!

I am not going to go into a theological debate or discuss the prophetic significance of Christ's sacrifice. There
are numerous books and volumes written on those subjects.
But I do want to paint a picture of the sacrifice that Jesus
endured for our sins. He took the punishment we deserved
and paid the price so we could be set free. For this reason,
it is my prayer that you will come to an understanding of
the love that Jesus poured out on the cross for you and me.
And, better yet, that you will comprehend that the physical cost of that sacrifice was sufficient to pay the price for
your sin both now and forever more.

In *The Cross of Jesus*, Warren Wiersbe writes, "On Sunday evening, February 19, 1882, Charles Haddon Spurgeon opened his message with these words: 'On whatever
subjects I may be called to preach, I feel it to be a duty
which I dare not neglect to be continually going back to
the doctrine of the cross. . . .' Unless we go back to the
cross, we can't go forward in our Christian life."[139] David
Hocking, a Bible teacher, adds, "I do believe at some point
in a Christian's life he should study the details of what hap-

pened in the suffering and torturing of Jesus Christ. No man has ever endured what He endured."[140]

The problem for many of us is that we have heard the story of the cross so often and we know it so well that it has lost some of its punch. As Pastor Jon Courson states, "We think, 'Oh, yeah. He was beaten. He was marred more than any man and eventually nailed to a tree.' But it would do us well, I think, to sometimes take a long walk in the evening or get up early in the morning and consider what Jesus really went through step by step with you on His mind, with you in His heart. . . . willingly walking in to the butchery that bruised and beat Him more than any other man—all for you. [Ponder this truth:] He really did it for me. I was on His mind. I was in His heart when He took those blows, when He felt that pain, when He endured that horrible suffering. It was all for me. It was all for you."[141]

As Weirsbe writes, "It was love that motivated the Father to give his Son to be the Savior of the world (John 3:16; Romans 5:8; 1 John 4:9-10), and it was love that motivated the Son to give his life for the sins of the world (John 15:13)."[142]

> Amazing love! How can it be? That Thou my God should'st die for me!
>
> —Charles Wesley

It was out of a love so deep for you and for me that God, in His infinite wisdom, devised a plan before the foundations of the world to save us from our sins.[143] As Weirsbe again states, "The cross was a divine assignment, not a human accident."[144] It was a divine assignment of love. Listen to these words of love from Jesus:

146

> I lay down my life for the sheep. . . . No one takes it
> from me, but I lay it down of my own accord. I have
> authority to lay it down and authority to take it up
> again.
>
> —John 10:15b,18a

Jesus willingly laid down His life in love. Weirsbe said
it best when he wrote, "The false impression that in his
death Jesus was a victim instead of the victor [is not the
truth]. . . . Our Lord was not murdered against his will; he
voluntarily gave himself to die for us."[145]

Approximately 700 years before Jesus was born, the
prophet Isaiah penned a portrait of the Suffering Savior. As
the *Halley Bible Handbook* explains, "It begins at [Isaiah]
52:13. [It is] so vivid in detail that one would almost think
of Isaiah as standing at the foot of the cross. . . . so clear in
his mind that he speaks of it in the past tense, as if it had
already come to pass. Yet it was written seven centuries
before Calvary. It cannot possibly fit any person in history
other than Christ."[146]

Let's take a closer look at the events that led up to Jesus literally laying His life down in love for you and me at
the cross. We will begin with the scene in the Garden of
Gethsemane. It is interesting to note that "Gethsemane"
means oil press. As Courson notes, "In an oil press, olives
were crushed, broken, and ground up so that oil might be
produced. Scripturally, oil is symbolic of the Holy Spirit.
The picture is clear: before the Holy Spirit could be given,
Someone had to be crushed and broken. And that Someone was Jesus Christ."[147]

> Then Jesus went with his disciples to a place called
> Gethsemane, and he said to them, "Sit here while I

> go over there and pray." He took Peter and the two
> sons of Zebedee along with him and he began to
> be sorrowful and troubled. Then he said to them,
> "My soul is overwhelmed with sorrow to the point of
> death. Stay here and keep watch with me."
>   —Matthew 26:36-38

Why was Jesus so overwhelmed with sorrow to the point of death? Because He knew what lay ahead. As Courson explains, "There was far more for Jesus than the physical agony of being crucified in a few hours. Should He go through with this plan to pay for your sins and my sins, He would not only feel the wrath of God poured upon Him as He died in place of us, but His suffering would go much farther and longer than what we could possibly imagine. Jesus didn't suffer for just a few hours on a Friday afternoon. Revelation 3:18 speaks of the Lamb slain before the foundation of the world. In other words, the suffering was eternal and incredible. Jesus understood this, and He could have bailed out in the Garden."[148] But He didn't. Instead, He submitted to the will of the Father and paid this incredible price for your sins and mine.

> Amazing love! How can it be? That Thou my God
> should'st die for me!
>   —Charles Wesley

After Jesus asked three of His disciples to keep watch and pray with Him, He walked about a stone's throw away and knelt down to pray. Soon, the three whom He had asked to pray were fast asleep. Meanwhile, Jesus, in agony, pleaded with the Father. Three times He cried out, "Abba, Father. . . . everything is possible for you. Take this cup from me. Yet not what I will, but what you will" (Mark

14:36). Can you hear His cry? Can you hear the crying and pleading of a man so filled with passion as He knelt down and thought of the events to come—as He thought of you and me in love? He is so overwhelmed, in fact, that we read "an angel from heaven appeared to him and strengthened him" (Luke 22:43).

Jesus clearly had a choice—a choice of faith to follow the will of the Father or a choice of the flesh to refuse and say the price was too high. It was a choice that caused Him great distress. As the physician Luke writes, "Being in anguish, he prayed more earnestly, and his sweat was like drops of blood falling to the ground" (Luke 22:44).

According to Dr. Frederick Zugibe, "The sweating of blood, called hematidrosis, is a clinical term because there have been many cases of it. It was first described by Aristotle. Around the sweat glands themselves there are multiple blood vessels in a net-like form."[149] Dr. Robert Beck explains, "It has been shown to occur in great stressful situations. What happens is that around the sweat glands [are] these very fragile capillaries, these are little vessels that only one blood cell can go through at a time, for some reason they rupture and the blood is mixed in with the sweat. Christ did not lose a large amount of blood during this time, but what it does, it makes the skin exquisitely sensitive and very tender to the touch."[150]

Imagine this anguish of love so deep for you and me. Yet Jesus said to the Father, "Not my will, but yours be done" (Luke 22:42b). David Hocking describes the scene like this: "It happened in a moment of great trial and torture as He sweat as it were drops of blood as He felt the agony, says the Bible, of all of the events that would come

against Him. The passion of Gethsemane was real and awful because Jesus *knew* what would happen."[151] Out of love,
Jesus set His face like flint[152] and walked toward His cap-
tors. Can you feel His love with each step He takes—steps
of love toward the cross?

It was a man named Judas, one of Jesus' own disciples,
who betrayed Him.[153] Imagine one of your closest friends,
with whom you had shared the last three years, betray-
ing you. That was what Judas did, and He betrayed His
Lord with a kiss![154] Let's pick up the story in the Gospel
of John:

> So Judas came to the grove, guiding a detachment
> of soldiers and some officials from the chief priests
> and Pharisees. They were carrying torches, lanterns
> and weapons.
>
> Jesus, knowing all that was going to happen
> to him, went out and asked them, "Who is it you
> want?"
>
> "Jesus of Nazareth," they replied.
>
> "I am he," Jesus said. (And Judas the traitor was
> standing there with them.) When Jesus said, "I am
> he," they drew back and fell to the ground.
>
> —John 18:3-6

As you picture this scene in your mind, realize that
a detachment of soldiers was 600 men! This was a huge
group of soldiers who had come to arrest Jesus. When Jesus
then says, "I am he," as Courson explains, "Jesus is actually saying, 'I AM,' *'Ego Eimi'*—a declaration of deity."[155]
Jesus was claiming, and rightfully so, that He was God.
But catch the picture. Can you see it? I like the way Courson goes onto to describe the scene: "With torches flying,

armor clanking, and swords falling, these guys go down under the sheer power of Jesus' proclamation."[156] The *NIV Study Bible* explains it this way: "They came to arrest a meek peasant and instead were met in the dim light by a majestic person."[157] Do you understand? Jesus was in complete control at all times. He gave up His life willingly out of His immeasurable love for you and me.

After the soldiers got up and brushed themselves off, they stepped forward, seized Jesus and arrested Him.[158] It was at this point that Peter decided to try and save the day. He whipped out his sword and cut off the ear of a servant of the high priest.[159] "Put your sword back in its place," Jesus said to him, "for all who draw the sword will die by the sword. Do you think I cannot call on my Father, and he will at once put at my disposal more than twelve legions of angels?" (Matthew 26:52-53).

As Courson teaches, "A legion being six thousand, Jesus was talking about seventy-two thousand angels at His disposal—quite a force, considering it took only one to wipe out 185,000 Babylonians (2 Kings 19:35). What a glorious day when you learn you don't have to defend Jesus Christ—that He is perfectly capable of defending Himself."[160] At any time, Jesus could have stopped these events from taking place. But He chose not to do so. Why? Because of His love for you and me! He chose to go to the cross out of a love so deep—a love to set you free! Given this, can we not be willing to choose love as well? Jesus made faith choices over flesh choices out of His love for us. Can we offer Him any less?

The disciples deserted Jesus, and He was led alone from the Garden of Gethsemane to stand before Caiaphas, the high priest that year. But remember, as Courson points out, "It was not the chains, the ropes, nor the soldiers which bound Jesus. It was love."[161] It was not the trial, the beating to come or the cross that Jesus was thinking about. He had already set His face like flint when He was led through the city of Jerusalem. He was thinking about you and how much He loves you. He knew this was the only way to set you free from the penalty of your sin.

Jesus was taken first to Annas (who was the former high priest) and then to Caiaphas (who was the son-in-law of Annas).[162] During this time, as Courson goes on to explain, "A meeting of the Sanhedrin was called. The Sanhedrin was the seventy-one member Jewish Supreme Court. From the very outset, however, the trial was illegal, since night meetings of the Sanhedrin were forbidden by Mosaic Law."[163]

> They were looking for false evidence against Jesus so that they could put him to death. But they did not find any, though many false witnesses came forward.
>
> —Matthew 26:59-60

During this illegal trial, "they all condemned him as worthy of death. Then some began to spit at him; they blindfolded him, struck him with their fists, and said, 'Prophesy!' And the guards took him and beat him" (Mark 14:64-65). Can you hear the guards' mockery? Imagine the spit running down Jesus' face. Can you hear their laughing? But there was only silence in reply from the Creator of the Universe. Even though Jesus was blindfolded, He knew exactly who was hitting Him, just as He knew the exact day we first denied His love. Even though He chose to be silent, He knew. In the same way as the palace guards struck Him and beat Him, we struck Him in His heart with our denial of Him in our lives. Can you hear the silence? Can you hear His heart break? He did it for you. He did it for me.

> Amazing love! How can it be? That Thou my God should'st die for me!
>
> —Charles Wesley

Courson continues, "It was now 5:00 A.M. After a night of agony in the Garden of Gethsemane, an illegal trial by the Sanhedrin, followed by a beating at the hands of the palace guards, Jesus was led before Pontius Pilate."[164] There, as the false accusations were told to Pilate, the Roman governor, Jesus remained silent, just as had been foretold seven centuries earlier:

> He was oppressed and afflicted, yet he did not open his mouth; he was led like a lamb to the slaughter, and as a sheep before her shearers is silent, so he did not open his mouth.
>
> —Isaiah 53:7

Christ's very silence in the midst of all the agony, the torture and the mockery fulfilled that prophecy. Pilate was amazed that Jesus did not utter one word in His defense.[165] In Luke's account, we read:

> Then Pilate announced to the chief priests and the crowd, "I find no basis for a charge against this man."
>
> —Luke 23:4

According to Courson, "The uniqueness of Jesus is verified by the fact that Pilate went on record, saying, 'I find no fault in Him'—a finding which has never been disputed by historian or cynic. According to many historian records, Pilate himself committed suicide in Sicily not long after this."[166]

Let's take a break in our depiction of Jesus to look a bit more in-depth at suicide. We read in the Gospel of Matthew that Judas committed suicide by hanging himself. Here, we learn from Courson that according to historical records, Pilate himself committed suicide not long after Jesus' crucifixion. The reason? These two men never grasped the depth of the love that God had for them. Likewise, many sinful folks have struggled with suicidal thoughts, fantasies or attempts because of the overwhelming feelings of guilt they have from their sinful lives.

Judas and Pilate both committed suicide because of their sin. Dear beloved, learn a lesson from these men. They did not take their sin, their guilt and their shame and kneel at Jesus' feet. They did not recognize who He was, nor did they give Him the rightful place in their lives. They denied Christ, even though He stood among them, and tried to carry their burdens all by themselves. We cannot forget that Jesus offered this wonderful invitation:

> Come to me, all you who are weary and burdened,
> and I will give you rest.
> —Matthew 11:28

Jesus came to carry the load. The only way you will be able to fully receive rest from your sin is to understand that the price has been paid, and paid in full!

Jesus stands in your midst. Will you accept the sacrifice He made in love for you, or will you, too, deny Christ though He stands before you? Perhaps you are realizing that you have never bowed your knee before Him. If so, it is not too late. He is waiting with open arms to receive you. When you finish reading this chapter, go back to the chapter titled "Are You Right with God?" and again read those words. Put your faith in Christ to be your Lord and Savior. He paid the price—in full!

Now, as if the beating and the mockery that Jesus had endured were not sufficient, Pilate, as a way to get rid of this problem, sent Jesus to Herod.[168] There, "Herod and his soldiers ridiculed and mocked him. Dressing him in an elegant robe, they sent him back to Pilate" (Luke 23:11). Can you imagine all the suffering Jesus had endured thus far—being sent first here, then there—and all the ridicule and mockery? He endured it for you. He endured it for me.

> Pilate called together the chief priests, other rulers and the people, and said to them, "You brought me this man as one who was inciting the people to rebellion. I have examined him in your presence and have found no basis for your charges against him. Neither has Herod, for he sent him back to us; as you can see, he has done nothing to deserve death. Therefore, I will punish him and then release him."
>
> —Luke 23:13-17

The punishment of which Pilate was speaking was scourging. As Courson describes, "Scourging was brutal. It was done with a Roman instrument of torture called a flagellum—a whip made of twelve or thirteen leather thongs. Lead balls were attached to the end of these thongs and pieces of glass and metal were embedded between the lead balls and the handle. . . . The accused would be tied by his wrists and dangled about a foot off the ground, rendering him helpless to protect himself in any way. Then the beating would begin—usually thirty-nine lashes."[169]

At this point, it's interesting to consider for a moment the nature of the typical Roman soldier. Dr. Beck illuminates their mindset for us: "They are veterans in battle, they know how to kill, they hate the Jews, they hate being in Israel, they hate everything and for them to finally get a hold of somebody and just beat them, is nothing but to their joy."[170] The courtyard was filled with these Roman soldiers. Can you hear them mocking Jesus? Can you see them inciting the soldier with the whip to beat Him as hard as he could? Can you hear them egging him on, saying, "Beat Him! Beat Him!"

So the beating began. Just think of Jesus' extra-sensitive skin from sweating drops of blood. Dr. James Strange describes the flagellum whip the Romans would have used as follows: "When flicked as it were, with considerable strength by the person doing the beating, it actually whips around the body and embeds in the flesh and then when it is pulled out one bleeds profusely."[171] Can you hear the snap of this whip? Can you hear Jesus' intake of breath with each stripe He received for you and each stripe He received for me?

> Amazing love! How can it be? That Thou my God should'st die for me!
>
> —Charles Wesley

Dr. Beck goes on to elaborate about the damage that would have been done to Jesus' body by the whip: "First, it ripped through the skin, then what we call the subcutaneous tissue, the fatty tissue under the skin. . . . Then they would continue to whip the individual not only on the back, but on the buttock, on the legs, on the feet. . . . They would love to see just shreds of flesh and muscle just hanging. Literally off the back or the back of the legs and also to expose the vertebrae and the ribs. Now the severity of the scourging was according to how long the individual would last. And with Christ they did a severe scourging."[172] Pastor Corson goes onto explain, "At the end of the beating, the accused would be cut down, and his body would fall to the ground, where he would lay in a pool of his own blood."[173]

Can you picture Christ lying there with His stripes of love for you and with His stripes of love for me? He endured this out of love, and it is by His stripes that we are healed.[174] As Courson states, "So brutal was the beating Jesus endured, Isaiah prophesied He would be more disfigured than any man who ever lived.[175] His beard would be plucked; His face would be swollen. The spit of His accusers would be running down His cheeks. He could have called ten thousand times ten thousand angels. But He didn't."[176] Why? Because of His deep love for you and His deep love for me.

> I offered my back to those who beat me, my cheeks to those who pulled out my beard; I did not hide my face from mocking and spitting.
> —Isaiah 50:6

Many men died as a result of such a beating. After the scourging, "the soldiers twisted together a crown of thorns and put it on his head. They clothed him in a purple robe and went up to him again and again, saying, 'Hail, king of the Jews!' And they struck him in the face" (John 19:2-3). The Roman soldiers draped this rough cloth robe across Jesus' raw and bleeding back, and in a moment of cruel mockery they fashioned a crown of thorns and pushed it down onto His head.[177] As Dr. Beck explains, "They forced that down through His scalp creating even more bleeding because the scalp itself has a large amount of blood supply. It is very vascular. You cut your scalp and it looks like you cut the major vessel in your body."[178]

I like the way Pastor David Hocking describes this scene: "Many people try to get us to relate to this by having a picture of Jesus on the cross.' . . . Often when they have that picture of Christ on the cross, invariably, you see maybe the crown of thorns on Him, with maybe a little blood trickling down, but His face always looks nice. I am sorry—that is not the Bible. Do you understand that Jesus' face was beat up so bad nobody could recognize who He was? And that bloody mess, that pulp, was led out in front of the people by Pilate. . . . 'Behold the man!' It was a mockery."[179] Pilate's statement was a joke! Jesus was marred and beaten beyond recognition. It was impossible to even identify He was a man. Listen to how John describes the scene:

> Pilate went out again and said to them, "See, I am bringing him out to you that you may know that I find no guilt in him." So Jesus came out, wearing the crown of thorns and the purple robe. Pilate said to them, *"Behold the man!"* When the chief priests and the officers saw him, they cried out, "Crucify him, crucify him" Pilate said to them, "Take him yourselves and crucify him, for I find no guilt in him."
> —John 19:4-6, ESV, emphasis added

Can you hear the cries of the crowd—the passion with which they yelled? Did our *own* actions of sin yell just as loudly to Christ, "Crucify Him! Crucify Him!"?

Wiersbe writes, "In spite of their [the Jews] careful attention to the study of the Old Testament, the people didn't recognize their Savior and King when he arrived. They mocked him as a prophet and said, 'Prophesy! Who is it that struck you?' They mocked him as a king, putting a robe on him, giving him a scepter, and placing a crown of thorns on his head. They shouted to Pilate, 'We have no king but Caesar!' They laughed at Christ's claim that he was the Son of God. 'He saved others; let Him save Himself if He is the Christ, the chosen of God!'"[180] Let us weigh our *own* actions carefully, lest we make the same mistake that they made.

Jesus endured hours of misery, but the worst of the ordeal was yet to come:

> Finally Pilate handed him over to them to be crucified. So the soldiers took charge of Jesus. Carrying his own cross, he went out to the place of the Skull (which in Aramaic is called Golgotha).
> —John 19:16-17

As Dr. John Bonica states, "I can't imagine how a person who was whipped or who was injured in [such] ways would be expected to carry a very heavy load. I would anticipate that the average individual would not be able to tolerate that for more than a few feet."[181] Dr. Strange goes onto explain, "The cross itself is a very heavy timber. . . . the objective is to make it last a long time. The timber is unfinished, it is not lovely, sanded down timber, it is just

159

cut out with adzes so it is quite rough and even injures the skin while it is being carried."[182] Keep this in mind as you read how Luke describes the scene:

> As they led Jesus away, Simon of Cyrene, who was coming in from the country just then, was forced to follow Jesus and carry his cross. Great crowds trailed along behind, including many grief-stricken women.
>
> —Luke 23:26-27, NLT

Imagine the scene. Imagine the people. Imagine the heartbreak. Once the Romans soldiers reached Golgotha, they threw Jesus down to the ground to prepare Him for the cross. They stripped Jesus of His clothing with brutal indifference to the gaping wounds that covered His body. Then, as John relates:

> They crucified him, and with him two others—one on each side and Jesus in the middle.
>
> —John 19:18

As Courson notes, "Crucifixion was developed by the Persians, today called the Iranians, around the year 1000 BC. Designed to be excruciatingly painful. . . . The Persians considered the ground of their country to be holy, they mandated that a crucified victim be elevated lest his cursing defile it. That is why when a man was crucified he was raised up usually three to four feet off the ground. When the Greeks took over the Persian Empire, they adopted crucifixion. And when the Romans came on the scene, they borrowed it from the Greeks."[183]

Dr. Beck explains, "Now the hand itself cannot support the full weight of the body. But in Greek when they mention [the] hand it also includes the wrist. So the one area that you could drive that nail was either through the wrist or between the two bones which make up the forearm."[184] The Romans pounded the nails quickly into Jesus' hands and feet. Can you hear the hammer hit the nail? Yet not a word did Jesus scream or mutter in pain. Pound, pound, pound . . . in love for you! In love for me!

Dr. Beck goes on to describe the areas of the hands and feet where the soldiers would drive the nails: "There is really not an arterial vessel in this area. . . . But what is there is a nerve called the median nerve. And as they were driving that [nail] through, it would cause the hand to go into a claw-like appearance with immense shooting pain in the hand and up the arm."[185] Dr. Zugibe explains, "If the median nerve is ruptured or injured [this] will cause severe excruciating, burning-like pain. Like lightening bolts traversing the arm into the spinal cord."[186] Can you imagine what Jesus endured in love for you and endured in love for me?

> Amazing love! How can it be? That Thou my God
> should'st die for me!
>
> —Charles Wesley

We know from the Gospel accounts that there were four women there at the scene of the cross. As Courson states, "It was not easy for them. It was not easy for Mary to watch her Son convulsing in pain, or for her sister to hear the curses hurled at Him. It was not easy for the wife of Cleophas to see the spit of the crowd running down His face, or for Mary Magdalene to see His blood flowing from His wounds. But these four women, [who loved the Lord and followed Him,] were there at the foot of the Cross, no matter how great the price, no matter how deep the pain."[187] Through it all, these women watched. Can you see the love in their eyes for their Savior? Imagine how you would feel if it were your son being crucified. Can you see the sorrow?

> When they had crucified him, they divided up his clothes by casting lots. And sitting down, they kept watch over him there.
>
> —Matthew 27:35-36

> And as prophesied in the Old Testament dogs have surrounded me; a band of evil men has encircled me, they have pierced my hands and my feet. I can count all my bones; people stare and gloat over me. They divide my garments among them and cast lots for my clothing.
>
> —Psalm 22:16-18

Can you imagine the pain Jesus endured—a pain so great that He could count all His bones because each one was crying out in a symphony of pain? Can you imagine the shame of hanging on a cross, practically naked, with people looking on in mockery and cruelty, casting lots and dividing up the clothes He wore? Can you see the flies swarming around His body and the vultures circling overhead? Why did He allow it? Out of His deep love for you and out of His deep love for me!

> Jesus said "Father forgive them; for they know not what they do."
>
> —Luke 23:34, KJV

Weirsbe writes, "Consider the wonder of the appeal. The tense of the verb 'said' indicates that our Lord repeated this prayer. As the soldiers nailed him to the cross, he prayed, 'Father, forgive them.' When they lifted the cross and placed it in the hole in the ground, our Lord prayed, 'Father, forgive them.' As he hung there between heaven and earth, and heard religious people mocking him, he repeatedly prayed, 'Father, forgive them.'"[188]

Beloved, as He looked upon you and upon me, He cried, "Father forgive them; for they know not what they do" (Luke 23:34, KJV). Imagine the look of love—a love so deep for you and a love so deep for me!

As Jesus hung on the cross, He would have literally had to fight for each breath He took. Jesus was hanging in a position called "inhalation." This is how Dr. Beck describes this torturous position: "Now to exhale He had to first of all flex His arms, in other words bend them, to pull up on those nails. At the same time as He was pulling up He had to push on that nail which was basically the weight-bearing nail. He would slide up the wood, which would again open up His back and wounds. And He would start bleeding again. With each movement the pain was absolutely excruciating."[189]

According to Weirsbe, "Close to the end of his ordeal, Jesus was forsaken by the Father and announced this fact in a loud voice: 'My God, My God, why have You forsaken Me?' (Matthew 27:46). This was the climax of the awful darkness that had shrouded the cross for three hours."[190] God the Father cannot look upon sin,[191] and it was at this point that Jesus became sin for us.[192] He took upon Himself the sin of the whole world—including our sin. Though He was without blemish or any iniquity at all, He took your sins and mine upon Himself. He took the punishment we deserved and literally laid down His life for you and for me. Why? Because of His deep and immeasurable love for us! He offered Himself as the penalty for our sin.

> Amazing love! How can it be? That Thou my God should'st die for me!
> —Charles Wesley

Then Jesus cried out in a loud voice, "It is finished!" (John 19:30). According to Weirsbe, "In the Greek language in which John wrote his Gospel, this statement was only one word of ten letters—tetelestai. In the Greek, it means, 'It is finished, it stands finished, and it always will be finished.'"[193] *Tetelestai* is a word that was familiar and commonly used in Jesus' day. To a merchant, the word would have meant that the debt had been fully paid. As Weirsbe notes, "Unbelieving sinners are in debt to God and can't pay their bill. Having broken God's law, they are bankrupt and unable to pay (Luke 7:36-50). But Jesus paid the debt when he died for us on the cross. That's what tetelestai means: the debt has been paid, it stands paid, and it always will be paid. When we turn to Christ in faith, our sins are forgiven and the debt is canceled forever."[194] It is interesting to note that the verses Wiersbe references in Luke 7 are from the story of the Sinful Woman. The price had been paid!

Soon, Jesus' ordeal was over. As Luke describes the scene:

> Then Jesus, calling out with a loud voice, said, "Father, into your hands I commit my spirit! And having said this he breathed his last.
> —Luke 23:46

Jesus' parting words prove to us that the Father and the Son are together again. Weirsbe said it best when he wrote, "He was forsaken by the Father that we might never be forsaken by God."[195]

Perhaps the next part of the story is the most inconceivable to me. It shows the depravity of humans in their religious endeavors. Oh, how we can twist up our sins to make them presentable! Courson describes the scene found in John 19:31 this way: "The next day being Passover, the Jews didn't want the bodies left on the crosses. 'Break their legs' the Jews said to Pilate, 'and speed up the death so we can move on with our holy convocation.' Incredible!"[196]

> The soldiers therefore came and broke the legs of the first man who had been crucified with Jesus, and then those of the other. But when they came to Jesus and found that he was already dead, they did not break his legs. Instead, one of the soldiers pierced Jesus' side with a spear, bringing a sudden flow of blood and water. . . . These things happened so that the scripture would be fulfilled. "Not one of his bones will be broken," and, as another scripture says, "They will look on the one they have pierced."
> —John 19:32-37

Ponder what Courson has to say for a moment: "Not a bone of Jesus was broken. Why is this such a big deal? Because where is the blood continually produced in the body? It's produced in the bone. Therefore, God mandated not a bone of His would be broken ensuring a perpetual and inexhaustible supply of blood. That's why Paul could later declare, 'Where sin abounds, grace abounds yet more' (Romans 5:20).' Truly, the blood of Jesus Christ is sufficient to cleanse you from every sin you have ever committed or will commit. Why? Because not a bone of His was broken."[197]

> In him we have redemption through his blood, the forgiveness of sins, in accordance with the riches of God's grace that he lavished on us with all wisdom and understanding.
>
> —Ephesians 1:7-8

It is the blood that cleanses us. Remember what we talked about at the beginning of this chapter? "Without the shedding of blood there is no forgiveness" (Hebrews 9:22).

According to the *Halley Bible Handbook*, "Jesus was already dead when the spear pierced his side, after being on the cross six hours. Some medical authorities have said that in the case of heart rupture, and in that case only, the blood collects in the pericardium, the lining around the wall of the heart, and divides into a sort of bloody clot and a watery serum. If this is a fact, then the actual immediate physical cause of Jesus' death was heart rupture. Under intense pain, and the pressure of his wildly raging blood, his heart burst open. It may be that Jesus, literally, died of a heart broken over the sin of the world. It may be that suffering for human sin is more than the human constitution can stand."[198]

Jesus died of a broken heart.

Perhaps, just perhaps, dear beloved, His heart did not break because the sin of the whole world was placed upon Him. Perhaps, just perhaps, His heart did not break because He was separated from the Father. Perhaps His heart broke from love—a love so deep for you and a love so deep for me that it literally broke His heart that we forsook His love.

Have you ever loved someone so deeply, but that love was not returned? Did your heart feel as if it would break? Did Christ's heart break because we denied His love?

> He was pierced for our transgressions, he was crushed for our iniquities; the punishment that brought us peace was upon him, and by his wounds we are healed.
>
> —Isaiah 53:5

> Amazing love! How can it be? That Thou my God should'st die for me!
>
> —Charles Wesley

Ponder this love over the next week or two when you feel you cannot forgive yourself. Ponder this love over the next month or so when you feel no one loves you. Ponder this love over the next year or so as you choose to live a life pleasing to God. And remember to ponder this love as you walk away from the side of the bridge into a whole new life filled with truth and meaning. He loves you more than you know!

Courson said it best: "According to the Word of God, if you open up your heart to Jesus Christ and believe in His work on the Cross, your sin is gone."[199] There is no reason you cannot forgive yourself. The price is paid!

But the story is not yet ended. In fact, the best is yet to come! At dawn, three women went to the tomb to anoint Jesus' body with spices. "As they entered the tomb, they saw a young man dressed in a white robe sitting on the right side, and they were alarmed. 'Don't be alarmed,' he said. 'You are looking for Jesus the Nazarene, who was crucified. He has risen! He is not here" (Mark 16:5-6a).

> On the evening of that first day of the week, when the disciples were together, with the doors locked for fear of the Jews, Jesus came and stood among them and said, "Peace be with you!" After he said this, he showed them his hands and side. The disciples were overjoyed when they saw the Lord.
>
> —John 20:19-20

The first words Jesus spoke to His disciples after the crucifixion and resurrection were "peace be with you!" Why do we choose to stand in the prison cell when the door is wide open? Accept the gift. The price is paid! He is the One who walked away from an empty tomb. Dear beloved, won't you join Him? Won't you *go in peace!*

Chapter Twelve

THE TEMPLE OF THE HOLY SPIRIT

> *Do you not know that your body is*
> *a temple of the Holy Spirit,*
> *who is in you, whom you have received from God?*
> *You are not your own; you were bought with a price.*
> *Therefore honor God with your body.*
> 1 CORINTHIANS 6:19-20

*N*ow that we have dealt with the issue of sin regarding abortion, it is time to address another matter: immorality. For those of us who chose to have sex outside of marriage, this is the sin that got us into this mess in the first place—our sin did not begin with the abortion. Furthermore, if you are one who chose abortion within the boundaries of marriage, you are also not exempt from this issue. You, too, will find something of value in this chapter, for you will discover that many times sin begins within the *mind*. Remember, God Word calls us to take every thought captive, including thoughts of romance and love. Pay attention to how quickly thoughts of love can turn into thoughts of lust. Listen to what Jesus taught:

> You have heard that it was said, "Do not commit adultery." But I tell you that anyone who looks at a woman lustfully has already committed adultery with her in his heart.
>
> —Matthew 5:27-28

169

This wasn't written to just men. Women can also commit adultery within their hearts when they look at a man (or even a woman) lustfully. Sin not only includes your wrong actions but also your wrong attitudes and even your wrong thoughts. With this in mind, you need to learn to take your thoughts captive, moment by moment, and make them obedient to Christ. For if you do not make your thoughts obedient to Christ, they can trigger your emotions, which can trigger your desires, and your desires, if allowed, can trigger your actions.

Because of this, it is important to know that many times the sin begins with the *second* thought. The reason I say this is because many times when the thought first enters your mind, it is not sin. Remember what the apostle Paul wrote in the book of Ephesians concerning Satan and the fiery darts he shoots at you:

> Above all, taking the shield of faith with which you will be able to quench all the fiery darts of the wicked one.
>
> —Ephesians 6:16, NKJV

The enemy wants to cause you to stumble and fall. He knows that if he can make you choose a life of habitual sin, it will cause you to fall away from the Lord. For this reason, the enemy (or one of his many cohorts) will shoot a fiery dart to play on your feelings and emotions, or he may even shoot a fiery dart filled with a sexual thought. This first thought is not sin, because it is something over which you have no control. But the moment you allow that thought to take hold and you choose to let your imagination run wild with it, then it becomes sin. This is why I believe Paul wrote the following:

> Finally, brothers, whatever is true, whatever is noble,
> whatever is right, whatever is pure, whatever is love-
> ly, whatever is admirable—if anything is excellent or
> praiseworthy—*think* about such things.
>
> —Philippians 4:8, emphasis added

When you choose to think on things that *aren't* true, or noble, or right, or pure, or lovely, or admirable, or excellent, or praiseworthy, many times it is sin you are thinking about. This is exactly what happened to Eve in the Garden of Eden. Remember the story?

> Now the serpent was more crafty than any of the
> wild animals the LORD God had made. He said to
> the woman, "Did God really say, 'You must not eat
> from any tree in the garden'?"
>
> The woman said to the serpent, "We may eat
> fruit from the trees in the garden, but God did say,
> 'You must not eat fruit from the tree that is in the
> middle of the garden, and you must not touch it, or
> you will die.'"
>
> "You will not surely die," the serpent said to the
> woman. "For God knows that when you eat of it
> your eyes will be opened, and you will be like God,
> knowing good and evil."
>
> When the woman saw that the fruit of the tree
> was good for food and pleasing to the eye, and also
> desirable for gaining wisdom, she took some and ate
> it. She also gave some to her husband, who was with
> her, and he ate it.
>
> —Genesis 3:1-6, emphasis added

Now, it is true that Adam and Eve sinned when they chose to eat the fruit. However, I believe that the sin in

171

their hearts began when they started *thinking* about eating the fruit. The sin began when Eve saw that the fruit was good.

The word "saw," as it appears in the original Hebrew, could actually be translated "to gaze at, to look intently at, to observe, to consider, to learn about, and to give attention to."[200] In fact, the tense of the word "saw" in this verse indicates that it relates "not so much as to one occasion, [but] as to a continued condition . . . frequent repetition."[201] In other words, Eve gazed at the fruit and considered eating it for some time. When she *saw* that the fruit was good, it means she took more than a casual glance—she *chose* to gaze at it and then *considered* and *thought* about eating it.

Can you picture the event? Imagine what might have happened. It was a beautiful day in the Garden of Eden. Eve was walking about when all of a sudden the serpent appeared and said, "Hey, Eve, come over here. Check this out." (Loosely paraphrased, of course.) I don't think Eve ate the fruit that day, because the tense of the word "saw" indicates she considered it for some time. Rather, I believe the serpent planted that seed by shooting a fiery dart into her mind with his words. That seed became a sin when Eve chose to start thinking about eating the fruit. Each time Eve walked passed the tree in the middle of the Garden, she began to gaze at it a little bit more intently. She saw that it was pleasing to the eye, and then she began to justify her desires of eating the fruit as a good thing, because it was desirable for gaining wisdom.

Do you see how Eve's thoughts triggered her emotions? The word "emotion" is just a fancy word for feelings. Her feelings then triggered her desires of gaining wisdom, and her desires triggered her actions. This same is true for us: sin begins with the second thought. It takes root when we begin to look at something intently and consider doing wrong. Sin begins to grow in our hearts and in our minds well before any action has taken place. If we don't stop our thoughts, this can be the beginning of the vicious downward spiral of sin, sin and more sin. So be warned. Be careful about not only what you look at but also what you think about.

Here's an example of how easily our thoughts can get out of control. Say you stop at the gas station to fill your tank and as you are walking into the station to pay, a nice looking guy walks by. You say "hi" in passing. He replies, "Hi!" and sort of flirts with you. You think, *Wow, he thinks I am cute.* Then you take a second look to see if he is still checking you out. That is the moment where sin comes in. The moment you allow the thought to play on your emotions and your desires, it triggers the action of the second look.

At this point you may be thinking, *Come on, that's not that big of a deal.* However, it is important to recognize that you have a choice when you are in a situation like that—a flesh choice or a faith choice. The flesh choice is to start thinking about it and dwelling on it, and then possibly taking the second look. While it might seem innocent—*just* a little flirt—and that no harm can come of it, it is still sin. The faith choice is to decide *not* to even allow your thoughts to go there so you don't take the second look and commit a sin. You can pick up your shield of faith to deflect the fiery darts and keep on walking.

Remember that God's Word says to be prepared to "take up the shield of faith, with which you can extinguish all the flaming arrows of the evil one" (Ephesians 6:16). As you choose to not allow your thoughts to run amuck, you are using the shield of faith in the manner God intended. Of course, making this faith choice is not as much fun at that moment, but it is the choice from which you will reap the blessings—the blessings of a content marriage, children who are walking with the Lord, and friends who consider you a woman of virtue. As for you single ones who may be arguing, *But he could be my future husband,* don't worry. If he is truly the one, God will work it out. Remember, you are the daughter of the King of kings. Your heavenly Father knows exactly whom He has picked for you if you are to marry, so relax and trust Him.

Unfortunately, all too often we tend to fall into this trap. We allow our thoughts to run wild, and soon our thoughts trigger our feelings and emotions of love and romance. We long to feel wanted and special, and these emotions trigger our desires—the desire (for those who are single) to be married, the desire (for those who are married) to have a husband who is caring and kind, the desire (for all of us) to live in a beautiful house with a white picket fence. Those desires, in turn, trigger an action—just a look, just a little flirt. We try to deceive ourselves into believing that flirting is innocent (especially if we are already married).

> Beloved, do not think it strange concerning the fiery trial which is to try you, as though some strange thing happened to you.
> —1 Peter 4:12, NKJV

Many married women I disciple deeply desire for their husband to be the spiritual leader in their house. One woman I knew desired this so strongly that the enemy was able to use it to get a foothold in her life. She thought every day that if only her husband were the spiritual leader in their home, they would be so much happier.

Soon, in all innocence (or so she thought), she began to communicate with a man via the Internet. The things he wrote to her triggered her emotions of having someone interested in her—a new love and a new romance. Then the emotions triggered her desires—the desire of wanting her husband to be the spiritual leader. Before long, she began to compare her husband to the romantic knight in shining armor who was sending her emails—a figure of her imagination with whom her husband could not compare. The woman began to think that her husband would *never* be the spiritual leader in their house, and this desire began to trigger an action—the action of building a friendship with the other man over the Internet, and then setting up a meeting.

Nothing had happened (she justified to herself deep within her heart) except that now she was considering leaving her husband for this man. Notice that the sin did not begin when she went so far as to arrange a meeting. The sin began with the second thought—the thought that perhaps this man would care for her and fulfill the desires of her heart. The sin began in her mind when she allowed the enemy's fiery darts to take root and grow into thoughts of romance and love.

My friend shared with me that this man was a believer and that she just knew in her heart that he would be the spiritual leader she so desired. I told her that this individual could never be the spiritual leader she was seeking. "But you don't know him," she said. "How can you say that?" I replied, "Because if he were, he would have fled from you and left his coat in your hands" (read the story of Joseph and Potiphar's wife in Genesis 39.) Praise the Lord! My friend broke off the relationship and stayed with her husband.

How many of us began relationships that *seemed* innocent but quickly went way too far and got out of control? My friend was ready to give up her family and her life for romantic thoughts. This is where the enemy so deceives us. Romantic thoughts never come true when they are outside of God's will. All they will ever be are thoughts—thoughts of sin. Yes, there is pleasure in sin for a short season,[202] but what then? Visitation rights to see your children every other weekend? Remarriage and then, after a couple of years, the same problems you had in your first marriage? A blended family with kids all struggling to fit in? For those of you who are single, this pattern—date one guy, dump that guy, date another guy, dump that guy—is a total setup for marriage and divorce, marriage and divorce. Sounds romantic, doesn't it? Were these real-life problems included in your thoughts of love and romance?

Have you ever looked up the definition of "romance"? According to the *Webster's Ninth New Collegiate Dictionary*, it is "a medieval *tale* based on *legend*; a prose narrative treating *imaginary characters* involved in events remote in time or place; something, as an *extravagant* story or account, that *lacks* basis in *fact*."[203] How about the definition of "romantic"? It means "consisting of or resembling a romance; having *no* basis in *fact*: *imaginary*; *impractical* in conception or plan."[204] It seems as if the enemy has twisted words once again. I know I was surprised at these definitions, and it gets even more interesting if you look up the words "romance" and "romantic" in a thesaurus. Some of the more interesting synonyms suggested in the *Roget's 21st Century Thesaurus* include "madman," "lunatic," "maniac," "crazy," "dreamer" and "seer."[205] I challenge you to look at a thesaurus and check it out yourself.

Another woman I knew had a tremendous struggle with thoughts of romance. When she was a young woman, both she and her husband loved the Lord with all their hearts. They went to church all the time and were actively involved in ministry. But her dreams of romance and love were so overpowering that she *felt* as if she were not able to control them. She did not realize that when those thoughts began, they represented a fiery trial for her to overcome and be victorious. Instead, she allowed them to run wild. Her thoughts triggered her emotions, and her emotions triggered her desires. Her husband was not able to fulfill the need that she had in her heart for romance, and soon he paled in comparison to the men she fantasized about. Real life did not compare to the romantic encounters she had in her mind.

She claimed she never acted on these thoughts, but because she did not take them captive and make them obedient to Christ, it caused her and her husband to stumble and not be victorious believers. Tragically, the enemy defeated them, and their marriage ended in divorce. This woman who loved the Lord and had a desire to be used by Him was rendered ineffective. It all began with the second thought—a thought not given over to God and made obedient to Christ.

When I met this woman years later, she was still in bondage, shackled and chained to thoughts of romance and love. The enemy had established a foothold in her life and kept her under lock and key for years. At this point, she was in a relationship with another man. She knew this was wrong and she was taking steps to break off the relationship, but the battle was fierce.

One time as I was teaching a workshop on the elements of repentance (godly sorrow on account of sin and repulsion toward sin followed by the actual forsaking of sin), she honestly shared with me, "But I like his kisses. How am I ever going to achieve this second element of repentance and be victorious?" What she said was so true. We all like the feelings we have when we are in a relationship—even one that is wrong. No matter how hard she struggled to forsake the sin, the truth was that she enjoyed his kisses. She had tried everything to end this relationship. She had moved far away from him, she was struggling daily not to call him, and she had become involved in church again. Yet she liked his kisses. How would she ever reach this second element of repentance?

I immediately asked God for wisdom, and He gave me some vivid verses to share with all the women in that workshop concerning this woman's question:

> The body is not meant for sexual immorality, but for the Lord, and the Lord for the body. By his power God raised the Lord from the dead, and he will raise us also. Do you not know that your bodies are members of Christ himself? *Shall I then take the members of Christ and unite them with a prostitute? Never!* Do you not know that he who unites himself with a prostitute is one with her in body? For it is said, "The two will become one flesh." But he who unites

himself with the Lord is one with him in spirit. Flee
from sexual immorality. All other sins a man com-
mits are outside his body, but he who sins sexually
sins against his own body. Do you not know that
your body is a temple of the Holy Spirit, who is in
you, whom you have received from God? You are
not your own; you were bought at a price. Therefore
honor God with your body.
        —1 Corinthians 6:13b-20, emphasis added

I told the ladies in that workshop of the shame I felt
when I first learned these verses—when it dawned on me
that every time I kissed a man outside of marriage (speaking of situations before I was married), I was placing Christ
in that situation! Oh, how I must have grieved Him! I was
seeking love, but only the love that He had to offer could
satisfy my longing. As Pastor John Courson states, "Forni-
cation not only jeopardizes one's eternal state, but it ago-
nizes our holy King. Paul says, 'Don't you understand that
you're bringing Jesus into that situation?' The concept is so
shocking that Paul doesn't even get into it very much except to say that if you're in an immoral situation, you place
Christ in that situation. God forbid."[206]

Now, please don't misunderstand. Paul is not saying
that Christ is a sinner. Remember, Jesus Christ is "the sinless, spotless Lamb of God" (1 Peter 1:19, NLT). Instead,
Paul is saying that my sin and your sin placed Jesus Christ
on the cross—He took our sin upon Himself, even though
He was sinless and spotless—and it places Him in that
situation every time we sin. Every time a woman kisses a
man outside of marriage, she is placing Christ in that situation. Every time a woman touches a man in the wrong
way outside of marriage, she is placing Christ in that situ-

ation. Ponder that for a moment. Does that change your perspective? Does it help you achieve that second element of repentance? Remember, even though you might be doing something in secret, Christ sees everything. Nothing is hidden from Him.

I know that in my situation, it helped me reach the second element of repentance: to be repulsed and repugnant toward my sin. Or, as my wonderful daughters so adeptly expressed it when hearing this from a recorded session, "Mom, that's so gross!" (I always prayed they would remember these words and make it to their wedding night, and both of our daughters walked down the aisle in purity. They married wonderful men who not only came to ask us if they could marry our daughters, but also if they could date them!) The truth, dear beloved, is that we must keep our actions within the boundaries of God's Word. When we look at our sin and see it the way Christ sees it, we can then reach the second element of repentance.

Some will say, "But how then can you have a relationship with your husband if you are a member of Christ's body?" All the way back in Genesis, God says that when two are married, they shall become one.[207] Therefore, you can be intimate with your husband because God sees you and your husband as one. It is for this relationship, marriage, that God created these powerful and wonderful emotions, desires and actions. It is His desire that we would be fruitful and multiply.[208]

Everything that God made beautiful the enemy wants to destroy. Remember, Satan is the thief who comes only to steal, kill and destroy, and that is exactly what he has done. He has taken something beautiful that God intended to be between a man and a woman within the boundaries of marriage and has twisted it into something ugly and hurtful. The result of this sin leads to so many consequences, such as sexually transmitted diseases, pregnancy outside of marriage (which oftentimes leads to abortion), emotionally giving one's heart to another who only wants a physical relationship, prior relationships that create thoughts and memories that are brought into a marriage, a broken family concerning the issue of adultery, hurting kids—the list goes on. There are so many terrible consequences that end up wreaking havoc in our lives. Listen to how Paul describes it:

> The acts of the sinful nature are obvious: sexual immorality, impurity and debauchery; idolatry and witchcraft; hatred, discord, jealousy, fits of rage, selfish ambition, dissensions, factions and envy; drunkenness, orgies, and the like. I warn you, as I did before, that those who live like this will not inherit the kingdom of God.
>
> —Galatians 5:19-21

Dear beloved, these are the results of living outside of God's will. For me, I know that I no longer want to walk in a life such as this. But how can we live in such a way that will honor God? It is only by taking our thoughts captive, moment by moment, and making them obedient to Christ.

The apostle Paul encourages us to "live by the Spirit" so that we "will not gratify the desires of the sinful nature" (Galatians 5:16). The term "live by" in the original Greek is in the present tense and means to "go on living"[209] —continually, moment by moment. As Ralph Earl states in *Word Meanings in the New Testament*, "The only way to avoid fulfilling fleshly desire is to keep walking in the Spirit."[210] That's why I believe King David wrote:

> Create in me a pure heart, O God, and renew a steadfast spirit within me.
>
> —Psalm 51:10

The word "create" in this verse is also written in the present tense, and it means to continue to create moment by moment. King David goes on to state, "Do not cast me from your presence or take your Holy Spirit from me" (Psalm 51:11). He knew that the only way to avoid fleshly desire was *to keep walking* in the Spirit. That's why he talked about being steadfast. "Steadfast" means firm, unshakeable, unbendable and steady. In this way, we see that while the principle of *taking our thoughts captive* may sound simple, it does not necessarily mean that it is easy to do. We must take every thought captive—moment by moment—and make it obedient to Christ.

Let me give you some practical ways to take your thoughts captive. First, when you realize that your thoughts are not ones that are pleasing to God, repent and give them over to Him. (He already knows what you are thinking anyway; He just wants you to be obedient. Remember, He knew what Simon was thinking concerning the Sinful Woman.) When you immediately give your wrongful thoughts over to Christ, you are making them obedient to Him. Then you must immediately replace those thoughts with His Word. Hopefully, by this point you have memorized some verses in the book (or at least know a praise song). Instead of dwelling on the wrongful thoughts, begin to dwell on a verse you are memorizing, or sing a praise song. It is amazing how fast the sinful thoughts will flee when you choose to change your thinking.

Second, avoid situations that cause desires. For me, I needed to stop reading romance novels and avoid watching certain programs on television. Please understand that I am not saying that you should *never again* read romance novels or watch television because they are sinful. What I am trying to relate to you is that if you find certain things are triggering wrong thoughts and causing you to stumble, you need to take action to avoid falling into sin—the sin of sinful thoughts.

Third, if you are single, set some guidelines—guidelines for success! Choose your friends wisely. You may even need to make new friends. As Proverbs states:

> The righteous should choose his [or her] friends carefully, For the way of the wicked leads them astray.
> —Proverbs 12:26, NKJV

Some of you may need to change your lifestyle. As Paul states in Ephesians 5:17-18, "Do not be foolish but understand what the Lord's will is. Do not get drunk on wine, which leads to debauchery. Instead be filled with the Spirit." "Debauchery" means "extreme indulgence in sensuality. Orgies or seduction from virtue or duty."[211] In view of this, do not allow yourself to get into situations that can get out of control.

Fourth, do not be unequally yoked. God has a plan for your life—a perfect plan. That's why Paul warned believers to "not be unequally yoked together with unbelievers" (2 Corinthians 6:14). The Lord already knows who your husband will be, if you are to be wed. You do not need to go out looking for him. In God's perfect timing, you will meet him.

Perhaps the most important guideline I could give you is what Paul states in Romans 12:2: "Do not conform any longer to the pattern of this world, but be transformed by the renewing of your mind." As Elisabeth Elliot so aptly expresses in *Passion and Purity*, "There is dullness, monotony, sheer boredom in all of life when virginity and purity are no longer protected and prized. By trying to grab fulfillment everywhere, we find it nowhere."[212]

Now, it doesn't mean that when you give these things over to God you will no longer be tempted. Remember what you learned in John 10:10: "The thief comes only to steal and kill and destroy." Satan, or one of his many cohorts, will try to seduce you and pull you away from your virtue. As Elisabeth Elliot goes on to state so beautifully, "If the yearnings went away, what would we have to offer up to the Lord? Aren't they given to us to offer? It is the control of passion, not its eradication, that is needed. How would we learn to submit to the authority of Christ if we had nothing to submit?"[213] This is why, as Paul writes:

It is God's will that you should be sanctified: that you should avoid sexual immorality; that each of you should learn to control his [or her] own body in a way that is holy and honorable, not in passionate lust like the heathen, who do not know God. . . . For God did not call us to be impure, but to live a holy life. Therefore, he [or she] who rejects this instruction does not reject man but God, who gives you the Holy Spirit.

—1 Thessalonians 4:3-5,7-8

184

Please do not reject this instruction, and do not think that you are "too far gone" and can never change. If you are like me when I was a teen and have blown it, you *can* start over again. Yes you can! Remember that you are no longer the bad guy you played in act one. As Paul again states:

> Forgetting what is behind and straining toward what is ahead, I press on toward the goal to win the prize for which God has called me heavenward in Christ Jesus.
>
> —Philippians 3:13b-14

You are a new creation, so learn to submit to the authority of Christ. *Live* by the Spirit moment by moment and allow Him to *create* in you a pure heart! Take every thought captive and make it obedient to Christ, and walk forth a new woman of virtue. As you do, you will *go in peace!*

Chapter Thirteen

BREPHOS

As soon as the sound of your greeting reached my ears,
the baby [brephos] in my womb leaped for joy.
LUKE 1:44

*A*s I mentioned in a previous chapter, many women who have had an abortion (even women who follow Christ) believe that abortion is acceptable. One of the main reasons they believe this is because to believe otherwise hurts too much. For many years I also needed to believe that lie, for to believe otherwise was just too painful to bear.

However, if you wish to lay all of your burdens concerning abortion at the feet of Jesus, then you must look at abortion as God sees it. Remember, the Wonderful Counselor, also known as the Prince of Peace, is always by your side. God, in His infinite wisdom, knew that we would have this controversial debate over this important question and that human life would depend on His answer. So, if you want to know the truth, open your heart and join with me as we take a look at the beautiful story of Jesus before His birth. This story is so awesome that it answers the age-old question, "Does life begin at birth or at conception?"

In the sixth month, God sent the angel Gabriel to Nazareth, a town in Galilee, to a virgin pledged to

187

be married to a man named Joseph, a descendant of David. The virgin's name was Mary. The angel went to her and said, "Greetings, you who are highly favored! The Lord is with you."

Mary was greatly troubled at his words and wondered what kind of greeting this might be. But the angel said to her, "Do not be afraid, Mary, you have found favor with God. You will be with child and give birth to a son, and you are to give him the name Jesus. He will be great and will be called the Son of the Most High. The Lord God will give him the throne of his father David, and he will reign over the house of Jacob forever; his kingdom will never end."

"How will this be," Mary asked the angel, "since I am a virgin?"

The angel answered, "The Holy Spirit will come upon you, and the power of the Most High will overshadow you. So the holy one to be born will be called the Son of God. Even Elizabeth your relative is going to have a child in her old age, and she who was said to be barren is in her sixth month. For nothing is impossible with God."

"I am the Lord's servant," Mary answered. "May it be to me as you have said." Then the angel left her.

At that time Mary got ready and hurried to a town in the hill country of Judea, where she entered Zechariah's home and greeted Elizabeth. When Elizabeth heard Mary's greeting, the baby leaped in her womb, and Elizabeth was filled with the Holy Spirit. In a loud voice she exclaimed: "Blessed are you among women, and blessed is the child you will bear! But why am I so favored, that the mother of my Lord should come to me? As soon as the sound of your greeting reached my ears, the baby in my womb leaped for joy. Blessed is she who has believed that what the Lord has said to her will be accomplished!" . . . Mary stayed with Elizabeth for about three months and then returned home.

—Luke 1:26-45,56

I would like to share with you some key points from these verses—points that I pray will confirm to you the truth of God's Word about the sanctity of life from the moment of conception. First, note that the angel told Mary that Elizabeth, her cousin, was going to bear a child and that she was six months pregnant at the time. The child to be born to Elizabeth was John the Baptist, and the child to be born to Mary, of course, was Jesus.

Notice that the passage says, "At that time Mary got ready and hurried to a town in the hill country of Judea" (Luke 1:39). As soon as this miraculous event occurred, Mary got ready and hurried to where Elizabeth lived. Upon hearing Mary's greeting, John the Baptist leaped for joy in Elizabeth's womb. He recognized and honored the life of Jesus in the womb.

At that same moment, Elizabeth was filled with the Holy Spirit and exclaimed to Mary, "Blessed are you among women, and blessed is the child you will bear!" (Luke 1:42). She went on to say, "But why am I so favored, that the mother of my Lord should come to me?" (verse 43). She, too, recognized that Jesus, her Lord, was present.

It is important to remember that Jesus had just been conceived. Judea was about 60 miles away, as the crow flies, from where the angel appeared to Mary. In biblical times, this journey would have taken Mary one to two weeks to travel. Therefore, we can safely say that Mary arrived at Elizabeth's house during the first month of her pregnancy. Mary stayed with Elizabeth for about three months, and then returned home. If Elizabeth was six months along when Mary arrived, then Mary stayed long enough (three months) to see the birth of Elizabeth's child. This, then, is another confirmation of Jesus just being conceived when John the Baptist and Elizabeth recognized and honored Him.

There is one more beautiful illustration that I would like to note. Sharon Pearce writes, "When writing this Gospel, Luke used a single word to describe children, born and unborn."[214] The Greek word he used is *brephos*. As the following verses illuminate:

> When Elizabeth heard Mary's greeting, the baby [*brephos*] leaped in her womb. . . . In a loud voice she [Elizabeth] exclaimed . . . "As soon as the sound of your greeting reached my ears, the baby [*brephos*] in my womb leaped for joy."
> —Luke 1:41-42,44

Luke, who was a doctor, used this same word to describe Jesus after His birth:

> This will be a sign to you: You will find a baby [*brephos*] wrapped in cloths, lying in a manger. . . . So they hurried off and found Mary and Joseph, and the baby [*brephos*], who was lying in the manger.
> —Luke 2:12,16

Luke, inspired by God, also used this word to describe other children:

People were also bringing babies [*brephos*] to Jesus to have him touch them.

—Luke 18:15

Now, I would be remiss in my teaching if I didn't include the words penned in Psalm 139:13-16, which represent some of the most beautiful verses about life before birth in the Bible. King David was truly inspired when he wrote:

> For you created my inmost being; you knit me together in my mother's womb. I praise you because I am fearfully and wonderfully made. Your works are wonderful, I know that full well. My frame was not hidden from you when I was made in the secret place. When I was woven together in the depths of the earth, your eyes saw my unformed body. All the days ordained for me were written in your book before one of them came to be.

In view of this wonderful truth found in God's Word, let's take a look at how God knit us together in our mother's womb. From the moment of conception, the new life inherits 23 chromosomes from each parent, for a total of 46 in all. This single cell contains the blueprint for every facet of that baby's development—its sex, hair color, eye color, height and skin tone.[215] From the moment of conception, the knowledge stored in the files of an individual's genetic hard disk is 50 times greater than the data contained in an entire set of the *Encyclopedia Britannica*.[216]

This cell begins to divide at a tremendous rate. One cell becomes two, then the two become four, and then four become eight. At some point, early during this stage of growth, the cells begin to specialize. Some cells begin to

191

form the respiratory system, some the skeletal system, others the nervous system, and on and on. To this day, medical science cannot explain how the cells know to begin to differentiate, but there is Someone who does:

> As you do not know the path of the wind, or how the body is formed in a mother's womb, so you cannot understand the work of God, the Maker of all things.
>
> —Ecclesiastes 11:5

The baby develops at an astronomical rate. In the third to fourth week, the baby's heart begins to beat, pumping its own blood, not the mother's. This circulation of blood means that the cardiovascular system is the first organ system to reach a functional stage.[217] Eyes, ears, arms and legs have just begun to show, and the foundation for the baby's brain, spinal cord and nervous system are also in place.[218]

During the sixth week, the baby's brain begins to function and control movements of the muscles and organs.[219] At seven weeks, the baby also acquires the ability to rotate its head and will frequently touch its hand to its face at the same time.[220] Seven-week embryos have been photographed sucking their thumbs.[221] Isn't that so cute!

At eight weeks, the medical term for the baby changes to "fetus," which is the Latin word for "young one" or "offspring." At this point, all of the organs that are found in a fully developed adult are present. The fetus' heart has been beating for more than a month, its stomach is producing digestive juices, and its body even responds to touch.[222] The fetus' diaphragm is fully completed by eight weeks' gestation (hiccups have even been observed at this early stage).[223] If you were to view a video of fetal development, you would be able to see that the baby's fingers and toes are fully formed by this point.

In the brochure *What They Never Told You About the Facts of Life*, Dr. Paul Rockwell describes an event that took place when he was presented with a fetus at approximately this stage of development: "While giving an anesthetic [medicine] for a ruptured ectopic [tubal] pregnancy . . . I was handed what I believe was the smallest human ever seen. . . . This tiny human was perfectly developed, with long, tapering fingers, feet and toes. . . . The baby was extremely alive and swam about the sac approximately one time per second, with a natural swimmer's stroke."[224]

During the third month of development, the fetus' fingerprints become evident,[225] and its fingernails also begin to develop.[226] If the mother goes to the doctor, she can now hear the baby's heartbeat. The fetus now sleeps, awakens and exercises its muscles. It can turn its head, curl its toes, open and close its mouth and make a tight fist with its hand.[227]

By the end of the fourth month, the fetus is now 8 to 10 inches in length and weighs half a pound or more. This is the point at which the mother begins to "show." The fetus' ears are functioning, and the available evidence suggests that it can even hear the mother's voice and heartbeat as well as other external noises.[228] The mother may be able to feel the baby move at this stage.

From the fifth month on, the infant continues to grow and store fat—just growing and waiting for its time to be born. Each stage of development is a part of the story of life—a story that begins at conception and continues until death. As the brochure *What They Never Told You About the Facts of Life* goes onto say, "Birth isn't the beginning of . . . life—it's just one chapter in a continuing story. In fact, the baby will continue to develop, just like [it] did in the womb, until [it] reaches the ancient age of approximately twenty-three years!"[229]

Dear beloved, you may be saying to yourself right now, *All of this is fine for her, but she has no idea of the situation I was in at the time. There was no way I could have kept my child.* Believe me, I do know. I had all the same arguments and reasons why I could not have a child at 16. But as I look back, I can see that it would have worked out. God would have provided somehow, either financially for me to raise the child or through providing loving parents who desired adoption. That fact—of being able to look back and see that everything would have worked out—was part of my pain. Why did I do it?

Do you know that there were two inspirational men in the Bible who at one time wished they had never been born? One of these men was the prophet Jeremiah. He states that he wished his mother's womb would have been his tomb:

> For you did not kill me in the womb, with my moth-
> er as my grave, her womb enlarged forever.
> —Jeremiah 20:17

The other man, Job, said the following during an extremely difficult time in his life:

> May the day of my birth perish, and the night it was
> said, "A boy is born!" That day—may it turn to dark-
> ness. . . . For it did not shut the doors of the womb

on me to hide trouble from my eyes. Why did I not perish at birth, and die as I came from the womb? Why were there knees to receive me and breasts that I might be nursed? For now I would be lying down in peace; I would be asleep and at rest.

—Job 3:3-4a,10-13

Imagine if these two men had died in their mother's womb. We wouldn't have the book of Job or the book of Jeremiah (and possibly not even the book of Lamentations, as many attribute that book to Jeremiah as well). Imagine how many lives these two men have touched! God had plans for Jeremiah and Job, just as He has plans for every baby in the womb. It is not God's will to put these children to death. We must remember that nothing is impossible with God!

In Acts 7:18-19, Luke quotes the following from Stephen's speech to the Sanhedrin:

Then another king, who knew nothing about Joseph, became ruler of Egypt. He dealt treacherously with our people and oppressed our forefathers by forcing them to throw out their newborn babies [*brephos*] so that they would die.

—Acts 7:18-19

Let us no longer throw out our babies in the womb. Many people believe that during the first three months of pregnancy the baby is not truly a life. But, as God's Word and the medical evidence shows, this is not the truth. So let us honor life—both born and pre-born—as God honors life.

For those of you who have chosen this abomination and today have realized the error of your ways, please know

195

that our God is a God of mercy and compassion—a God of love and forgiveness. Today, give over the sin of abortion to Him, the God of all creation. Let Him cleanse you from all unrighteousness.

Deep down, every woman knows that abortion is wrong. We were created to love and nurture our children. To have an abortion requires us to go against the way we were created and shut down our God-given maternal instincts. For many of us, we have been shutting down those instincts for years. It is time to stop.

The first important step that you must take in regard to your healing is to admit that abortion is wrong. No more excuses. Of course, to admit that abortion is wrong means that you must admit that what *you did* was wrong. Yes, what you did was wrong! This is difficult and painful to admit, especially if you are able to remember at what stage of development your baby was when it was aborted. As you can see from the scientific evidence, it was not *just* a product of conception or a fetal tissue mass—it was a baby, your baby—your *brephos*.

I know how painful this is for you to admit, and my heart breaks for the hurt you feel. But take to heart these words from Paul:

> Even if I caused you sorrow by my letter, I do not regret it. Though I did regret it—I see that my letter hurt you, but only for a little while—yet now I am happy, not because you were made sorry, but because your sorrow led you to repentance. For you became sorrowful as God intended.
> —2 Corinthians 7:8-9

If I could sit beside you today, I would say, "Let me come in where you are weeping, friend . . . for I have known a sorrow such as yours, and understand."[230] And remember to not stop the tears, they bring relief. As the psalmist states:

> Weeping may remain for a night, but rejoicing comes in the morning.
>
> —Psalm 30:5b

I am comforted to know that though I cannot be with you, my Best Friend—the Wonderful Counselor—is by your side, lovingly and patiently healing and cleansing you. So turn to Him. Let Him soothe your wounds. Gain your strength from Him, for the Prince of Peace will restore to you a peace that surpasses understanding as long as you don't give up and lose heart. As you kneel at His feet just as the Sinful Woman did, you will *go in peace!*

Chapter Fourteen

WEEPING MAY LAST FOR THE NIGHT

Weeping may last for the night,
but a shout of joy comes in the morning.
PSALM 30:5B, NASB

here are many issues in life that cause us to grieve. Of course, a normal grief issue is the death of a loved one. But we can also grieve many other situations—divorce, loss of our childhood innocence due to abuse, and even issues that are self-inflicted, such as abortion. Yet God's Word gives us both hope and comfort.

In the book of Ecclesiastes, we learn that there is a time for everything:

> A time to weep, and a time to laugh; a time to mourn, and a time to dance.
> —Ecclesiastes 3:4, NKJV

Most of us desire that our lives fall only under the categories of laughing and dancing. We shy away from any situation that may cause us to weep or to mourn. Yet grief is a normal part of life. Grief, like the other issues we have covered in this book—hurt, anger, bitterness and unforgiveness—can also keep us from becoming all that God intends us to be.

199

It wasn't until I admitted to myself that I was grieving the loss of my children because of the abortions and that I was grieving some other issues from my childhood that I was finally set free. By allowing myself to grieve, I was able to go in peace. It was then that I felt true joy and happiness. This was the first time I had felt these things in years—in fact, since the time of my childhood. What was even more amazing was that I didn't even realize that the joy and happiness were missing in my life until they were restored.

The Lord gave me an interesting word picture years ago of abortion as a terrible wound—a wound so deep and so painful that when the trauma first took place we were afraid to touch it or cleanse it properly. That picture reminds me of one of my daughters who is fearful of pain. When she was a child, if she had a little splinter that needed to be removed, we literally had to hold her down to remove it. To our neighbors, it must have sounded as if we were beating her, as she would cry and scream at the top of her lungs. But as her parents we loved her, and we knew that the splinter had to be removed and the injury cleansed. If not, infection would set in.

For many of us who have had an abortion, we acted much like my daughter. Because we were so fearful of the pain, we tried to ignore the wound. We left it untreated, without the proper cleansing, and intended to never look at it again. At first, we covered it up—placing a bandage over our uncleansed wound—and deceived ourselves into believing it was completely healed. But soon the wound festered and oozed. It was too painful to touch, so we tried even harder to ignore it, hoping and praying that the pain would go away. Then, when we least expected it, we hit the wound on something, and pus and infection gushed out in an outburst of anger or a moment of anxiety.

Still afraid of the true cost of healing, we continued to cover the wound and tried to go on with our lives. But then came the constant pounding ache, in sync with our heartbeat. Oh, how we tried to ignore it, but it was always there, always present, deep within our hearts. It caused us to experience the many consequences we were so desperately trying to avoid. Listen how God spoke through the prophet Isaiah:

> Why should you be beaten anymore? Why do you persist in rebellion? Your whole head is injured, your whole heart afflicted. From the sole of your foot to the top of your head there is no soundness—*only wounds and welts and open sores, not cleansed or bandaged or soothed with oil.*
> —Isaiah 1:5-6, emphasis added

If this picture describes you, then it is time to approach the Great Physician, who is the Only One who can bring true healing. Yes, beloved, He can even heal this. But you have to tend to the wound and drain the infection so that it can be cleansed. Will pain be involved? Yes! But until you truly reach the depth of the valleys, you will never see the majesty of the heights. As the Lord declared through the prophet Jeremiah:

> I will restore you to health and heal your wounds.
> . . I will bring health and healing to it; *I will heal my people and will let them enjoy abundant peace* and security. . . . I will cleanse them from all the sin they

have committed against me and will forgive all their
sins of rebellion against me.
    —Jeremiah 30:17; 33:6-8, emphasis added

Grieving is a normal and important part of life. The
problems begin when we do not grieve properly. As believers, we need to model our lives after Christ. The prophet
Isaiah wrote that Jesus was "a man of sorrows and ac-
quainted with grief" (Isaiah 53:3, NKJV). According to
Charles Spurgeon's description of Jesus, "He carried out to
the full that. . . . precept, *weep with those who weep*."[231] We
see evidence of this when we read the story of how Mary
and Martha mourned the loss of their brother, Lazarus.
Scripture tells us that when Jesus saw Mary weeping, "He
was deeply moved in spirit and troubled" (John 11:33). In
fact, Scripture goes on to tell us that "Jesus wept" (John
11:35).

Jesus came to set us free, and many times freedom is
found through tears. In Luke 4:18, Jesus said:

> The Spirit of the Lord is on me, because he has
> anointed me to preach good news to the poor. He
> has sent me to proclaim freedom for the prisoners
> and recovery of sight for the blind, to release the op-
> pressed, to proclaim the year of the Lord's favor.

Many of us who have not allowed ourselves to grieve
properly are prisoners who have become oppressed by not
allowing ourselves the freedom to express our emotions.
For years we have kept our emotions under lock and key,
so afraid that if we allowed ourselves a moment of grief,
we would lose control and never be able to stop crying.
Please know, beloved, that it is only by allowing ourselves
to grieve that we will unshackle the chains that hold us

fast. I wish I could be beside you as you enter the Valley of the Shadow of Death,[232] but I am comforted to know that the Prince of Peace, the Wonderful Counselor, is there by your side, for He is your Comforter in sorrow.[233]

In *Comforting the Bereaved*, Wiersbe and Wiersbe (yes, father and son) write, "In the hour of sorrow, the prayer that comforts is the one that leads everybody into the presence of the loving Father where His peace can come to troubled hearts."[234] Our hearts have been troubled for years because we never grieved the loss of our child (or children) properly.

As we discussed in the last chapter, our society does not acknowledge abortion as a loss of life. It is considered a surgical procedure—the fetus is just a tissue mass or a product of conception. Many times, a woman who has chosen abortion is told, "You took care of the problem, so get on with your life." Abortion is not considered to be a socially acceptable loss over which a woman should grieve.

There are other reasons why a woman who has had an abortion may feel she is unable to grieve. She may feel the need to be punished for the choice she made. Or she may feel that she does not have the right to feel bad or to grieve, as she was the one who was responsible. If this is something with which you struggle, remember that the price was paid! Paid in full! God's Word teaches:

> When we were overwhelmed by sins, [God] forgave our transgressions.
>
> —Psalm 65:3

> As far as the east is from the west, so far has He removed our transgressions from us.
>
> —Psalm 103:12

> Though your sins are like scarlet, they shall be as
> white as snow; though they are red as crimson, they
> shall be like wool.
>
> —Isaiah 1:18

But perhaps the main reason why a woman chooses
not to grieve the loss of her child (or children) is fear. She
is afraid of facing her grief. She may fear that her feelings
will be too intense and that she will lose control. In a previous chapter, I shared about a woman who hadn't cried
about anything in more than 15 years. This was the issue
with which she struggled. She kept her feelings of grief
locked tight deep within her heart, deep within her inmost
being.

Dear beloved, once again, the Lord wants you to deal
with what is hidden in the depths of your heart, to take
every thought captive (including the thoughts of grief),
and make them obedient to Christ. Remember the list you
made of all the things you do and feel when you are guilty?
Well, I want you to take that list out again. But this time,
I want you to make a second list on the other side of the
paper—a list of all the things you do (the actions) and all
the things you feel (the emotions) when you are grieving.

If you have denied the feelings associated with the loss
of your child (or children) through abortion and are just
considering it for the first time, you may find it difficult
to identify what you do when you grieve. If so, just try to
think of another grief situation in your life—perhaps the
death of a loved one or a friend. What were some of the
things you felt and did during that time? I know that for
me, I cried, I felt sick and I was depressed, angry and fearful. Do not forget to list the spiritual aspects as well, such

as feeling separated from God or perhaps being angry with God. You will probably end up with a list of about 20 to 30 different kinds of feelings and actions.

After you have finished, compare the two lists. Do you see any patterns? Are they both the same? If so, perhaps all those years you were feeling guilty you were also grieving—yes, dear beloved, grieving the loss of your child (or children). However, you no longer need to punish yourself with feeling guilty. Jesus paid the price! He came to set you free! He forgave you the moment you asked Him to do so. In view of this amazing truth, it is time to grieve in the manner He intended, because He wants you to *go in peace!* As God's Word states:

> Grieve, mourn and wail. Change your laughter to mourning and your joy to gloom. Humble yourself before the Lord and he will lift you up.
> —James 4:9-10

> For he wounds, but he also binds up; he injures, but his hands also heal.
> —Job 5:18

> Though he brings grief, he will bring compassion, so great is his unfailing love.
> —Lamentations 3:32

Note that as you begin to experience this loss, you will go through stages of grief. To understand these different stages, we are going to take a look at some of the eloquent verses concerning grief contained in the book of Lamentations. This book of mourning portrays the events of the destruction of the city of Jerusalem and the Temple in 586 BC. This poetic book of the Bible, as the *NIV Study Bible* points out, "poignantly shares the overwhelming sense of loss that accompanied the destruction of the city, temple and ritual as well as the exile of Judah's inhabitants."[235]

According to the *Illustrated Encyclopedia of Bible Facts*, "The Jewish name of this book literally means 'Ah, how!'"[236] The name can also mean, "How?"[237] Our English word "lament" means "to mourn aloud, wail, to express sorrow or mourning, to regret strongly."[238] Yes, beloved, it is acceptable to strongly regret the decisions we made in the past. That is part of grieving.

It is believed that Jeremiah was the author of this book. As Wiersbe and Wiersebe state, "The fact that Jeremiah expressed these deep emotions in an inspired book of the Bible would indicate that God expects us to grieve, and that He accepts our expressions of grief."[239] So, using this information as a backdrop, let us compare this book of grief to the normal stages of grief seen as a result of death.

The first stage of grief is *shock*. Listen to how Jeremiah first described the destruction of Jerusalem in Lamentations 1:1:

> *How* deserted lies the city, once so full of people!
> *How* like a widow is she (emphasis added).

When we compare our grief over an abortion to a normal grief situation, such as the death of a loved one, we see that asking "how" and "why" is a typical response. The *NIV Study Bible* explains that "how! expresses a mixture of shock and despair."[240] Wiersbe describes it like this: "There is an emotional numbness when we hear a loved one has died. This is a normal response triggered by the nervous system of the body. It is God's way of anesthetizing the person so that he or she might be able to face the reality of death and handle the difficulties to come. Of course, if this stage lasts too long, it is abnormal and will create problems."[241] Emotional numbness for a woman who has had an abortion is a response that allows her to get through the first few days and weeks after the abortion. However, many post-abortive women stay stuck there, too afraid to move on to the next stage of grief.

This next stage is *strong emotions.* Listen to how Jeremiah describes it:

> Bitterly she weeps at night, tears are upon her cheeks.
>
> —Lamentations 1:2

He goes on to describe his own reaction of grieving:

> My eyes fail from weeping, I am in torment within, my heart is poured out on the ground.
>
> —Lamentations 2:11a

Perhaps Weirsbe described it best when he wrote, "God made us to weep, and tears are always in order when there is a broken heart. The foolish counsel 'Now, don't cry!' is based on both bad psychology and bad theology. Jesus wept, and so did the saints of God named in the Scriptures (Genesis 23:2; 50:1; 2 Samuel 18:33; Acts 8:2). *We are not told that it is wrong to sorrow. We are told that our sorrow should not be hopeless,* like the sorrow of the world (1 Thessalonians 4:13-18)."[242] We see this foolish counsel of "don't cry" at work whenever someone tells a woman who has had an abortion that the problem has been solved and she should "get on with her life."

207

For the woman in this stage of grief, her emotions may be so overwhelming that she continues to deny that the abortion has had any affect on her or that she did anything wrong. For her to admit otherwise would create emotions too strong to endure. However, we must remember that "weeping may last for the night, but a shout of joy comes in the morning" (Psalm 30:5a, NASB).

The stage of grief that follows strong emotions is *depression*. Listen to what Jeremiah writes on this subject:

> This is why I weep and my eyes overflow with tears. No one is near to comfort me, no one to restore my spirit.
> —Lamentations 1:16a

> He has besieged me and surrounded me with bitterness and hardship. . . . He has walled me in so I cannot escape; he has weighed me down with chains. Even when I call out or cry for help, he shuts out my prayer. . . . He pierced my heart with arrows from his quiver. . . . and my soul is downcast within me.
> —Lamentations 3:5-20

For many women, there is no one with whom they can share why they are depressed. They may have fallen into depression because they cannot change the past and they may feel the need to be punished for what they have done for the rest of their lives. According to Weirsbe, "Sometimes there are even symptoms of physical problems. If the grief is not fully worked out, it could lead to real physical problems."[243] It is true, dear beloved, that we are powerless to change the past, but we can change the future! And there is a Friend closer than a brother[244] with whom we can share our deepest hurts.

Next is *fear*. Even Jeremiah states that he felt fear in the midst of his grief:

> What I see brings grief to my soul because of all the women of my city. Those who were my enemies without cause hunted me like a bird. They tried to end my life in a pit and threw stones at me; the waters closed over my head, and I thought I was about to be cut off. I called on your name, O LORD, from the depths of the pit. You heard my plea. . . . You came near when I called you, and you said, "Do not fear."
>
> —Lamentations 3:51-57

As Wiersbe goes on to explain, "The bereaved person finds it difficult to think, to concentrate, and then becomes afraid and panicky. Life seems to be falling apart both on the outside and the inside. Sometimes well-meaning people misunderstand what the grief-stricken person is saying or doing, and this only leads to more fear and disorientation."[245] For the woman who has had an abortion, many of those close to her have no idea what she has been through and therefore do not understand how to help. Again, the woman may be fearful of her reactions if she allows herself to grieve—and, of course, she worries about what others would think.

The next stage of grief is *guilt*. Listen to how Jeremiah describes it:

> Let him sit alone in silence, for the LORD has laid it on him . . . and let him be filled with disgrace.
>
> —Lamentations 3:28 & 30b

A woman who is working through the stages of grief over her abortion often feels guilty because she is finally

209

taking responsibility for the death of her child. The woman continually plays the scenario over and over in her mind and thinks, *If only I had done things differently.* As Weirsbe explains, "This 'if only' response is a normal expression of grief: the bereaved person takes all the blame."[246]

Soon, the depression, fear and guilt turn into *anger* and *rebellion*. Once again, listen to how Jeremiah describes these same feelings of grief:

> Is any suffering like my suffering that was inflicted on me, that the LORD brought on me in the day of his fierce anger? . . . See, O LORD, how distressed I am! I am in torment within, and in my heart I am disturbed, for I have been most rebellious.
>
> —Lamentations 1:12,20

Wiersbe writes, "Along with blaming himself or herself, the sorrowing person will also blame others. . . . We remember old resentments and negative experiences, and these become a confusing part of our hurt feelings. We can do nothing about the loss of the loved one, and this frustration only creates more hostility. Sometimes people show this hostility by blaming God and even saying all kinds of blasphemous things. It is this feeling of guilt and anger that helps to cause some of the family problems."[247]

Delores Kuenning, in her book *Helping People Through Grief*, writes, "It is not uncommon during the grief process to feel anger towards God. . . . These feelings against God usually add to the problem because we then feel guilty for our anger."[248] Our anger and rebellion separate us from God and enable a bitter root to grow into a bitter poison in our lives. This is why it is so important to learn what Weirsbe writes in *Why Us? When Bad Things Happen to*

God's People: "Bitterness only makes suffering worse and closes the spiritual channels through which God can pour his grace."[249] Dear beloved, take every thought captive and make it obedient to Christ so that God can pour out His grace in your life.

The next stage of grief is *apathy*. "Apathy" means "lack of feeling or emotion."[250] We can see this stage of grief in what Jeremiah writes:

> The LORD has done what he planned; he has ful-filled his word, which he decreed long ago.
> —Lamentations 2:17a

Weirsbe states, "It seems strange that [anger and] hos-tility can be replaced by apathy, but this is often the case. 'Nobody understands how I feel. . . . Life is not worth liv-ing.' The bereaved person finds it painful to relate to real life and wants to withdraw into his or her own shell and be left alone. Certainly it is normal for a hurting person to be left alone; but if this withdrawal continues too long, it becomes dangerous."[251]

The final stage of grief is *adjustment* and *acceptance*. Even Jeremiah described this:

> Because of the LORD's great love we are not con-sumed, for his compassions never fail. They are new every morning; great is your faithfulness. . . . The LORD is good to those whose hope is in him, to the one who seeks him. . . . For men are not cast off by the LORD forever. Though he brings grief, he will show compassion, so great is his unfailing love.
> —Lamentations 3:22-32

Weirsbe describes it this way: "Slowly the person learns to accept the loss, rearrange his or her life, and comes to

211

grips with reality. This does not mean the total absence of grief, loneliness, or bewilderment; but it does mean that the bereaved person recognizes what is happening and is able to cope with it. . . . . There are definite signs when this adjustment is taking place: the bereaved person can openly and easily talk about [the past in the proper place]. . . . The person no longer gives vent to hostility but, instead, seeks for ways to minister to others when they suffer loss."[252] The woman comes to the place where she wants to help others. She is ready for ministry work.

Now that we have learned that it is normal and acceptable to grieve, let's explore how we can do so in a healthy manner. One time when I was listening to a radio program, I heard a woman share a story of grief about the tragic death of her son due to an unfortunate accident. The woman stated that though she knew it was important to grieve the loss of her son, it was just as important to God for her to move on with her life. She knew that she couldn't stay stuck in shock or depression for the rest of her life.

So this woman set aside a time each day—literally with a timer—to be alone with the Lord. She would go to her room, close the door and let out all the emotions and feelings associated with her terrible grief. She would share all of her feelings of anger, depression and fear with God and pour out her heart and her tears. Then, after the timer went off, she would get up and go on with her day. Every day she did this, she would deduct one minute from her allotted time to grieve. She used this as a means to get through the normal cycle of grief and still move on with her life so that she could bring glory and honor to God.

There will be times when you will feel depressed or sad. This is normal. When you notice this in your life, take time with the Lord and ask Him to reveal to you the reason for your feelings. When I am feeling blue, I like to find a quiet place and honestly search my heart. I ask God to "search me . . . and know my heart; try me and know my anxious thoughts; and see if there be any hurtful way in me, and lead me in the everlasting way" (Psalm 139:23-24, NASB).

During such times of searching, the Lord might remind you of how an issue associated with abortion or abuse or some other hurtful issue came up recently in a movie or a discussion, and that deep down you are grieving over that matter once again. When this happens, allow yourself to grieve so that you do not become stuck in one part of the normal pattern of grief. It is all right to take time alone and shed a few tears—remember that the problems will develop when you try to stuff everything deep down inside. It is amazing the comfort and release you will feel when you learn to recognize what is really going on and allow yourself time to grieve. As God promises:

> Weeping may last for the night, but a shout of joy comes in the morning.
> —Psalm 30:5b, NASB

Many who have had an abortion or lost a baby through miscarriage or stillbirth wonder if their child is in heaven. If you have had these thoughts, it is important to take comfort in knowing the heart of God. He desires that none shall perish.[253] The verses that I find bring the most comfort to me are the ones that describe the death of King David's infant son. Let me give you the background to the story, which is found in 2 Samuel 11–12.

King David had an adulterous affair with Bathsheba, and she became pregnant. David tried to cover his sin of adultery by calling Uriah, Bathsheba's husband, back from war. David thought that if he sent Uriah home for the evening, Uriah would sleep with his wife and later think the child was his own. But Uriah did not go home. He didn't feel that it was right to do so with his men still on the battlefield, so he slept at the entrance to the palace. David, still trying to cover his sin, decided to get Uriah drunk. He figured that this would make Uriah go home for the evening and lie with his wife. But, once again, Uriah did not go home. So King David sent Uriah back to the battlefield. David wrote a letter to the commander of the army and instructed him to put Uriah in the front line, where the fighting was the fiercest. Then the commander was to withdraw, leaving Uriah alone so he would be struck down.

King David was now not only guilty of adultery but also responsible for the death of Uriah—and he did all of this as a means to cover his sin with Bathsheba. After Uriah's death, David married Bathsheba. and she bore a son. "But the thing David had done displeased the LORD" (2 Samuel 11:27).

Nathan, a prophet of the Lord, was sent to rebuke David for what he had done. Ultimately, King David recognized his guilt and confessed his sin, saying to Nathan, "I have sinned against the LORD" (2 Samuel 12:13). Nathan explained to David that because his sin had made the enemies of the Lord despise God, his son would die. (We reap what we sow.)

King David's child was ill for seven days. During this time, David fasted and wept and prayed for the child. When the child died, David's servants were afraid to tell him the news. The king had been so distraught while the child was alive that they were concerned he might now do something desperate. David overheard his servants whispering, and he asked if the child was dead. Let's pick up the story:

> "Yes," they replied, "he is dead."
>
> Then David got up from the ground. After he had washed, put on lotions and changed his clothes, he went into the house of the LORD and worshipped. Then he went to his own house, and at his request they served him food, and he ate.
>
> His servants asked him, "Why are you acting this way? While the child was alive, you fasted and wept, but now that the child is dead, you get up and eat!"
>
> He answered, "While the child was still alive, I fasted and wept. I thought, 'Who knows? The LORD may be gracious to me and let the child live.' But now that he is dead, why should I fast? Can I bring him back again? *I will go to him, but he will not return to me.*"
>
> —2 Samuel 12:19-23, emphasis added

I believe that all children under the age of accountability—whether the parents are saved or not—go to heaven. As we read in Matthew 19:14, Jesus said, "Let the little children come to me, and do not hinder them, for the kingdom of heaven belongs to such as these." These words of Jesus are repeated in three of the four gospels. The only requirement for us to join our children in heaven, as King David stated in 2 Samuel, is for us to have accepted Jesus Christ as our Lord and Savior. Then, at the moment that God takes us home, we will join them there. I am so thankful that we have these beautiful verses in the Bible. God knows there are many grieving parents in this world, and He left us with His comfort in these inspired words.

Let's go back to what we learned about Adam and Eve's sin in the Garden of Eden for a moment. For those of us whose lives have been impacted by abortion, the *covering* of our shame and nakedness (perhaps a pregnancy outside of marriage or the abortion itself), *blame* (believing others talked us into it), *hiding* (rationalizing the baby is just a fetal tissue mass) and *fear* (worry about what others would think if they found out) caused us to depersonalize our children. Our healing cannot continue with this depersonalization. We must realize and admit the baby (*brephos*) was a child. Our child!

Many women who embark on this journey to mourn and heal find different ways of comfort. Some who are artistic enjoy drawing or painting a picture of a small infant. Others find comfort in writing a poem or a letter to or about their children. (Of course, in saying this I am not suggesting that you are able to talk to the dead. God's Word says this is impossible, as seen in the parable of the rich man and the poor man.[254] But you can write a letter about what you *would* say to your child if you could.) Some have even written songs about a child lost to abortion. Some women instinctively know if their child was a boy or a girl, while others desire to know. If you ask, the Lord, in His timing, will reveal to you whether your child was a boy or a girl. Many times, He will even impress upon you his or her name.

Many women find comfort in tangible ways for healing. One woman, to help her sister heal, purchased two beautiful rose bushes. After completing the *Go in Peace* workshop, she and her sister planted the rose bushes on each side of a memorial plate at her church as a way of honoring the unborn. I thought it was interesting that the name of the two rose bushes they planted was "peace." What a beautiful memorial to the memory of her children.

There is also a National Memorial for the Unborn in Chattanooga, Tennessee. This memorial is at a facility that, from April of 1975 to May of 1993, was an abortion clinic. God, in His sovereignty, led a small group of believers to pray regularly at this clinic, and when the group discovered that the property was to be sold in bankruptcy court and that the abortionist was planning to buy it, God supernaturally opened the door for the Pro-Life Majority Coalition of Chattanooga to purchase the property. The property was then turned into a memorial for the unborn. As the organization's brochure states, "The National Memorial for the Unborn is dedicated to healing generations of pain associated with the loss of aborted children. On the site where 35,000 babies died, the memory of unborn children is honored."[255]

Beloved, if you run to Jesus and kneel at His feet just like the Sinful Woman did, eventually your wound will be healed completely. There will be no more pain, no more infection and no more sadness. However, there will be a scar—a scar that is touchable, a scar to remember. But do not ever forget the scars on the hands and feet of the Prince of Peace—the scars that set you free, the scars of love! He loves you more than you know. So *go in peace!*

Chapter Fifteen

YOUR WORTH IN CHRIST

*It is because of Him that you are in Christ Jesus,
who has become for us wisdom from God—
that is our righteousness, holiness and redemption.*
1 CORINTHIANS 1:30

I want to tell you a story about a very special woman named Hidajete (He-da'-ye-tay). When I met her in 1999, I was a missionary in Macedonia, Eastern Europe, and she was an Albanian refugee who had fled from Kosovo because of the war in Serbia. She became a special friend to me. I truly believe that God loved her so much that He literally sent me halfway around the world to tell her just how much.

One evening, Hidajete shared with me that in Albania there is a custom in which the oldest child, whether male or female, is considered to be the one who is *worthy*. She went on to explain that even though she, as the oldest child, was culturally declared to be worthy, she had never felt that way—and she was now almost 50 years old. I smiled and said to her, "You are worthy simply because God says you are worthy!"

Now, I know some of you will argue that none of us are truly worthy. That's true! Only God is worthy.[256] In fact, as Paul says in Romans:

> As the Scriptures say, "No one is good—not even one."
>
> — Romans 3:10, NLT

Let me lay the foundation for my statement to Hidajete. On our own, we are nothing. Not one of us is good—not even one. Many mighty men of God knew this to be true. John the Baptist said, "After me will come one more powerful than I, the thongs of whose sandals I am not worthy to stoop down and untie" (Mark 1:7). He was speaking, of course, of Jesus. I think the apostle Paul said it best: "I know nothing good lives in me, that is, in my sinful nature. For I have the desire to do what is good, but I cannot carry it out. . . . What a wretched man I am!" (Romans 7:18,24a).

I think it's interesting to note that before his decision to follow Christ, Paul was named Saul. "Saul" means "requested one," whereas "Paul" means "little." Why did Paul change his name from Requested One to Little?[257] According to Pastor Jon Courson, "Some say it was the result of his humility. As Saul, he was a proud Pharisee who looked down on other men. But when he was converted, he was broken."[258]

Self-esteem is an issue that is very prevalent in our society today. Most of the authors who write post-abortion books and workbooks state that it is important to build up a woman's self-esteem to help her overcome the issues with which she is struggling. They believe that part of the woman's problem is that her self-esteem is too low. Some of what these authors say is right, but most of what they say is so wrong!

220

Yes, a woman who has had an abortion does have low self-esteem—and I praise the Lord for it! That is exactly where God wants us. Our ailment brings us to the foot of the cross where we kneel at Jesus' feet. The Sinful Woman knew this truth, and deep down we know it as well. It is our conscience whispering to us that we are wretched sinners, just as Paul says in Romans: "What a wretched man I am!" (Romans 7:18).

Praise the Lord for this conviction of sin that points us to the foot of the cross! This is the only way in which we can truly deal with our sin. But remember that we have an enemy who likes to tell us lies about ourselves. Satan thinks up the lie, the world sells the lie, and we—the flesh—buy the lie. The enemy tries to get us to buy the lie of self-esteem by playing on our feelings, emotions and desires of wanting to feel good about ourselves. Heaven forbid, the world cries, if we have to admit that we are sinners!

In view of this, it is important to understand exactly what *esteem* means. According to Pastor Bob Hoekstra, "Esteem means to hold in high regard. Self-esteem [then is] learning to hold *yourself* in high regard."[259] That is just a politically correct word for pride! There are so many verses that speak of this evil of pride. God's Word warns that pride goes before destruction.[260] A person who is full of pride does not seek God[261] but only breeds quarrels.[262] Proverbs 11:2 clearly shows what happens because of pride:

> When pride comes, then comes disgrace, but with humility comes wisdom.

Could this be why Paul changed his name from Requested One to Little? He realized that *with pride* comes *disgrace*, but with *humility* (being little) comes *wisdom*. I know that I surely don't want any more disgrace in my life. Do you? It would be so wrong for me to teach you a lie—to teach you "man's way." Remember Proverbs 16:25, which I shared with you in the beginning of the book:

> There is a way that seems right to a man, but in the end it leads to death.

I want to teach you, dear beloved, the way that leads to life! I want to teach you God's way, not man's way or human philosophy or human psychology. In view of this, you must humble yourself to the will of God. He has great plans for you! But I'm getting ahead of myself. Let's step back a bit and look at what Jesus says about self-esteem in the book of Luke:

> To some who were confident of their *own* righteousness and looked down on everybody else, Jesus told this parable: "Two men went up to the temple to pray, one a Pharisee and the other a tax collector. The Pharisee stood up and prayed about himself: 'God I thank you that I am not like other men—robbers, evildoers, adulterers—or even like this tax collector. I fast twice a week and give a tenth of all I get.'
>
> But the tax collector stood at a distance. He would not even look up to heaven, but beat his breast and said, 'God, have mercy on me, a sinner.'
>
> I tell you that this man, rather than the other, went home justified before God. For everyone, [pay attention] who exalts himself will be humbled, and he who humbles himself will be exalted."
>
> —Luke 18:9-14, emphasis added

"Justified" means just as if you had never sinned. Listen to what the *NIV Study Bible* has to say about this parable: "God reckoned him [the tax collector] to be righteous, his sins were forgiven and he was credited with righteousness—not his own but that which comes from God."[263]

So what did I mean when I said to Hidajete, "You are worthy simply because God says you are worthy"? I think Paul said it best when he wrote:

> What a wretched man I am! Who will rescue me from this body of death? Thanks be to God— through Jesus Christ our Lord!
> —Romans 7:24-25

The answer is that we have worth through Jesus Christ our Lord! Hidajete's worth and our worth is not in ourselves, but is based on who we are *in Christ*. As Paul again writes:

> It is because of *Him* that you are *in* Christ Jesus, who has become for us wisdom from God—that is, our righteousness, holiness and redemption. Therefore, as it is written: "Let him who boasts boast in the Lord."
> —1 Corinthians 1:30-31, emphasis added

Our worth is not based on anything we have done. All that we are is based on the grace of God. God's Word goes on to say:

> Therefore, if anyone is *in* Christ, [she] is a new creation; the old has gone, the new has come!
> —2 Corinthians 5:17, emphasis added

God knit Hidajete together in her mother's womb. Her life had worth and meaning simply because God said it did. And so does yours! For 50 years Hidajete had tried to be worthy, but there was nothing—NOTHING—she could do on her own to become worthy. It didn't matter if the Albanians had a custom that said the oldest was worthy, because she knew deep within her heart that on her own she would *never* be so. But God loves her so much and she is so very special to Him that because of who she is *in* Him, she is worthy. And so are you, beloved.

Listen to how special Hidajete is. Out of the 750,000 refugees from the war in Serbia—350,000 refugees from Kosovo went to Macedonia and another 400,000 refugees went to Albania—God picked three special ones to come and live in our house. God *knew* that even though Hidajete had been born a Muslim, she would come to accept Jesus as her Lord and Savior.[264] The moment she did, she became someone of worth simply because of who she was in Christ. In view of this truth, she was worthy of all that God wanted to bestow upon her. This is true for you as well. The moment you accepted Jesus as your Lord and Savior, you became someone special. I don't think you realize just how special you are. In view of this, let's look at 1 Corinthians 1:30 a bit more in-depth:

> It is because of *Him* that you are *in* Christ Jesus, who has become for us wisdom from God—that is, our righteousness, holiness and redemption (emphasis added).

The word "righteousness" means free from guilt or sin.[265] Did you know that because of who you are in Christ, you are forgiven? You are washed clean from your sins, set free and justified. God sees you just as if you had never sinned. You are the righteousness of God and are free from guilt and sin.

The word "holiness" means to be separated or to be set apart. The *Unger's Bible Dictionary* describes it this way: "Holiness is. . . . used to indicate sanctity or separation from all that is sinful, impure or morally imperfect. . . . Holiness, so far as it appears in man, is an outcome of God's gracious work in salvation and yet not without the proper exertion of one's own free will."[266] Paul described it this way:

> You were taught with regard to your former way of life, to put off your old self. . . . and to put on the new self, created to be like God in true righteousness and holiness.
>
> —Ephesians 4:22-24

In Christ, He is your holiness. Praise the Lord! God sees you just as if you never sinned and you are white as snow. That is why you are of worth!

This verse also says that Christ is your redemption. Because of who you are *in* Christ, you are redeemed. There are a few definitions of "redeemed" in the dictionary that I found interesting, including: to buy back or repurchase; to free from what distresses or harms; to free from captivity by payment of ransom; to free from the consequences of sin; to repair or restore.[267] All of these are true of what Christ did on the cross for you and me.

Redemption, then, is being set free from the bondage of death as a penalty of sin.[268] As Paul writes, "For the wages of sin is death, but the gift of God is eternal life *in* Christ Jesus our Lord" (Romans 6:23, emphasis added).

You are redeemed by the blood of the Lamb and are free from condemnation. All of your sins are washed away. You are dressed in His righteousness, His holiness and His redemption.

To sum up the main ideas in this chapter, I want to show you just exactly what God's Word says about your worth as a woman *in* Christ. Therefore, I am going to list who you are *in* Christ, and as I do, I want you to repeat each one out loud. Please also remember at the end of this chapter to go back and look up each Bible verse in the footnotes. It will bless your socks off!

Are you ready? You better get some tissues, because you are going to see just how special you are to God. Okay, let's begin.

You are loved by God![269] Let Him hear you say, *"I am loved by God."*

You are valued by God.[270] Cherish it: *"I am valued by God."*

You are saved.[271] Praise Him as you declare, *"I am saved."*

You are complete in Him.[272] Shout it out loud as you accept it: *"I am complete in Him."*

You are a citizen of the kingdom of God.[273] Richly declare it: *"I am a citizen of the kingdom of God."*

Your royalty is sealed with the Holy Spirit.[274] Grandly proclaim it: *"I am sealed with the Holy Spirit."*

You are a child of God.[275] Let me hear you giggle it: *"I am a child of God."*

You are created in His image.[276] Imagine the magnitude of this statement as you say, *"I am created in His image."*

As His child, you are always in His thoughts.[277] Ponder it as you whisper it: *"I am always in God's thoughts."*

Because of His wonderful love for you, you are blessed by God.[278] Applaud Him as you praise it: *"I am blessed by God."*

As a precious child of the King, you are the apple of His eye.[279] Refreshingly recite it: *"I am the apple of His eye."*

As a child of God, you are promised rest.[280] Try not to yawn as you snuggle it: *"I am promised rest."*

In fact, you are able to sleep without fear.[281] Pray it as you lie down to sleep: *"I am able to sleep without fear."*

You are forgiven![282] Have confidence as you claim it: *"I am forgiven."*

You are washed clean from your sins.[283] God's Word says, "I will sprinkle clean water on you, and you will be clean" (Ezekiel 36:25). Feel His Spirit wash over you, believe it and say it out loud: *"I am washed clean from my sins."*

You are redeemed.[284] That's surely something good to boast in: *"I am redeemed."*

You are crucified with Christ.[285] Recite after me: *"I am crucified with Christ."*

You are dead to sin.[286] Affirm it: *"I am dead to sin."*

You are set free.[287] Gleefully shout it: *"I am set free!"*

You are reconciled to God.[288] Repeat it: *"I am reconciled to God."*

You are free from condemnation.[289] Cheer it out loud: *"I am free from condemnation."*

As you blossomed in His love, you became His workmanship.[290] "For we are God's workmanship, created *in* Christ Jesus to do good works" (Ephesians 2:10, emphasis added). So quote it: *"I am God's workmanship."*

You are a new creature in Christ.[291] Delight in it: *"I am a new creature in Christ."*

You are chosen to go and bear fruit.[292] Celebrate Him as you say it: *"I am chosen."*

You are called of God.[293] Magnify Him as you memorize it: *"I am called of God."*

You are the salt of the earth and the light of the world.[294] Sparkle as you claim it: *"I am the salt of the earth and the light of the world."*

You are an ambassador for Christ.[295] State it in a grand manner: *"I am an ambassador for Christ."*

You are always near to God.[296] Delight in it: *"I am near to God."*

In fact, when you are brokenhearted He is there for you. "The LORD is close to the brokenhearted and saves those who are crushed in spirit" (Psalm 34:18). You are protected by God.[297] So shout it out loud, in strength: *"I am protected by God."*

You are strong in the Lord,[298] even to the end.[299] Declare it: *"I am strong in the Lord."*

228

You are more than a conqueror.[300] Claim it in His name: *"I am more than a conqueror."*

You are a partaker of His divine nature.[301] Receive it and sing it with joy: *"I am a partaker of His divine nature."*

You are the temple of the Holy Spirit.[302] Whisper it in reverence: *"I am the temple of the Holy Spirit."*

And you are at *peace* with God.[303] Weep it with joy as you let His Spirit overflow you: *"I am at peace with God!"* As the Lord told the prophet Isaiah, "Though the mountains be shaken and the hills be removed, yet my unfailing love for you will not be shaken nor my covenant of *peace* be removed" (Isaiah 54:10, emphasis added). So . . .

Beloved,

repeat it,

believe it,

shout it,

weep it:

He loves you.

Whisper it,

laugh it,

joyfully say it, and

don't ever forget it.

Shout it one more time: *"I am loved by God! I am somebody special, simply because He says I am. I am free to go in peace!"*

Chapter Sixteen

SET APART

But know that the LORD
has set apart the godly for himself;
the LORD hears when I call to him.
PSALM 4:3, ESV

*N*ow that you have learned about who you are in Christ, it is time to learn about the deep, intimate, personal relationship that God desires to have with you. He wants to meet with you in the depths of your innermost being, and it is in this secret place that you will become all that He intends you to be.

There is an interesting statement that I think oftentimes we overlook in the first half of Psalm 139:13. It says:

For you created my inmost being.

What do you think that means? I believe that God created our inmost being as the secret place He wants to meet with us in intimacy, but many times (as you have learned in the previous chapters of this book) our innermost being is so stuffed full of hurt, pain, anger, bitterness and unforgiveness that there is no room to meet with Him. Remember, He is a jealous God, and He does not want to share that secret place with anyone or anything.

231

In view of this, let me share an interesting story I read recently about Queen Victoria's life. She was England's longest-ruling monarch. She became queen when she was only 18 years old and ruled for 64 years. As the account I read stated:

> When she was young, Victoria was shielded from the fact that she would be the next ruling monarch of England lest his knowledge spoil her. When her teacher finally did let her discover for herself that she would one day be Queen of England, Victoria's response was, "Then I will be good!" Her life would be controlled by her position. No matter where she was, Victoria was governed by the fact that she sat on the throne of England.[304]

From the moment Queen Victoria discovered the truth of who she was, she determined in her heart and mind to be good. She determined to walk worthy of her calling.

Well, much like Queen Victoria's teacher, I would like to help you not only discover who you are in Christ (as we talked about in the last chapter) but also live who you are in Christ! For you, too, are royalty. You are a child of the King of kings. For this reason, you are sanctified. "Sanctified" means to be "set apart"[305] and "to be free from sin."[306] There are two aspects to sanctification—a positional aspect and a practical aspect. The *positional aspect* has to do with the moment of your salvation. When you decide to give your heart to God and follow Him, you have immediately been set apart. The *practical aspect* has to do with how you live out your salvation. Each day, you must choose to make wise choices to be set free from sin. Therefore, sanctification is both a *one-time event* and an *ongoing process* throughout your life.

We see these two aspects in Queen Victoria's life. Because of her royal birth, she knew that she would one day be the future queen of England. This was the positional aspect of her monarchy—the moment she was born, she was immediately in line to rule the country. However, the practical aspect of her rule occurred when she learned that she would one day be queen and made the declaration, "Then I will be good!" From the moment she learned who she was and determined in her heart and in her mind to be good—to be the person that her birth and her position called her to be—she began the ongoing process of conducting her life in the way a queen should. In fact, on June 20, 1837, the day that Victoria was told that King William IV had died and she was now Queen of England, she wrote in her journal, "Since it has pleased Providence [God] to place me in this station, I shall do my utmost to fulfill my duty towards my country."[307]

I pray that you will also desire to fulfill your duty to be all that God intends you to be. If you do, you will have a life filled with purpose and meaning and have lasting peace and contentment. In this chapter, we will look at who you are in Christ *positionally* and also learn about the special privileges that are yours because of who you are in Christ.

As you learned in the previous chapter, you are loved by God, created in Christ Jesus, and complete in Him. You are not a mistake, for you are His workmanship, created in His image. You are His beloved. The moment you become born again and accept Christ as your Lord and Savior, you become a citizen of the kingdom of God. You become His child, chosen by Him, and are forever protected by Him. You are forgiven, redeemed, justified and washed clean from your sins. You are a partaker of His divine nature. You are His and are always in His thoughts.

Now, because of this truth of who you are in Christ, God desires to have a real, personal and *intimate* relationship with you. The word "intimate" means familiar, close, dear, personal, confidential, private, trusted, secret, deep and detailed. These words describe the type of relationship that God truly desires to have with you—yes, you! He wants to be your friend, your confidant, your advocate, your supporter, your provider, your sympathizer and your companion. These are other words that can be used to describe intimate. God desires to be your all-in-all, your best friend—the lover of your soul.

Now, because of the deep love He has for you, He has given you a choice: You can choose to dwell within the Holy of Holies at the foot of His throne and learn how to be all that He intends you to be, or you can choose to settle for second or even third best. Let me explain about the Holy of Holies in which you are invited to dwell.

It has always been God's desire to dwell among His people. Yet ever since the Garden of Eden when Adam and Eve chose to sin, mankind has wandered from God's presence. Then, at Mount Sinai, God returned His presence and reestablished the long-lost relationship with His people.

It was at this time that God spoke to Moses and said:

> Then have them make a sanctuary for me, and I will dwell among them.
>
> —Exodus 25:8

This was to be a place where God's chosen people could come to hear from Him. It was a place where they could receive His love, forgiveness and guidance. And so they made the Tabernacle. It is important to have a basic understanding of the pattern of this Tabernacle, because found within it was the Holy of Holies, and the clue to unlocking the secret of how to have a deep, personal and intimate relationship with God.

God loves you so much that He wants to speak to you. Exodus 33:11a tells us:

> The LORD would speak to Moses face to face, as a man speaks with his friend.

Psalm 84:2 shows how the psalmist yearned to meet with God:

> My soul yearns, even faints, for the courts of the LORD; my heart and my flesh cry out for the living God.

Have you ever spent one day—or even one moment—in the presence of God? If you have, then your soul will yearn to be there again. What is more amazing is that you can spend every day in the Holy of Holies with God.

Many times when you are studying God's Word, you will see that God speaks to His people with pictures and parables (which is a biblical name for stories) so that they can picture the spiritual lesson He desires to teach. The Tabernacle is a visual picture of the intimate relationship that God desires to have with you. This visual picture can show you where your heart is spiritually concerning your relationship with God.

THE TABERNACLE
Exodus 25:8

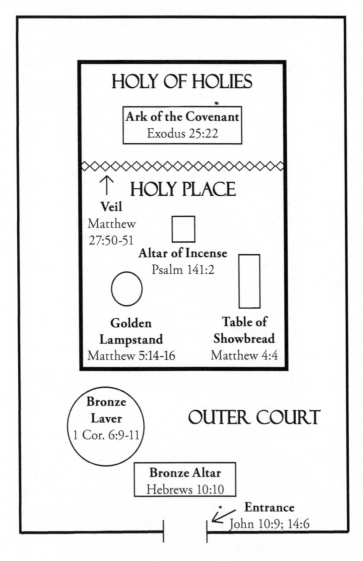

HOLY OF HOLIES

Ark of the Covenant
Exodus 25:22

↑ HOLY PLACE

Veil
Matthew
27:50-51

Altar of Incense
Psalm 141:2

**Golden
Lampstand**
Matthew 5:14-16

**Table of
Showbread**
Matthew 4:4

**Bronze
Laver**
1 Cor. 6:9-11

OUTER COURT

Bronze Altar
Hebrews 10:10

Entrance
John 10:9; 14:6

In her study "Dwelling in the Holy of Holies," Kay Smith states that there are three types of believers in regard to where they live spiritually. We can draw this picture of the three types of believers by relating them to the Tabernacle.[308] Basically, the Tabernacle had three parts: (1) the outer court, (2) the Holy Place and (3) the Holy of Holies. The Holy of Holies was the place where God dwelt.

There was only one entrance to the Tabernacle, and that was through the door that led into the *outer court.* Now, remember, the Tabernacle can be a visual picture of our relationship with God. In the same way that there was only one way to God in the Tabernacle, there is only one way to God in our lives, and that is by accepting Jesus Christ as our Lord and Savior. In John 14:6, Jesus said:

> I am the way and the truth and the life. No one comes to the Father except through me.

He also said:

> I am the door. If anyone enters by me, he will be saved.
>
> —John 10:9a, ESV

So the moment that you accepted Jesus Christ as your Lord and Savior, you entered the outer court in your relationship with Him.

Unfortunately, many believers remain in the outer court and never go any deeper. They never enter into the deep, personal, intimate relationship that God desires to have with them. They have experienced the positional aspect of salvation, but they are not living out their life on a practical day-by-day basis of following Christ. They are not being all that God intends them to be.

Let's explore this by taking a look at the two items found within the outer court: the Bronze Altar and the Bronze Laver. The *Bronze Altar*, also known as the Altar of Sacrifice, was a large piece of furniture that was used to make sacrifices in Old Testament days before Jesus came.[309] As John Schmitt and Carl Laney explain, "The position of the altar near the entrance of the Tabernacle reminds us of our need for atonement [our need to have our sins paid for by Christ's death] as the basis for approaching a holy God. The altar serves as a visual lesson, anticipating the perfect sacrifice that Christ offered on the cross."[310]

Once Christ died on the cross, there was no longer any need to offer sacrifices for man's sin. The sacrifice was made once, for all. Hebrews 10:10 teaches about this sacrifice that Jesus made so that we can enter into the outer court:

> And by that will we have been sanctified through the offering of the body of Jesus Christ once for all.
>
> —ESV

The *Bronze Laver* was the second item in the outer court. It was filled with water and was used for ceremonial washings. The Bronze Laver illustrates our need for spiritual cleansing from sin.[311] Remember, we are all sinners. First Corinthians 6:9-11 explains clearly what would happen to each of us if we were not washed by the blood of Jesus Christ:

> Do you not know that the wicked will not inherit the kingdom of God? Do not be deceived: Neither the sexually immoral nor idolaters nor adulterers nor male prostitutes nor homosexual offenders nor thieves nor the greedy nor drunkards nor slanderers

nor swindlers will inherit the kingdom of God. And that is what some of you were. *But you were washed, you were sanctified, you were justified in the name of the Lord Jesus Christ and by the Spirit of our God* (emphasis added).

Keeping these two objects in mind, let's go back to our picture of the Tabernacle and where each type of believer is spiritually in his or her relationship with God. *Outer Court Believers* are those who have received salvation but have gone no further in their relationship with God. They have received the sacrifice that Jesus Christ made on the cross when He died for their sins (as the Bronze Altar represents) and have been washed clean (as the Bronze Laver represents), but that's it. It's as if they entered through the door to the outer court when they accepted Jesus Christ and just stopped there. They have experienced the *positional aspect of salvation,* but are not practically living out their salvation in the manner God intended.

These believers are not becoming all God desires them to be. They are missing out. They have no witness for God and continue to live their lives by their feelings and their fleshly desires. They will never find purpose, meaning or lasting peace and contentment by remaining in the outer court. They are right where Satan wants them to be.

Remember, there is a battle going on that we cannot see—a battle that includes you and me. Satan does not want us to draw near to God and become all that He desires us to be. Satan wants to keep us ineffective so that we will not be a light and impact others for Christ. In view of his schemes, it is important to know that God does not want us to live our lives in the outer court. He has so much more for us. He wants a personal and intimate relationship with you and me. Do you desire to be an Outer Court Believer? Or do you want more in your relationship with God?

Now, let's return to our picture of the Tabernacle. Beyond the outer courts was the *Holy Place*. There were three items of furniture in the Holy Place that apply to our lives: (1) the Table of Showbread, (2) the Altar of Incense and (3) the Golden Lampstand.

The purpose of the *Table of Showbread* was to display 12 loaves of bread as a continual thank offering to God for His many blessings. Here again is another spiritual lesson.[312] In Matthew 4:4, Jesus said:

> It is written: "Man does not live on bread alone, but on every word that comes from the mouth of God."

This is why the Bible is referred to as "the Bread of Life." It is important to read the Bible daily. We cannot survive on just physical food. We need spiritual food as well.

The *Altar of Incense*, as the name implies, was the place in which the priests burned incense as an offering to the Lord. In Scripture, incense often symbolizes prayer.[313] Psalm 141:2 teaches:

> May my prayer be set before you like incense; may the lifting up of my hands be like the evening sacrifice.

Prayer is the way in which we talk to God.

The oil lamps in the *Golden Lampstand* provided light to the priests who ministered within the darkened interior of the Holy Place. Matthew 5:14-16 explains how this applies to the believer's life.[314] Jesus said:

> You are the light of the world. A city on a hill cannot be hidden. Neither do people light a lamp and put it under a bowl. Instead they put it on its stand, and it gives light to everyone in the house. In the same way, let your light shine before men, that they may see your good deeds and praise your Father in heaven.

As we read God's Word each day and pray, we begin to become a light unto the Lord. Others begin to see Christ in us.

Let's go back to our visual of the three types of believers. Unlike the Outer Court Believer, the *Holy Place Believer* enters into the Holy Place by spending time in prayer and reading God's Word. Thus, his or her life begins to become a light unto God. But this believer is still missing the most important aspect of his or her relationship with God: *intimacy.* Because of this, the Holy Place Believer still lives by his or her feelings and desires, which causes no purpose, meaning, or lasting peace and contentment in his or her life.

"Contentment" means "happiness with one's situation in life."[315] In other words, it means being fulfilled and satisfied regardless of what is happening. Holy Place Believers are not truly fulfilled and satisfied. They are not content. They spend some time with the Lord, which is a good thing, but then go about their day in their own strength. They try to find peace and contentment in things and situations, instead of in God. They are still living their lives by feelings and fleshly desires. They are not living by the truth of God's Word or seeking Him for His love, forgiveness and guidance. As Kay Smith notes, "They will give the Lord an hour or two, but that's it. They want the rest of the time for self."[315] Elisabeth Elliot also explains, "By trying to grab fulfillment everywhere, [they] find it nowhere."[317]

Like the Outer Court Believer, the Holy Place Believer is also missing out. And you and I will be missing out as well if we remain in the Holy Place. We will not find true purpose and meaning or lasting peace and contentment in our lives if we remain in the Holy Place. God desires a deeper intimate relationship with us. In fact, He desires to be involved in every aspect of our lives. He wants to be our all-in-all.

Do you desire to be a Holy Place Believer? Or do you want more in your relationship with God?

This brings us to the *Holy of Holies*. This was the place where God dwelt. The high priest could only enter the Holy of Holies one day each year. That day was called Yom Kippur, the Day of Atonement. On this day, the high priest would go in and make atonement for the sins of the people.

Because the Holy of Holies was so holy, only the high priest could enter, and he had to go through a whole ritual to cleanse himself beforehand. If the priest wasn't cleansed or his heart wasn't right before God, God could zap him right on the spot. For this reason, the high priest wore bells on his robe so that the others could hear him walking around in the Holy of Holies and know that he was still alive. In addition, because no one else could enter, they tied a rope to his leg in case he got zapped so they could pull him out.

Now, pay attention to this next part—Satan would love for you to miss what you are about to learn. Separating the Holy Place from the Holy of Holies was the *veil*. This also has significance in our lives. The moment that Jesus Christ died on the cross for you and me, the veil was torn in two. Matthew 27:50-51 states it this way:

> And Jesus cried out again with a loud voice, and yielded up His spirit. Then, behold, the veil of the temple was torn in two from top to bottom.
>
> —NKJV

This is a visual picture that shows you and me that we are now able to enter into the Holy of Holies and meet with God personally. No matter what we have done or how bad we have been God wants to meet with us! Listen to what Charles Spurgeon said back in the 1800s concerning the veil:

> Yet the rending [tearing] of the veil of the temple is not a miracle to be lightly passed over. It was made of "fine twined linen. . . ." This gives the idea of a substantial fabric, a piece of lasting tapestry, which would have endured the severest strain. No human hands could have torn that sacred covering; and it could not have been divided in the midst by any accidental cause; yet, strange to say, on the instant when the holy person of Jesus was rent by death, the great veil which concealed the holiest of all [the Holy of Holies] was "rent in twain [torn in two] from top to the bottom." What did it mean? It meant much more than I can tell you now.[318]

This was a miracle—that's what it means! There was no way that the veil could have been torn by anyone other than God. When the veil was torn in two, it proved that God desires a deep, personal and intimate relationship with you and me. We no longer have to go through some cleansing ritual like the high priest had to do to enter the presence of God. No matter where we have been or what we have done, we won't be zapped! God simply wants us to come and spend intimate time with Him in fellowship. He doesn't want us to be satisfied by only reading His Word and praying. He wants more.

He desires an intimate relationship with you and with me. He loves us. He wants to be our all-in-all, our best friend, the lover of our souls. That is why He made a way for us to enter the Holy of Holies—so we can be near to Him.

There was one piece of furniture in the Holy of Holies, and that was the *Ark of the Covenant* (also known as the Ark of the Testimony). The Ark was a reminder to the Israelite people of God's personal presence. He desired to meet with them and speak to them.[319] In Exodus 25:22, God declared:

> There, above the cover between the two cherubim that are over the ark of the Testimony, *I will meet with you* (emphasis added).

Let's go back to our visual of the three types of believers. Unlike the Outer Court Believer or even the Holy Place Believer, the *Holy of Holies Believer* desires to become all that God intends him or her to be. Holy of Holies Believers desire for God to be their all-in-all. They live by the truth of God's Word, not by their feeling and desires.

The Holy of Holies is not just a place but also an attitude of the heart. This is where our relationship with God moves from our heads to our hearts. It is here in the Holy of Holies that we realize who God is—He is amazing, the almighty God, the King of glory. He is all-powerful, all-knowing and unchanging, yet He loves us and wants to be involved in every aspect of our lives.

It is in the Holy of Holies that we seek God daily, sometimes moment by moment, to receive His love, forgiveness and guidance. It is here that He sees the yuck of our hearts and decides to love us anyway. It is here that we fall to our knees and offer our heart to Him to be changed. When we become Holy of Holies Believers we realize that sin builds a wall between us and God and breaks our fellowship with Him. Therefore, we are continually aware of the sins in our own hearts and take immediate action to admit, confess and repent of it so that our intimate relationship with God is restored. Psalm 139:23-24 becomes a way of life:

> Search me, O God, and know my heart; test me and know my anxious thoughts. See if there is any offensive way in me, and lead me in the way everlasting.

It is in the Holy of Holies that God takes our hearts and molds us into all He desires us to be when we come to Him in truth. It is here that we find our purpose and meaning for life. It is here that we discover lasting peace and contentment for every situation in life.

God wants to be involved in every aspect of our lives—in our living, breathing, waking and sleeping; in our hurting, weeping, cleansing and healing; in our laughing, hoping, dreaming and waiting. He wants to be our best friend—the lover of our souls. It is only in the Holy of Holies that we can meet Him and grow to become all that

He intends for us to be. It is here where we will learn how to practically live out who we are in Christ.

Beloved, where have you been dwelling? Which would best describe your relationship with God?

- *Outer Court Believer*—You are saved, but that's it! You have received the sacrifice that Jesus made on the cross for you. You are washed clean from your sins, but you are missing out on all that God has for you.

- *Holy Place Believer*—You spend time reading God's Word and praying. However, you are still missing the most important aspect of your relationship with God: intimacy. Because of this, there is no lasting contentment in your life. You continue to run after this or that to find satisfaction and pleasure. You don't look to God to be your all and all.

- *Holy of Holies Believer*—You desire to know God intimately. You realize that sin breaks fellowship with God, and because of this, you search your heart daily to make sure that there is no offensive way in you. You desire to be all that God intends for you to be. You have purpose, meaning, lasting peace and contentment in your life.

Which are you? Is this where you desire to be? If not, what can you do to become a Holy of Holies Believer?

In Anna and the King, one of my favorite movies, there is a scene that beautifully illustrates exactly the kind of relationship God desires to have with us. The movie is based on a true story about an English schoolteacher named Anna Leonowens.[320] In the movie, Anna has been hired to tutor the son of the King of Siam. Shortly after she arrives in Siam, she finds that she isn't being treated in the manner she was promised before she took the job. Her patience begins to wear thin, and she demands to meet with the king.

Each day, Anna goes to the court and waits to meet with the king to discuss this lack of manners. Each day, her hopes are dashed when court ends and she hasn't been allowed to speak to the king. So, one day she decides to take matters into her own hands. She approaches the king without permission—a stunt that almost costs Anna and her son their lives. The king's guards react immediately. They raise their swords to protect their king and strike them dead. Because of who she was positionally—an unknown English schoolteacher—she was unable to approach the king.

Yet, when Anna's son and king's oldest son later get into a fight, the king's favorite daughter is so troubled that she takes off to find her daddy. The king is holding court, seated on his throne, taking care of all the important business for the country of Siam, when his precious little daughter runs in past all the guards, through their legs, past all the court officials and up the steps to her daddy. She jumps into his lap and whispers in his ear. He stops everything. He bends down to listen in love to her concern, and then he carries her away to go off to solve her problem.

This is a beautiful picture of how our relationship with the King of kings can be. He loves us. Because of who we are in Christ positionally, you and I have the right to enter into the King's presence. We are His children. No one will stop us as we enter into the Holy of Holies, because we have every right to be there. We will not be zapped.

247

God loves us and, according to His Word, we are able to approach Him with confidence. But He gives us a choice: We can choose to sit at His feet in the Holy of Holies and become all He wants us to be, or we can choose to live our lives by our feelings and fleshly desires, running after this or that but never being truly satisfied. The choice is ours.

God truly desires to have a deep, personal, intimate relationship with you. You have the privilege to come into His presence. In fact, because of who you are in Christ positionally, you not only have the privilege but also the right to draw near to Him. You are able to approach the King with confidence.

Satan will do everything in his power to keep you from becoming all that God intends for you to be. Satan is hoping that you will not become a Holy of Holies Believer. In view of this, take some time today to enter the Holy of Holies in your relationship with God. Spend some quiet time reading His Word and in prayer. But don't stop there. Go deeper and enter into the Holy of Holies! Spend time just sitting at God's feet, meeting with Him and listening to His still, small voice. Ask Him to mold you and make you into the person He desires you to be. Ask Him to lead you and guide you. Ask Him to search your heart to see if there is any offensive way in you. Remember, it is sin which breaks fellowship with Him. It is the sin within your heart that places the veil between you and Him. Therefore, get your heart right with Him today.

Then take some blank paper or grab a journal and write whatever God puts on your heart. He wants to talk to you. Are you willing to listen? If you are, you will *go in peace!*

IN VIEW OF GOD'S MERCY

Therefore, I urge you, brothers [and sisters],
in view of God's mercy,
to offer your bodies as living sacrifices.
ROMANS 12:1A

*I*n a previous chapter, we learned that there are three elements of repentance. The first is a *genuine sorrow* toward God on account of our sin. The second is an *inward repugnance* to sin, which is necessarily followed by the actual *forsaking* of it. Now that we have discussed who we are in Christ *positionally*, it is time to look at the third element of repentance: "Humble self-surrender to the will and service of God."[321] In other words, the third element is about *walking worthy of our calling* so that we can live out who we are in Christ *practically*. This is the *practical aspect* of our sanctification.

To set the stage, let's go back to our story of Queen Victoria. Remember that when Victoria discovered for the first time that she would one day be queen of England, she said, "Then I will be good!"[322] The moment she discovered the truth of who she was, she determined to be the person whom her birth and position called her to be. In her heart and her mind, she determined to walk worthy of her calling in a *practical* manner. Her choice would greatly impact her life and the lives of everyone around her.

You and I also have a choice. We can make the wise choice to live up to our position in Christ by determining in our hearts and minds to humbly die to self and live for Christ, or we can make the foolish choice to live our lives by our feelings and desires. Our choices will greatly impact our lives and the lives of those around us.

I know that for me, I no longer want to live my life by my feelings and my desires. I have discovered that feelings are fickle and that when I choose to live by them, I usually make wrong choices—choices that often have devastating results. Therefore, I have decided to be like Queen Victoria and determine in my heart and mind to live up to the person that my position in Christ calls me to be. I have determined in my heart and mind to live out the third element of repentance by humbly surrendering my will for the service of God. Listen to what Jeremiah 15:19a says:

> Therefore this is what the LORD says: "If you repent, I will restore you that you may serve me."

You and I have been restored; therefore, it is time for us to serve the Lord. It's time for us to live out the *practical aspect* of our sanctification. Perhaps the thought that most helped me to make this final decision to offer myself as a living sacrifice to God was this: *In view of what God did for me—can I offer Him anything less than my life?* In view of the fact that He took my most horrible guilt and shame and set me free, can I offer Him anything less than my life? In view of the fact that He forgave me, can I offer Him anything less than my life? In view of the fact that

He healed my heart, can I offer Him anything less than my life? Likewise, in view of what He did for you, can you offer Him anything less than your life? I think the apostle Paul said it best:

> Therefore, I urge you, brothers, in view of God's mercy, to *offer* your bodies as living sacrifices, holy and pleasing to God—this is your spiritual act of worship. Do not conform any longer to the pattern of this world, but be transformed by the renewing of your mind. Then you will be able to test and approve what God's will is—his good, pleasing and perfect will.
>
> —Romans 12:1-2, emphasis added

In view of God's mercy! But what exactly does that mean? Mercy is "a form of love."[323] It is "kindness towards the helpless."[324] It is to have compassion on the suffering.[325] The word itself actually means that the price has been paid.[326] Remember, dear beloved, that during the final 18 hours of Christ's life, He paid the ultimate price for our sin with His life. He paid this price so that you and I could be set free. Out of His mercy, love, kindness and compassion toward us when we were lost and suffering, He came and saved us, restored us and set us free. In view of this, how can we offer Him anything less than our lives?

To "offer" means "'by a once-for-all presentation to place your bodies [your life] at the disposal of God.' The language here clearly refers to the crisis of complete consecration."[327] To be "consecrated" means to be dedicated.[328] It means complete dedication to your Lord and Savior. His sacrifice was complete, and all He wants from you is the same. In view of this, how can you *not* express your faith in

251

Him through love? As Paul wrote in Galatians 5:6b, "The only thing that counts is faith expressing itself through love." God's perfect will for you is to express your faith through love as you offer yourself to Him and serve Him. He has amazing plans for your life! For this reason, as Paul states, it is time to be an imitator of God:

> Be imitators of God. . . and live a life of love, just as Christ loved us and gave himself up for us as a fragrant offering and sacrifice to God.
> —Ephesians 5:1-2

According to Weirsbe in *Be Compassionate*, "What was the proof of [the Sinful Woman's] salvation? Her love for Christ [was] expressed in sacrificial devotion to Him. For the first time in her life she had *peace with God*."[329] Dear beloved, do you wish to go forth from this day forward in total peace with God? If so, it is time to offer yourself to Him. As Paul writes:

> He died for all, that those who live should live no longer for themselves, but for him who died for them and was raised again.
> —2 Corinthians 5:15

It is death to self that is necessary here. It is time to deny yourself and no longer live according to your own plans. It is time to shift your interest from self to Christ. It is time to say no to self-will and self-effort. It is time to take up your cross and live for Christ. Listen to what Jesus said:

> If anyone would come after me, he must deny himself and take up his cross *daily* and follow me. For

> whoever wants to save his life will lose it, but who-
> ever loses his life for me will save it.
> —Luke 9:23-24, emphasis added

Now, to deny yourself daily, moment by moment you have to make faith choices over flesh choices. To accomplish this, you must have the attitude of one who believes that it is not about *you* but all about *Christ.* The pity-party attitude of "life is not fair" or "no one loves me" is no longer acceptable. So what if people aren't nice to you? You be the one who is nice no matter what. So what if people don't care about you? You be the one who cares for others no matter what. So what if life isn't fair? You be the one who is fair in every situation. This is what it means to die to self and live for Christ, and it is when you reach this place that you will bear fruit. Remember that you have been chosen to go and bear such fruit—fruit that will last—because you are Christ's ambassador here on earth. As Jesus said in John 12:24:

> I tell you the truth, unless a kernel of wheat falls to
> the ground and dies, it remains only a single seed.
> But if it dies, it produces many seeds.

It is time to deny self and die to your wants and desires, for when you deny yourself and live for Him, others will see Christ in you! So let's turn once again to the story of the Sinful Woman to see how she denied herself and lived for Christ. According to Wiersbe, we learn that "Jesus did not reject either the woman's tears or her gift of ointment, because her works were the evidence of her faith."[330] In fact, some say that the gift she brought was worth a years' wage. As we discussed, it was an alabaster jar that had to be broken in order to be opened. In the book of James, we learn that "faith without works is dead" (James 2:20, NKJV). So, in other words, you are called to do things for God to work out your salvation.

However, it is important to know that works—the things you do for God—cannot save you. These works are merely the result of your salvation. In fact, many times it is because of what God has done in your life that you can begin to do such powerful works. Listen to what Pastor Jon Courson has to say: "[God] takes those of us who have missed the mark or messed up in a certain area, and He delights in using us to bring ministry to others at a later time. He heals the hurts. He restores and rebuilds, renews and revives—and then He releases powerful ministry in the very area where we blew it previously."[331]

So, are you ready to deny yourself and live for Christ? Are you ready to offer yourself as a living sacrifice? For months now as I have been writing this book, my prayer has been that you would come to know just what Jesus meant when He told the Sinful Woman to "go in peace" and that you would experience that peace in your own life. Well, one morning as I was praying about the title *Go in Peace!* the word "go" jumped off the page at me. God calls us to *go*. In fact, one of the last things Jesus said to His disciples before He was taken up into a cloud to heaven was to go:

> All authority in heaven and on earth has been given to me. Therefore *go* and make disciples of all nations, baptizing them in the name of the Father and of the Son and of the Holy Spirit, and teaching them to obey everything I have commanded you. And surely I am with you always, to the very end of the age.
>
> —Matthew 28:18-20, emphasis added

Now, some of you may be arguing with me right now and saying, *What could I possibly do for the Lord? I do not know how to share or teach. I have no gifts. I am afraid.* I know the different thoughts that go through a person's mind because, if you remember, I said those same things. But look for a moment at the types of people that God chooses to use. God used Moses mightily, even though he had killed a man.[332] Moses was fearful and said he could not speak, so God gave him Aaron as his spokesman.[333] King David, also a murderer,[334] led the nation of Israel to follow the Lord. God's Word says that he was a man after God's own heart.[335] Look at Saul in the New Testament. He was a man who had persecuted believers and condemned them to death. Yet he became Paul, a man whom God also used mightily.[336] God even used a donkey to speak to Balaam.[337] God truly uses the foolish things of this world to confound the wise.[338] He even used me, a sinful woman.

I know that God also used the Sinful Woman, because Jesus said, "I tell you, her many sins have been forgiven—*for she loved much*" (Luke 7:47a, emphasis added). From the moment Jesus forgave the Sinful Woman of her sins, she was filled with a deep love. To this day, this deep love still touches many lives. How is it possible that a person could stand in God's presence and be washed clean and forgiven and not *go* out and touch lives?

Dear beloved, we should not question how God could possibly use us when He calls us to serve but instead eagerly respond, "Here I am. Send me!" (Isaiah 6:8b). Jesus Christ said the following before He ascended to heaven:

> But you will receive power when the Holy Spirit comes on you; and you will be my witnesses in

255

> Jerusalem, and in all Judea and Samaria, and to the ends of the earth.
>
> —Acts 1:8

Dear beloved, God's Word says that you will receive power when the Holy Spirit comes on you and that you will be His witnesses in *Jerusalem* (which represents your home), *Judea* (which represents your neighborhood), *Samaria* (which represents the unlovables) and to *the ends of the earth* (which represents other countries). So, in view of God's mercy, offer yourself as a living sacrifice and *go* and do whatever He calls you to do. It might be in *Jerusalem*—right in your own home. If so, go and be a living sacrifice in your home. If you have a family, raise up your children as unto the Lord and be the wife that God calls you to be. Deny yourself and to live as Christ. Perhaps the Lord will call some of you to homeschool your children. Perhaps He will call some of you to raise foster children, adopt or provide shelter for an unwed mother. For some of you, perhaps your husband is not a believer and God will call you to be the wife described in 1 Peter 3:1-5.

For others, the call is to *go* into *Judea*, which means to *go* out into your neighborhood to be a light for Christ. He wants you to *go* where He sends you and say whatever He commands you to say. If you offer yourself as a living sacrifice, He will be faithful to show you what His good, pleasing and perfect will is. You are now ready to *go*! Perhaps He wants you to be a Sunday School teacher or work with the youth group. We definitely need the truth of purity and the sanctity of life taught to our youth, as there are many teens—even teens who are believers—who find themselves in crisis pregnancies. Or perhaps He wants you to work at a local crisis pregnancy center which honors life—both born and pre-born. Or perhaps He is calling you to help set the captives free and minister to hurting women. You are ready! You can do it!

For some of you, the call is to *go* to *Samaria* and work with the unlovables. How many women end up in juvenile hall or in prison or on the streets because they were looking for love but found it in all the wrong places? The choices they made to feel loved led them to make some poor choices. Dear beloved, you know the truth. You may be the only one who will ever share the truth with these women. Is that scary? Yes! But a courageous woman is not someone who has no fear; rather, she is someone who is obedient to Christ in spite of that fear! So *go* for it! *Go in peace!*

And for some of you, like for me, the call is to *go* to *the ends of the earth*—to another country. If you feel such a call on your life, remember what Isaiah 26:3 says: "[God] will keep in perfect *peace* him whose mind is steadfast." He will simply amaze you with the perfect peace He gives no matter where He sends you. In 1999 when I went to Macedonia to help the Albanian refugees, we were often about 15 miles from the Serbian border, and sometimes less. We could hear the bombs falling and see the smoke from the fires. In fact, the first bomb we heard was so close that we could feel the concussion. But God's tremendous *peace* was always with us, and never once did I lose that peace. This is because—listen carefully—there is no place safer than in His perfect will! Wherever God sends you—whether it is in your home, your neighborhood, a ghetto, a prison, a different state or even a war-torn country—you are nowhere safer than in God's perfect will!

257

So, beloved, get ready! Your life will never be the same! He will take you to places and have you do things that you could never even have imagined. Oh, the plans I had for my life years ago, but they did not compare to the plans He had for me. Remember God's wonderful promise in Jeremiah:

> "For I know the plans I have for you," declares the LORD, "plans to prosper you and not to harm you, plans to give you hope and a future."
>
> —Jeremiah 29:11

I wish I had a dollar for every time I heard a woman say, "What is God's will for my life?" You have the answer: *In view of God's mercy*, offer yourself as a living sacrifice, for this is your spiritual act of worship, so that you will know what His good, pleasing and perfect will is for your life. Do what He calls you to do, whether it is something little or something big. As you do this, you will continually discover God's will for your life.

There is one more thing that I would like to ask you to write. This time it is not a letter but a contract. I was at a missionary conference once and Dr. Harold Sala was telling the story of a man. This man decided to enter into a contract with God over all the things he would do for the Lord that year. After he completed his list, he signed it and went into the church sanctuary. He kneeled at the altar and gave the contract to God. But as he was praying, he didn't feel God's presence. So he prayed, "God, here is a list of all the things I can do for You this year. Why do I feel as if You won't accept it?" The Lord began to impress upon his heart, "Those are the things you want to do for Me, not the things I want *you* to do for Me. Are you willing to offer yourself as a living sacrifice? Then sign your name to the bottom of a blank sheet of paper."

Dear beloved, are you willing to offer yourself as a living sacrifice? Are you willing to sign your name at the bottom of a blank sheet of paper? We have done a lot of kneeling throughout this book. Won't you, yet again, come and kneel at the altar and offer yourself as a living sacrifice? As Dr. Sala went onto say, "This is as serious as anything you have ever done. Are you willing to sign your name at the bottom [of a blank sheet of paper] and let God fill it in? The most exciting life in all the world is that of the person who has simply said, 'Lord, I'm Yours! No strings attached, no regrets, no reservations, no bargaining. I'm Yours, period!'"[339]

So I encourage you today to take a piece of paper, date it and write the words of Romans 12:1-2 at the top:

> Therefore, I urge you, brothers, in view of God's mercy, to offer your bodies as living sacrifices, holy and pleasing to God—this is your spiritual act of worship. Do not conform any longer to the pattern of this world, but be transformed by the renewing of your mind. Then you will be able to test and approve what God's will is—his good, pleasing and perfect will.

Leave the rest of the paper blank and sign the bottom. Keep it in your Bible, and throughout the year as God uses *you*, fill in the blanks. You will be amazed at how He uses and blesses yet another sinful woman. I challenge you each year on January 1st to sign another contract and watch God work in your life.

May your life never be the same as you live your life worthy of your calling. Serve Him to the best of your ability, and know that "God's gifts and his call are irrevocable" (Romans 11:29). As you live your life worthy of your calling, you will *go in peace!*

PROFILE OF AN ABUSER

Then Asa was angry with the seer
[the Lord's prophet Hanani]
and put him in the stocks in prison,
for he was in a rage with him because of this.
And Asa inflicted cruelties upon some of the people
at the same time
2 CHRONICLES 16:10, ESV

Unfortunately, because of people's sinful behavior, there will be those, both male and female, who will not control their anger and rage and, as a result, will inflict their cruelties on those around them. The issue of abuse is so prevalent in society today that you must know what to look for so you do not end up in an abusive relationship. Abuse is not only physical, such as hitting or slapping, but it can also be verbal, emotional and/or sexual. By knowing what to look for at the beginning of a relationship, you can get out before it is too late. And for those of you who may already be in an abusive relationship, know that there is help. Get out before the relationship goes any longer, especially before you bring babies into it.

The profile you are about to read has been compiled from many different sources.[340] Although some of the profiles varied somewhat, I have listed only those traits that

261

were repeated continually. If you would like more information, do an Internet search on the words *profile of an abuser.* You can also visit the website thesheepfold.org, which is a ministry providing help to abuse victims.

If after reading this profile you,believe that you are in an abusive relationship, get help! God loves you more than you know, and He does not want you to remain in such a relationship!

Character Traits

Charismatic, Romantic, Devoted and Protective

Is the person charming in public, but degrades you in private? Beware! An abuser is often "charismatic, romantic, devoted and protective. Everyone likes him. On the surface he seems great, so you accept a date with him. He is wonderful. After a few months, you start to notice things but you dismiss them."[314]

Jealous and Possessive

Is the person possessive and jealous? Be careful! Many abusers are often so jealous they could be described as paranoid. They often have trouble trusting people, especially you. They may continually tell you to "tell the truth" even when you are not lying. Yet, they would describe their possessiveness of you as love.

Controlling

Is the person controlling? Watch out! An abuser likes to be in control at all times. And he likes things his way.

He may keep you somewhere against your will or even take away your cell phone. He continually wants to know where you are, who you are with and what you are doing.

Manipulative

Is the person manipulative? Take heed! An abuser will, often times, tell you that he cannot live without you. Or that he would die if you left the relationship. He may talk about hurting or killing himself as a means of keeping you in the relationship. Or he may even threaten to harm or kill you if you leave.

Denies Wrongdoing or Blames Others for Wrongful Behavior

Is the person always blaming someone or something else for their own actions? Or do they act as if nothing happened after a terrible rage? Think twice! An abuser will deny their wrongdoing or blame others and situations for what caused the outburst. Often times, the person will even say that it is your fault.

Other Behavioral Traits

Does the person tease and say things that hurt? Or force you to have sex? Get out! Many times an abuser has an aggressive attitude. Often times, he will try to make others appear less significant than he feels by putting a person down in front of other people. And he may even be so aggressive that he forces you to have sex with him against your will.

Do friends and family members say this person is not good for you? Listen to what friends and family are saying. Sometimes others will see a situation more clearly than you will when you are "in love." The saying "love is blind" is often true. In addition, it is important to remember who you are in Christ. You are the child of the King of kings. God does not want you in an abusive relationship. He has plans to give you a hope and a future.

If you answered yes to many of these questions, please get out of the relationship immediately! If you need to go visit a friend or relative away from home for a while, do it! Get away and get help! There are also shelters and other resources available for abuse victims. Do not allow yourself to be manipulated back into the relationship. Rely on God to be your shield. Ask Him to protect you as you take the steps to protect yourself.

> The Lord is my rock, my fortress, and my savior; my God is my rock, in whom I find protection. He is my shield, the strength of my salvation, and my strong- hold, my high tower, my savior, the one who saves me from violence
>
> —2 Samuel 22:2-3, NLT

ENDNOTES

Acknowledgements

1. Who is Lappidoth? Read Judges 4. In Hebrew, his name means "torch."

Introduction

2. See Deuteronomy 33:12; 1 John 4:7.
3. See Psalm 139:10.
4. See Jeremiah 31:13.
5. See Deuteronomy 31:6.
6. See Jeremiah 30:17; 33:6.
7. See Isaiah 9:6.
8. See Isaiah 9:6.
9. See John 8:32.
10. See Galatians 5:22.

Chapter 1: What a Shame

11. *Webster's Ninth New Collegiate Dictionary* (Springfield, MA: Merriam-Webster, 1988), s.v. "adultery."
12. See 1 Corinthians 6:18.
13. See Psalm 30:3; 40:2.
14. See 1 John 1:9.
15. See Philippians 3:13b-14.
16. See 2 Corinthians 5:17.
17. See Psalm 3:3.

Chapter 2: For His Glory

18. See Jeremiah 29:11.
19. John C. Broger, general editor, *Self-Confrontation—A Manual for In-Depth Discipleship* (Rancho Mirage, CA: Biblical Counseling Foundation, 1991).
20. See Ephesians 6:10-18.
21. See Ecclesiastes 3:11.
22. Valentina Mincheva, "1998—A Year of No Risk For the Mothers," Shumenska Zarja (a newspaper in Shumen, Bulgaria), September 7, 1998.

Chapter 3: A Sinful Woman

23. Warren W. Wiersbe, *Be Compassionate* (Colorado Springs, CO: Chariot Victor Publishing, 1988), p. 80.
24. Wiersbe, *Be Compassionate*, pp. 79-80.
25. See Luke 10:38-42; also see Matthew 26:6-13; Mark 14:3-9; John 12:1-8.
26. Jon Courson, "Their Couch or His Table," lecture on cassette tape (Jacksonville, OR: Applegate Christian Fellowship, 1990).
27. Mark 16:9; Luke 8:2.
28. Ralph Earle, *Word Meaning in the New Testament* (Peabody, MA: Hendrickson Publishers, 1998), p. 61.
29. Wiersbe, *Be Compassionate*, p. 80.
30. Ibid.
31. *The NIV Study Bible* (Grand Rapids, MI: Zondervan Bible Publishers, 1985), "Simon," footnote on p. 1552.
32. Courson, "Their Couch or His Table."
33. Chuck Smith, "Luke 7–8," lecture on cassette tape (Santa Ana, CA: The Word for Today).
34. J.I Packer, Merrill C. Tenney and William White, Jr., *Illustrated Encyclopedia of Bible Facts*.(Nashville, TN: Thomas Nelson Publishers, 1995), p. 488.

35. Smith, "Luke 7-8."
36. Wiersbe, *Be Compassionate*, p. 81.
37. See Philippians 4:7.
38. See 1 John 1:9.

Chapter 4: Are You Right with God?

39. "History of Psychology" Wikipedia, December 28, 2010. http://en.wikipedia.org/wiki/History_of_psychology#The_word_itself. (accessed 1/27/2011).
40. "History of Psychology" Wikipedia, December 28, 2010. http://en.wikipedia.org/wiki/History_of_psychology#The_word_itself. (accessed 1/27/2011).
41. Jon Courson, "Their Couch or His Table," lecture on cassette tape (Jacksonville, OR: Applegate Christian Fellowship, 1990).
42. *Webster's Ninth New Collegiate Dictionary* (Springfield, MA: Merriam-Webster, 1988), s.v. "neurosis." Neurosis is defined as a mental and emotional disorder that affects only part of the personality, is accompanied by a less distorted perception of reality than in a psychosis, does not result in disturbance of the use of language, and is accompanied by various physical, physiological and mental disturbances (as visceral symptoms, anxieties, or phobias).
43. Jon Courson, "Their Couch or His Table."
44. See 1 Corinthians 3:11.
45. See Luke 5:21.
46. Warren W. Wiersbe, *Be Compassionate* (Colorado Springs, CO: Chariot Victor Publishing, 1988), p. 81.
47. See Romans 6:23.
48. Warren W. Wiersbe, *Be Compassionate*, pp. 80-81.
49. See John 1:1,14,
50. See Genesis 2:17; Genesis 3.

51. See Psalm 51:5.

52. See Romans 5:12.

53. See John 3:3.

54. Sheri Snyder, letter to a friend, 1998. Used by permission.

55. See John 3:16-17.

56. See Genesis 3:21.

57. See Hebrews 9:24-28.

58. Snyder, letter to a friend.

59. See Romans 6:10.

60. See Hebrews 10:19-23.

61. Snyder, letter to a friend.

62. See 1 Corinthians 15:3-5.

63. See 1 Corinthians 15:13-14.

64. Snyder, letter to a friend.

65. See John 14:6.

66. See Ephesians 2:8-9.

67. Snyder, letter to a friend.

Chapter 5: Do Not Be Deceived

68. James Strong, *Strong's Exhaustive Concordance of the Bible* (Peabody, MA: Hendrickson Publishers), G2799.

69. Ralph Earle, *Word Meanings in the New Testament* (Peabody, MA: Hendrickson Publishers, 1998), p. 61.

70. *Webster's Ninth New Collegiate Dictionary,* (Springfield, MA: A Merriam-Webster, 1988), s.v. "hope."

71. *Merriam-Webster Dictionary,* (Springfield, MA: Merriam-Webster, Inc. 2004), s.v. "depression."

72. Ibid., s.v. "anxiety,"

73. Ibid., s.v. "rage,"

74. Gary L. Bauer, Gracie S. Hsu and Robert G. Morrison, Our Better Angels: The Care of Human Life (Washing-

ton, DC: Family Research Council, BL021), p. 14. The Alan Guttmacher Institute, "Abortion in the United States," Facts in Brief, August 31, 1994.

Chapter 6: Take Every Thought Captive

75. Dictionary.com. The American Heritage® Stedman's Medical Dictionary. Houghton Mifflin Company, s.v. "suppression." http://dictionary.reference.com/browse/suppression. (accessed: February 1, 2011).

76. *Webster's Ninth New Collegiate Dictionary* (Springfield, MA: A Merriam-Webster, 1988), s.v. "rationalization."

77. Dictionary.com. Collins English Dictionary—Complete & Unabridged 10th Edition. HarperCollins Publishers, s.v. "denial." https://dictionary.reference.com/browse/denial. (accessed: February 1, 2011).

78. *Webster's Ninth New Collegiate Dictionary* (Springfield, MA: A Merriam-Webster, 1988), s.v. "denial."

79. Fillmore H. Sanford and Lawrence S. Wrightsman, "Reaction Formation," Psychology: A Scientific Study of Man, 3rd edition (Belmont, CA: Brooks/Cole Pub. Co., 1970).

80. See 1 John 1:9.

81. Charles H. Spurgeon, Jesus the Substitute for His People, booklet vol. 21, no 1223 (Pensacola, FL: Chapel Library), p. 3.

82. "Conscious"—"Aware of the surrounding world. Aware of some specific thing." Webster's 21st Century Dictionary (Nashville, TN: Thomas Nelson Publishers, 1993).

83. "Subconscious"—"Part of the mind beyond consciousness." Webster's 21st Century Dictionary (Nashville, TN: Thomas Nelson Publishers, 1993).

84. "Conscious," c. 1600, from Latin conscious, knowing, aware," from conscire; probably a loan-translation of Greek syneidos. A word adopted from the Latin poets and much mocked at first. The sense of "active and awake" is from 1837.

85. Douglas Harper, historian, Dictionary.com. Online Etymology Dictionary, s.v. "subconscious." http://dictionary.reference.com/browse/subconscious (accessed: February 21, 2011).

Chapter 7: Deprived of Peace

86. Jon Courson, "Ten Commandments: Do Not Murder—Part Two," lecture on cassette tape (Jacksonville, OR: Applegate Christian Fellowship, 1999).

87. Blue Letter Bible, s.v. "captive," dictionary and word search for aichmalōtizo (Strong's Hebrew # 163). https://cf.blueletterbible.org/lang/lexicon/lexicon.cfm?Strongs=G163&Version-kjv.

88. *Webster's 21st Century Dictionary* (Nashville, TN: Thomas Nelson Publisher, 1993), s.v. "tangible."

89. Blue Letter Bible, s.v. "offensive," dictionary and word search for otseb (Strong's Hebrew # 06090). http://cf.blueletterbible.org/lang/lexicon/lexicon.cfm?strongs=H06090&Version=kjv.

Chapter 8: Forgiveness Is Not an Option

90. Blue Letter Bible, s.v. "bitterness," dictionary and word search for la'anah (Strong's Hebrew #3939). http://cf.blueletterbible.org/lang/lexicon/lexicon.cfm?Strongs=H03939&Version=kjv.

91. Blue Letter Bible, s.v. "bitterness," dictionary and word search for pikria (Strong's Greek #4088).

http://cf.blueletterbible.org/lang/lexicon/lexicon.
cfm?Strongs=G4088&Version=kjv.

92. See Deuteronomy 29:18.

93. Blue Letter Bible, s.v. "forgive," dictionary and
    word search for aphiēmi (Strong's Greek #863).
    http://cf.blueletterbible.org/lang/lexicon/lexicon.
    cfm?Strongs=G863&Version=kjv.

94. Warren W. Wiersbe, *The Cross of Jesus* (Grand Rapids,
    MI: Baker Books, 1997), p. 54.

95. The idea for the phrases "forgiveness is and forgiveness
    in not" was adapted from Sharon Pearce, Silent Voices
    Post Abortion Syndrome Healing and Recovery Lead-
    er's Manual (Chula Vista, CA: Silent Voices, 1993), pp.
    53-55.

96. *The Wesley Bible New King James Version* (Nashville,
    TN: Thomas Nelson, Inc., 1990), p. 1447.

97. Jay Adams, *From Forgiven to Forgiving* (Amityville, NY:
    Calvary Press, 1994), p. 12.

98. Ibid., p.11.

99. Kathleen White, *Corrie ten Boom* (Minneapolis, MN:
    Bethany House Publishers, 1983), pp. 106-107.

100. *Merriam-Webster Dictionary* (Springfield, MA: Merri-
     am-Webster, Inc., 2004), s.v. "grudge."

101. Blue Letter Bible, s.v. "grudge," dictionary and
     word search for natar (Strong's Hebrew #05201).
     http://cf.blueletterbible.org/lang/lexicon/lexicon.
     cfm?Strongs=H05201&Version=kjv.

102. Lewis B. Smedes, *Forgive and Forget* (New York, NY:
     Pocket Books, 1984), p. 57.

103. WordNet® 3.0 (Princeton, NJ: Princeton University,
     2007), s.v. "tolerate." http://dictionary.reference.com/
     browse/tolerate.

104. Adams, *From Forgiven to Forgiving*, p. 57.

105. See Isaiah 43:25; Jeremiah 31:34.

106. Adams, *From Forgiven to Forgiving*, p. 12.

107. Wiersbe, *The Cross of Jesus*, p. 53.

Chapter 9: The Weapons of Victory

108. See 1 Timothy 6:11-14; 2 Timothy 4:7.

109. Warren W. Wiersbe, *The Strategy of Satan* (Wheaton, IL: Tyndale House, 1979). p. 11.

110. *The NIV Study Bible*, study notes on Revelation 12:10 (Grand Rapids, MI: Zondervan Bible Publishers, 1985).

111. *The NIV Study Bible*, study notes on Revelation 2:10.

112. Job 1:6-11; Revelation 12:7-11.

113. Holman Bible Dictionary on CD-ROM, Quick Verse 6.0 (Hiawatha, Iowa: Parsons Technology, 1999), s.v. "satan."

114. See Matthew 4:1-3.

115. See Genesis 3:1; Revelation 12:9.

116. See 1 Peter 5:8.

117. See 2 Corinthians 4:4.

118. See 2 Corinthians 11:13-15.

119. See Revelation 1:8; 21:6; 22:13.

120. See Revelation 1:17; 22:13.

121. See Psalm 91:1; Revelation 1:8.

122. See Psalm 24:10.

123. See Psalm 32:7; 2 Thessalonians 3:3.

124. See Psalm 18:1-2.

125. *The NIV Study Bible*, study notes on Isaiah 14:12 (see also Daniel 12:1).

126. Warren W. Wiersbe, *Be Rich* (Colorado Springs, CO: Chariot Victor Publishing, 1998), p. 164.

127. See John 12:31; 14:30-31.

128. See Revelation 12:4,7-9.

129. See Daniel 10:12-20.

130. Dictionary.com Unabridged, v 1.1 (New York: Random House, Inc., 2007), s.v. "faith." http://dictionary.reference.com/browse/faith.

131. Lance Wubbels, ed., Charles Spurgeon on Prayer: A 30-day Devotional Treasury (Lynnwood, WA: Emerald Books, 1998), Day 6.

Chapter 10: A Broken and Contrite Heart

132. Dictionary.com, Collins English Dictionary—Complete & Unabridged 10th Edition (HarperCollins Publishers.), s.v. "contrite." http://dictionary.reference.com/browse/contrite.

133. Ralph Earle, *Word Meanings in the New Testament.* (Peabody, MA: Hendrickson Publisher, 1998), p. 30.

134. Merrill F. Unger, *The New Unger's Bible Dictionary* (Chicago, IL: Moody Press, 1988), p. 1073.

135. Unger, *The New Unger's Bible Dictionary*, p. 1073.

136. *The Merriam-Webster Dictionary* (Springfield, MA: Merriam-Webster, Inc., 2004), s.v. "repugnance."

137. *Roget's 21st Century Thesaurus* (Nashville, TN: Thomas Nelson Publishers, 1992), "repugnant."

138. Unger, *The New Unger's Bible Dictionary*, p. 1073.

Chapter 11: The Price Is Paid

139. Warren W. Wiersbe, *The Cross of Jesus* (Grand Rapids, MI: Baker Books, 1997), p. 8.

140. David Hocking, "The Execution of the Messiah," (Tustin, CA: Hope for Today, 1999), lecture on tape.

141. Jon Courson, *The Gospel According to John, Volume III* (Jacksonville, OR: Olive Press, 1997). pp. 109-110.

142. Wiersbe, *The Cross of Jesus*, p. 32.

143. See Revelation 13:8.

144. Wiersbe, *The Cross of Jesus*, p. 12.

145. Ibid., p. 16.

146. Henry H. Halley, *Halley's Bible Handbook* (Grand Rapids, MI: Zondervan Publishing House, 1980), p. 303.

147. Jon Courson, *Jon Courson's Application Commentary New Testament* (Nashville, TN: Thomas Nelson, Inc., 2003), p. 193.

148. Jon Courson, *The Gospel According to Matthew*, Volume II (Jacksonville, OR: Olive Press, 1997), p. 241.

149. Dr. Frederick Zugibe (Chief Medical Examiner, Rockland County, New York) How Jesus Died: The Final Eighteen Hours. Trinity Pictures, 1994.

150. Robert Beck, M.D., "A Physician's Look at the Death of Jesus" (Temecula, CA: Calvary Chapel Temecula Valley, 1991), lecture on tape.

151. Hocking, "The Execution of the Messiah."

152. See Isaiah 50:7.

153. See Psalm 41:9.

154. See Matthew 26:48-49; Luke 22:48; John 18:3-4.

155. Jon Courson, *The Gospel According to John, Volume III*, p. 93.

156. Jon Courson, *Jon Courson's Application Commentary New Testament*, p. 582.

157. *The NIV Study Bible* (Grand Rapids, MI: Zondervan Bible Publishers, 1985), p. 1631.

158. See Matthew 26:50b

159. See Matthew 26:51; Mark 14:47: Luke 22:50; John 18:10.

160. Jon Courson, *The Gospel According to Matthew, Volume II*, p. 246.

161. Jon Courson, *The Gospel According to John, Volume III*, p. 96.

162. See John 18:13,24.

163. Jon Courson, *The Gospel According to Matthew, Volume II*, p. 248.

164. Ibid., p. 261.

165. See Mark 15:3-5.

166. Jon Courson, *The Gospel According to John, Volume III*, p. 110.

167. See Matthew 27:3-5.

168. See Luke 23:7.

169. Courson, *The Gospel According to Matthew, Volume II*, p. 268.

170. Beck, "A Physician's Look at the Death of Jesus."

171. Dr. James Strange, (Professor of Religious Science University of Southern Florida), How Jesus Died: The Final Eighteen Hours. Trinity Pictures, 1994.

172. Beck, "A Physician's Look at the Death of Jesus."

173. Courson, *The Gospel According to Matthew, Volume II*, p. 268.

174. See Isaiah 53:5.

175. See Isaiah 52:14.

176. Courson, *The Gospel According to Matthew, Volume II*, p. 250.

177. Strange, How Jesus Died: The Final Eighteen Hours, Trinity Pictures, 1994.

178. Beck, "A Physician's Look at the Death of Jesus."

179. Hocking, "The Execution of the Messiah."

180. Wiersbe, *The Cross of Jesus*, p. 56.

181. Dr. John Bonica (pain specialist), How Jesus Died: The Final Eighteen Hours. Trinity Pictures, 1994.

182. Strange, How Jesus Died: The Final Eighteen Hours.

183. Courson, p. 125.

184. Beck, "A Physician's Look at the Death of Jesus."

185. Ibid.

186. Zugibe, How Jesus Died: The Final Eighteen Hours.

187. Courson, *The Gospel According to Matthew, Volume II*, p. 115.
188. Wiersbe, *The Cross of Jesus*, p. 53.
189. Beck, "A Physician's Look at the Death of Jesus."
190. Wiersbe, The Cross of Jesus, p. 42.
191. See Habakkuk 1:13.
192. See 2 Corinthians 5:21.
193. Wiersbe, *The Cross of Jesus*, p. 105.
194. Ibid., p. 109.
195. Ibid., p. 42.
196. Courson, *The Gospel According to Matthew, Volume II*, p. 120.
197. Ibid., p. 121.
198. Halley, *Halley's Bible Handbook*, p. 549.
199. Courson, *The Gospel According to Matthew, Volume II*, p. 142.

Chapter 12: The Temple of the Holy Spirit

200. Blue Letter Bible, s.v. "saw" (Strong's Hebrew #07200, dictionary and word search for ra'ah.) http://cf.blueletterbible.orglang/lexicon/lexicon.cfm?Strongs=H07200&Version=kjv.
201. Ibid. http://cf.blueletterbible.orglang/lexicon/lexicon.cfm?Strongs=H07200&Version=kjv [Mood-Imperfect See 08811].
202. See Hebrews 11:25.
203. *Webster's Ninth New Collegiate Dictionary* (Springfield, MA: Merriam-Webster, 1988), s.v. "romance," emphasis added.
204. Ibid., s.v. "romantic," emphasis added.
205. *Roget's 21st Century Thesaurus* (Nashville, TN: Thomas Nelson Publishers, 1992), s.v. "romantic."
206. Jon Courson, *Jon Courson's Application Commentary*

(Nashville, TN: Thomas Nelson Publishers, 2003) p. 1038.

207. See Genesis 2:23-24.

208. See Genesis 1:28.

209. "Live by," *The NIV Study Bible*, (Grand Rapids, MI: Zondervan Bible Publishers, 1985), study note on p. 1787.

210. Ralph Earl, *Word Meaning in the New Testament* (Peabody, MA: Hendrickson Publishers, 1998), p. 284.

211. *Webster's Ninth New Collegiate Dictionary* (Springfield, MA: A Merrian-Webster, 1988), s.v. "debauchery."

212. Elisabeth Elliot, *Passion and Purity* (Grand Rapids, MI: Fleming H. Revell, 1984). p. 21.

213. Ibid., p. 90.

Chapter 13: Brephos

214. Sharon Pearce, *Silent Voices: Post Abortion Syndrome Healing and Recovery Leader's Manual* (Chula Vista, CA: Silent Voices, 1993), p. 70.

215. The First Nine Months, Booklet LF177/3608 (Colorado Springs, CO: Focus on the Family, Rev. 12/93), Day 1.

216. Bart T. Hefferman, M.D., "The Early Biography of Everyman," a chapter within F.J. Beckwith, Politically Correct Death (Grand Rapids, CO: Baker Books House Co., 1993), pp. 43-44.

217. Keith Moore, *Before We Are Born: Basic Embryology and Birth Defects, 5th ed.* (Philadelphia, PA: W.B. Saunders Company, 1989), p. 52.

218. The First Nine Months, Day 20.

219. The First Nine Months, Day 40 and Week 6.

220. J.I.P. de Vries, G.H.A. Visser and H.F.R. Prechtl, "The Emergence of Fetal Behavior I. Qualitative Aspects," Early Human Development 7 (1982), p. 311.

221. William A. Liley, M.D., "The Fetus as a Personality," Fetal Therapy 1, (1986), pp. 8-17.
222. The First Nine Months, Week 8.
223. de Vries, Visser, and Prechtl, The Emergence of Fetal Behavior I. Qualitative Aspects," pp. 301-322.
224. What They Never Told You About the Facts of Life (Norcross, GA: Human Development Resource Council, Inc., 1992), brochure.
225. The First Nine Months, Week 9.
226. K.L. Moore, Ph.D. and T.V.N. Persaud, M.D., The Developing Human: Clinically Oriented Embryology, 5th ed. (Philadelphia, PA: W.B. Saunders Company, 1993), p. 95.
227. The First Nine Months, Week 12.
228. The First Nine Months, Month 4.
229. What They Never Told You About the Facts of Life.
230. Grace Noll Crowell, "To One in Sorrow," from Songs of Hope, © 1938.

Chapter 14: Weeping May Last for the Night

231. Lance Wubbels, ed., Charles Spurgeon The Power of Christ's Tears (Lynnwood, WA: Emerald Books, 1996), p. 16.
232. See Psalm 23.
233. See Jeremiah 8:18.
234. Warren W. Wiersbe and David W. Wiersbe, *Comforting the Bereaved* (Chicago, IL: Moody Press, 1985), p. 9.
235. *The NIV Study Bible* (Grand Rapids, MI: Zondervan Bible Publishers, 1985), study notes p. 1215.
236. J.I. Packer, Merrill C. Tenney and William White, Jr., *Illustrated Encyclopedia of Bible Facts* (Nashville, TN: Thomas Nelson Publishers, 1995), p. 580.

237. James Strong, *Strong's Exhaustive Concordance of the Bible* (Peabody, MA: Hendrickson Publishers), Hebrew #349, p. 11 in the Hebrew and Chaldee Dictionary portion.

238. *Webster's Ninth New Collegiate Dictionary* (Springfield, MA: A Merrian-Webster, 1988), s.v. "lament."

239. Wiersbe and Wiersbe, *Comforting the Bereaved*, p. 131.

240. *The NIV Study Bible*, p. 1217.

241. Wiersbe and Wiersbe, *Comforting the Bereaved*, p. 22.

242. Ibid.

243. Ibid.

244. See Proverbs 18:24.

245. Wiersbe and Wiersbe, *Comforting the Bereaved*, p. 22.

246. Ibid.

247. Ibid.

248. Delores Kuenning, *Helping People Through Grief* (Minneapolis, MI: Bethany House Publishers, 1987), p. 25.

249. Warren W. Wiersbe, *Why Us? When Bad Things Happen to God's People* (Old Tappan, NJ: Fleming H. Revell Company, 1984), p. 96.

250. *Webster's Ninth New Collegiate Dictionary* (Springfield, MA: A Merrian-Webster, 1988), s.v. "apathy."

251. Wiersbe and Wiersbe, *Comforting the Bereaved*, p. 23.

252. Ibid.

253. See 2 Peter 3:9.

254. See Luke 16:19-31.

255. National Memorial for the Unborn (Chattanooga, TN: National Memorial for the Unborn), brochure.

Chapter 15: Your Worth in Christ

256. See Revelation 4:11; 5:11-14.

257. Jon Courson, *Jon Courson's Application Commentary*

New Testament (Nashville, TN: Thomas Nelson Publishers, 2003), p. 720.

258. Jon Courson, *Tree of Life Bible Commentary Romans* (Jacksonville, OR: Tree of Life Publishing, 1995), p. 1.

259. Bob Hoekstra, "The Exaltation of Self" (Murrieta, CA: Living in Christ Ministries), lecture on cassette tape.

260. See Proverbs 16:18.

261. See Psalm 10:4.

262. See Proverbs 13:10.

263. *The NIV Study Bible* (Grand Rapids, MI: Zondervan Bible Publishers, 1985), study notes p. 1575.

264. See Ephesians 1:4-5,11.

265. *Webster's Ninth New Collegiate Dictionary* (Springfield, MA: A Merriam-Webster, 1988), s.v. "righteousness."

266. Unger, *The New Unger's Bible Dictionary*, p. 582.

267. *Webster's Ninth New Collegiate Dictionary* (Springfield, MA: A Merriam-Webster, 1988), s.v. "redeemed."

268. Unger, *The New Unger's Bible Dictionary*, p. 986.

269. See Ephesians 3:17-19; 1 John 4:16-19.

270. See Matthew 10:29-31.

271. See 1 Thessalonians 5:9; Titus 3:5; Hebrews 7:25.

272. See Colossians 2:10.

273. See Ephesians 2:19.

274. See Ephesians 1:13.

275. See Psalm 68:5; John 1:12-13; Romans 8:14-15; 1 John 3:1.

276. See Genesis 1:26-27.

277. See Psalm 139:17-18; Isaiah 49:15-16; Jeremiah 29:11.

278. See Deuteronomy 28:2-14; Psalm 1:1; Psalm 65:4; Ephesians 1:3.

279. See Deuteronomy 32:10; Psalm 17:8.

280. See Exodus 33:14; Matthew 11:28-29.

281. See Psalm 3:5; Psalm 4:8; Proverbs 3:24.

282. See 2 Samuel 12:13; Colossians 1:14; Hebrews 9:14; 1 John 1:9; 1 John 2:12.

283. See Isaiah 1:18.

284. See Galatians 3:13; 1 Peter 1:18-19.

285. See Galatians 2:20.

286. See Romans 6:1-4,17-18.

287. See Psalm 119:32; John 8:31-32; Galatians 5:13.

288. See 2 Corinthians 5:18.

289. See Romans 8:1; Colossians 1:22.

290. See 2 Corinthians 5:17.

291. See Deuteronomy 7:6-8; Ephesians 1:4-5; 1 Thessalonians 1:4; 1 Peter 2:9.

292. See John 15:16.

293. See 2 Timothy 1:9.

294. See Matthew 5:13-14.

295. See 2 Corinthians 5:20.

296. See Psalm 145:18; Ephesians 2:13; Hebrews 10:22; James 4:8.

297. See Deuteronomy 33:12,27; Joshua 1:3-9; 2 Chronicles 14:11; Isaiah 43:2.

298. See Psalm 18:1-2; Psalm 27:1; Isaiah 40:29-31; Ephesians 6:10.

299. See 1 Corinthians 1:8; Jude 1:24-25.

300. See Romans 8:37.

301. See 2 Peter 1:4.

302. See 1 Corinthians 6:19-20.

303. See Romans 5:1; Psalm 29:11; Psalm 85:8; Psalm 119:165; Isaiah 26:3.

Chapter 16: Set Apart

304. Warren W. Wiersbe, *Be Rich* (Colorado Springs, CO: Chariot Victor Publishing, 1998), pp. 13-14.

305. Ibid., p. 10.

306. *Webster's Ninth New Collegiate Dictionary* (Springfield, MA: Merriam-Webster, 1988), s.v. "sanctified."

307. "Historic Royal Speeches and Writings Victoria (r. 1837-1901)," The British Monarchy website, November 11 2007. http://royal.gov.uk/files/pdf/victoria.pdf.

308. Kay Smith, "Dwelling in the Holy of Holies" (Santa Ana, CA: The Word of Today, 2003), lecture on CD.

309. Stephen F. Olford, *The Tabernacle Camping with God* (Grand Rapids, MI: Kregel Publications, 2004), p. 76.

310. John W. Schmitt and J. Carl Laney, *Messiah's Coming Temple: Ezekiel's Prophetic Vision of the Future Temple* (Grand Rapids, MI: Kregel Publications, 1997), p. 28.

311. Ibid., p. 28.

312. Ibid., p. 29.

313. Ibid., p. 30.

314. Ibid.

315. WordNet® 3.0 (Princeton, NJ: Princeton University, 2007), s.v. "contentment." http://dictionary.reference.com/browse/contentment.

316. Smith, "Dwelling in the Holy of Holies."

317. Elisabeth Elliot, *Passion and Purity* (Grand Rapids, MI: Fleming H. Revell, 1984), p. 21.

318. Charles Spurgeon, "The Rent Veil," sermon delivered at the Metropolitan Tabernacle Pulpit, March 25, 1888. http://www.blueletterbible.org/Comm/charles_spurgeon/sermons/2015.html.

319. Schmitt and Laney, *Messiah's Coming Temple: Ezekiel's Prophetic Vision of the Future Temple,* p. 31.

320. Anna and the King (New York: 20th Century Fox, 1999).

Chapter 17: In View of God's Mercy

321. Merrill F. Unger, *The New Unger's Bible Dictionary* (Chicago, IL: Moody Press, 1988), p. 1073.

322. Warren W. Wiersbe, *Be Rich* (Colorado Springs, CO: Chariot Victor Publishing, 1998), pp. 13-14.

323. Unger, *The New Unger's Bible Dictionary,* p. 835.

324. *Webster's 21st Century Dictionary* (Nashville, TN: Thomas Nelson Publishers, 1993), s.v. "mercy."

325. Ralph Earle, *Word Meaning in the New Testament* (Peabody, MA: Hendrickson Publishers, 1998), p. 191.

326. *Webster's Ninth New Collegiate Dictionary* (Springfield, MA: Merriam-Webster, 1988), s.v. "mercy."

327. Earle, quoting Kenneth S. Wuest, *The New Testament: An Expanded Translation*, p. 198.

328. *Webster's 21st Century Dictionary* (Nashville, TN: Thomas Nelson Publisher, 1993), s.v. "consecrated."

329. Warren W. Wiersbe, *Be Compassionate* (Colorado Springs, CO: Chariot Victor Publishing, 1988), p. 81. emphasis added.

330. Wiersbe, *Be Compassionate,* p. 81.

331. Jon Courson, *The Gospel According to Matthew, Volume II,* Jacksonville, OR: Olive Press, 1997), p. 312.

332. See Exodus 2:11-12.

333. See Exodus 4:1-17.

334. See 2 Samuel 11:14-17.

335. See Acts 13:22.

336. See Acts 13:9; 22:1-10

337. See Numbers 22:28-30.

338. See 1 Corinthians 1:27.

339. Dr. Harold Sala, "Why Unlikely Candidates" (Murrieta, CA: Missions Conference 1999), lecture on tape.

Appendix 1: Profile of an Abuser

340. Adapted from www.tearmann.net/defndv.htm; www.brokenspirits.com/information/the_abuser.asp; www.paralumun.com/issuesabuser.htm> researched on

3/12/2008. Additional resources Gaddis, Patricia Riddle Dangerous Dating. Colorado Springs, Colorado: Waterbrook Press, 2000:p. 117-119.

341. The Sheepfold, "Profile of a Batterer," June 24, 2008. http://www.thesheepfold.org/victim/victim-batterer. htm.

About the Author

*I*n 1988, Cherie rededicated her life to the Lord, and soon after, God began performing His gentle surgery deep within her heart to heal her of her deep heart hurts. After leading her through a process of recovery, God began impressing on her that she needed to help others with similar hurts and show them how to apply His Word to their lives. In 1993, she co-founded Strong-ARM (Abortion Recovery Ministry) to help women deal with issues of abortion and teaching purity seminars to help teens make wiser choices. When many women began to attend her workshops for issues other than abortion, she changed the name to the Truth and Hope Ministry to better encompass the scope of the work.

In 1999, Cherie wrote her first book titled *Go in Peace!* to help women deal with post-abortion issues. You are reading the revised addition of that book. When she was unable to find a curriculum for her workshop that was 100 percent biblically-based, she began writing the *Go in Peace Leader's Manual* and *Go in Peace Student Workbook*. This curriculum was written for individuals attending her seminars who were suffering from any deep heart hurt issues—such as rejection, rape, abortion and abuse, to name just a few.

In 2001, Cherie and her husband, Keith, opened the non-profit Truth and Hope Foundation in Sofia, Bulgaria, to help women and teens heal from their deep heart hurts. In 2006, she joined the staff of Calvary Chapel Murrieta, where she is the overseer and trainer of the women's biblical counseling ministry. Today, in addition to writing, Cherie loves to travel and teach God's Word and can often be found teaching various topics at women's retreats and teen's seminars. Cherie has two daughters, who are both married to godly young men. And they have one grandson.

The sale of this book helps to further Cherie and her family's ministry work in the United States, Eastern Europe and wherever God sends them.

For more information about Cherie's books, products or teaching schedule, visit

www.cheriefresonke.com

www.sunflowerpress.net

For more information about the Truth and Hope Foundation in Sofia, Bulgaria, visit

www.truthandhope.net

If you want to know what Cherie is up to follow her on Facebook or Twitter at

www.facebook.com/cherie.fresonke

www.twitter.com/CherieFresonke

To order additional copies of this title please visit our website at

www.sunflowerpress.net

or write to

Sunflower Press

P.O. Box 813

Seal Beach, CA 90740